The
LEGITIMACY
of
BASTARDS

The
LEGITIMACY
of
BASTARDS

The Place of Illegitimate Children in
Later Medieval England

HELEN MATTHEWS

PEN & SWORD
HISTORY

AN IMPRINT OF PEN & SWORD BOOKS LTD.
YORKSHIRE – PHILADELPHIA

First published in Great Britain in 2019 by
PEN AND SWORD History
An imprint of
Pen & Sword Books Ltd
Yorkshire - Philadelphia

Hardback ISBN: 978 1 52671 655 2
Paperback ISBN: 978 1 52675 762 3

Typeset in Ehrhardt 11/13.5
by Aura Technology and Software Services, India

Printed and bound in UK by TJ International Ltd.

Pen & Sword Books Ltd incorporates the Imprints of Pen & Sword Books
Archaeology, Atlas, Aviation, Battleground, Discovery, Family History, History,
Maritime, Military, Naval, Politics, Railways, Select, Transport, True Crime, Fiction,
Frontline Books, Leo Cooper, Praetorian Press, Seaforth Publishing, Wharncliffe and
White Owl.

For a complete list of Pen & Sword titles please contact

PEN & SWORD BOOKS LIMITED
47 Church Street, Barnsley, South Yorkshire, S70 2AS, England
E-mail: enquiries@pen-and-sword.co.uk
Website: www.pen-and-sword.co.uk

Or
PEN AND SWORD BOOKS
1950 Lawrence Rd, Havertown, PA 19083, USA
E-mail: Uspen-and-sword@casematepublishers.com
Website: www.penandswordbooks.com

Contents

Acknowledgements

I am indebted to the staff of the National Archives and various local record offices for their assistance, and also to the many individuals who been involved in the digitization of primary and secondary texts, many of which have become available since I first started researching medieval bastards.

I would like to thank my PhD supervisor, Professor Nigel Saul, for providing the initial inspiration for this project and for his support and guidance throughout my research. I would also like to thank Mr David Morgan, Professor David d'Avray, Dr Nigel Ramsay and Bridget Wells-Furby for their advice at various stages of my research. Any errors are of course my own.

I would also like to thank Danna Messer and Claire Hopkins at Pen & Sword for giving me the opportunity to write this book.

Most of all I would like to thank my husband, Neil, for his encouragement and many cups of tea.

Foreword

If asked to name a life-changing book few people are likely to suggest *Scenes from Provincial Life*, Nigel's Saul's study of the Sussex gentry, but I can honestly say that it really did change my life. I was wondering what I might write my Masters dissertation about when I came across the following footnote: 'Reviewing S. M. Wright, *The Derbyshire Gentry in the Fifteenth Century*, Colin Richmond asks, "Would my impression that virtually every Derbyshire gentleman had a mistress and bastards be substantiated?" (*Medieval Prosopography* 6 (1985) 121). If the Sussex evidence is anything to go by, the answer is yes.'

This seemed to me to be both a hypothesis in need of further testing and a challenge I could not resist. One thing led to another and many years and a PhD later, I may not be able to agree that <u>every</u> English gentleman had a mistress and bastards, but many of them certainly did. Along the way, I have learned a lot about how the medieval landed classes managed their estates, their families and their sex lives.

When I first started researching the topic, it was necessary to spend weeks and months in libraries, ploughing through dusty tomes (some of them even with their pages still uncut), in order to find clues to illegitimate children. This is much easier now as more and more research resources are digitized and it is easier to make connections. Many more examples of bastards will surely be uncovered over time. This book is not and cannot be a comprehensive study of bastards in late medieval England, but it is an introduction to what I have found to be a fascinating subject that brings the medieval world to life.

*There are no footnotes/endnotes for this book.

Helen Matthews
April 2019

Introduction

In January 1236 a Great Council was held at Merton Priory in Surrey. One of the items of discussion was a request from the bishops that children born before the marriage of their parents be treated as legitimate by English law, just as they were according to the canon law of the Church. The assembled barons were having none of it. '*Nolumus mutare leges Angliae*' ('we do not wish to change the laws of England'), they replied and the law remained unchanged for almost 700 years. It was not until the Legitimacy Act of 1926 that English law allowed the legitimation of children following the marriage of their parents, provided that neither parent had been married to someone else at the time of the birth. Were the barons particularly concerned about the law relating to legitimacy? Perhaps not. The attitude of the landed classes towards illegitimate children over the following three centuries suggests that pragmatism, rather than principle, was the defining approach. They may have been voicing more general concerns about foreign influences in the realm, given that a power struggle between native magnates and those they saw as foreign interlopers was a defining feature of the long reign of Henry III (1216–72). From the perspective of the second decade of the twenty-first century this desire to maintain the distinctiveness of English law in the face of interference from a supranational organisation based on the Continent may seem strangely familiar.

Whilst it would obviously be anachronistic to view the political tensions of the thirteenth century as a form of proto-Brexit, illegitimacy is a subject which allows us to explore contrasts and similarities in attitudes between the medieval world and our own. There are obvious differences: modern science has made it possible to determine biological parentage accurately via DNA testing, whereas in the medieval period a simpler approach was needed. In general terms, the test for legitimacy in English law was simply whether or not the mother was married. Whether she was married to the biological father of the child was rather more difficult to prove and, except in very limited circumstances, the law did not unduly concern itself with this distinction. In terms of social attitudes, however, there are perhaps greater similarities between the medieval world and the twenty-first century than the intervening period between the sixteenth and twentieth centuries, during which illegitimacy carried a greater social stigma. During the sixteenth century, the introduction of the Poor Law, making parishes responsible for the costs of unwanted children, together with the activities of religious reformers combined to harden attitudes towards sexual misconduct and illegitimate children.

As illegitimacy affects rights of inheritance and therefore social status, it is the children of those with wealth and high status on whom illegitimate birth would be expected to have had the greatest impact. This book will therefore focus mainly on bastards of the landowning classes, as well as some wealthier townsmen. For the purposes of this book 'nobility' refers to the parliamentary peerage, i.e. those receiving an individual summons to parliament (the barons, earls, marquesses and dukes) whereas gentry refers to the lesser nobility of knights, esquires and gentlemen. The reason for the inclusion of town-dwellers, as well as nobles and county gentry, is that distinction between the two classes was not clear cut but permeable. Members of the nobility and gentry also owned town properties and often represented boroughs in Parliament, whilst successful townsmen purchased rural properties in order to demonstrate their status and proceeded to intermarry with the gentry. For example, Nicholas Potyn (d. 1398) managed to have a foot in both camps; originally a London fuller and draper, he continued to be described as a 'citizen of London' long after he had become an established landowner in Kent. Richard Whittington (d. 1423), Mayor of London and perhaps the most famous burgess of the age, came of gentry stock, the youngest son of a knightly landowner from Gloucestershire, Sir William Whittington. His brother Robert (d. 1423/4) served as a knight of the shire for that county on six occasions. Sir William Pecche of Lullingstone (d. 1399), who was elected a knight of the shire for Kent in 1394 and 1397, was the son of a London fishmonger who had built up a landed estate in several counties. Robert Hebburn (c. 1415) was a member of a family that had owned an estate at Newton-by-the-Sea (Northumberland) since the early-thirteenth century, and had acquired further landed estates through his mother, but derived most of his income from his mercantile activities, exporting wool and hides from Newcastle-upon-Tyne. Aside from the difficulty in drawing a clear line of demarcation between the gentry and the wealthier townsmen, it is in any case helpful to include burgesses within the scope of the study for comparative purposes. Property held in boroughs, unlike rural landed estates, could be devised by will, thus making it easier, potentially at least, to make provisions for illegitimate offspring.

What do we mean by 'illegitimate'?

Before going too much further, it would be useful to think about what illegitimacy actually is. It is a legal status, which can only be understood in relation to its opposite, legitimacy. A legitimate child is defined as one born in lawful wedlock and with full filial rights. An illegitimate child, or bastard, is one not born as a result of a lawful marriage and without the legal status that brings. Illegitimacy relies on being able to determine whether a couple were legally married or not and therefore became more significant as the rules as to what constituted a valid marriage became codified during the thirteenth century.

'Bastard' is defined by the *Oxford English Dictionary* as 'one begotten and born out of wedlock; an illegitimate or natural child.' Whilst this dictionary definition provides a useful starting point, it does not address the complexities of illegitimacy. It also adds a potential element of confusion, since the term 'natural child' was not exclusively used to denote illegitimacy in the medieval period, but could refer to any child with a genetic relationship to the parent, without any implications regarding legal status, for example to make a distinction between a 'natural' child and a step-child. This would appear to be the case in the will made by Jane Strangways on 28 October 1500. She bequeathed to her 'naturall son', Laurence Dutton, all the money that she had previously lent to him on condition that he would be content with it and trouble her executors no further. Her first husband was Roger Dutton, and Laurence was in all probability her legitimate son from this first marriage. The word 'bastard' has a superficial similarity to 'base', and the two terms seem often to have been associated, particularly in literature, but this probably stems from a mistaken assumption that they derive from the same source. The word 'bastard' actually comes from the Old French, and is believed to have originated from a combination of 'bast', a pack-saddle used as a bed by muleteers at inns, with the generally pejorative suffix '-ard', to imply a 'pack-saddle child' as opposed to a legitimate child of the marriage bed. The same word appears in Provencal, Italian, Portuguese and Spanish, and was also Latinised as '*bastardus*'—a term which tends to occur in English medieval Latin wills rather more frequently than the more correct Latin '*illegitimus*'. The word 'bastard' to describe an illegitimate child will be used throughout this book as it was the most commonly used term in medieval documents. No offence is intended.

It is important to understand that all bastards were not the same. The circumstances of the birth were relevant, and could make a significant difference to the child's prospects. It may be tempting to think of medieval bastards of the landed classes being the result of the lord of the manor exercising his privilege with the local peasant girls, but the reality was more complex. Whilst some of the examples in this book are clearly children born to low status women, others were born from stable relationships between social equals who were simply unable to marry. As well as the relative social position of the parents, there are

xii   The Legitimacy of Bastards

other ways of categorizing medieval illegitimate children. For legal purposes medieval bastards can be divided into: those born to an unmarried couple who were free to marry; those born as a result of an adulterous relationship; those born of marriages that were later dissolved because the couple were subsequently found to be too closely related ('consanguinity'); those born of marriages dissolved as a result of pre-contract; and children of the clergy. These children could be treated in different ways, as will be explained in Chapter One.

Fictional Bastards

In literature medieval bastards are frequently portrayed as villains, like Edmund in *King Lear,* or Don John, the 'plain dealing villain' of *Much Ado About Nothing*, jealously plotting evil schemes against their legitimate siblings. This notion of the villainous bastard was a common theme of Elizabethan and Jacobean drama, linking illegitimacy of birth with illegitimacy of power. Some illegitimate characters, like Spurio from Middleton's *The Revenger's Tragedy*, were even given names that indicated their illegitimacy. But illegitimate offspring in literature do not always play the part of villains. Contemporary medieval texts often displayed a more tolerant attitude. The audience of Chaucer's *Reeve's Tale* is meant to be amused by the social pretensions of the miller's wife, who is proud of her noble blood despite being the illegitimate daughter of the parson. In Malory's *Morte D'Arthur*, Arthur's legitimacy is questionable to say the least. Mordred, on the other hand, is a villain.

The fondness for villainous bastard characters in Renaissance drama has more to do with the hardening of social attitudes in the sixteenth century. The scheming bastard characters are overwhelmingly male. This is almost certainly a reflection of the fact that illegitimacy affected inheritance, and therefore had the greatest impact on first-born sons, who would otherwise have been their father's heir. By the eighteenth century, literary representations of illegitimacy had once more undergone a transformation. Whilst illegitimacy was still a common plot device, the villainous bastard had been superseded by the 'virtuous foundling' described by Lisa Zunshine.

Whether as evil schemers or wronged heroines, the frequent appearance of bastards in literature reflects their usefulness as a literary or dramatic plot device. Bastards are useful to writers because they are, in theory at least, outsiders, and as such can be seen as a disruptive element, threatening the natural order. Whilst it would not be appropriate to draw conclusions relating to the actual status and experience of bastards in later medieval England from later drama, the conception of bastards as being somehow apart from normal society, which makes them such a useful plot device, also makes them an interesting group to study. As the sociologist Kingsley Davis put it, the bastard is one of 'that motley crowd of disreputable social types which society has generally resented, always endured'. The Bastard in Shakespeare's *King John*, an illegitimate son of King Richard, plays a pivotal role in the drama precisely because his illegitimacy leaves him without a fixed identity or place in society.

Bastards and Heraldry

Whether villainous bastards, virtuous foundlings, or even real historic figures, illegitimate characters in literature often have a tendency to refer to the 'bar sinister' in their coat of arms. This notion is largely the fault of romantically inclined novelists with an imperfect knowledge of heraldry. The association of the inaccurate heraldic term 'bar sinister' with illegitimacy may first have appeared in Sir Walter Scott's 1823 novel *Quentin Durward*, where it is used by the Bastard Dunois (the illegitimate son of the Duke of Orleans) to renounce any claim to marrying the heroine, leaving the way free for Durward. The hero of John Buchan's historical novel *The Blanket of the Dark*, set in the sixteenth century, on being told that he is the son of Lady Elinor Percy, is reassured that 'there is no bar sinister on your shield. You were born in lawful wedlock, a second son.' Romantically-minded antiquarians were not immune from this interpretation of illegitimacy, either. William l'Anson, writing in 1913 of the career of the notorious Lucy Thweng, some-time wife of William Lord Latimer, and mistress of Nicholas Meinill and others, observed that the lady was responsible for introducing the 'bar sinister' to two noble families. The expression no doubt gained currency because of the negative connotations in English of the words 'bar' and 'sinister', but despite its popularity in literary contexts, in heraldry the term 'bar sinister' does not exist, or even make any sense. 'Sinister' means left, and a 'bar' is a horizontal line across the field of a shield, which obviously appears the same from left to right and right to left. 'Bar sinister' probably originates from a mistranslation of the French *'barre sinister'* which actually refers to different heraldic term, *'bend sinister'*. A *bend* is a diagonal line across the field of a shield and a *bend sinister* is one that crosses the shield from left to right rather than right to left from the point of view of the person holding the shield.

There is, however, no evidence even that the *bend sinister* was used during this period as a specific heraldic mark of disgrace for an illegitimate son. It was normal for differencing to be used in order to distinguish the arms of junior members of the same family, known as cadency, but there was originally no standard rule as to how these should be employed. Over the course of the fourteenth and fifteenth centuries heraldry evolved from its origin as a practical system for identification on the battlefield so that by the sixteenth century possession of a coat of arms had come to be regarded as a status symbol, denoting nobility or gentility in the wider sense. The ways in which illegitimacy was, or was not, signalled in coats of arms is thus relevant to more general public perceptions of illegitimacy.

One of the earliest known coats of arms for an illegitimate son were those of William Longspée, Earl of Salisbury (*c.* 1176–1226), the bastard son of Henry II (1154–89) and his mistress Fair Rosamund, but his arms of *azure, six lions rampant or*, may have been assumed in the right of his wife, Ela, Countess of Salisbury. Until the late fourteenth century there do not seem to have been any particular methods for differencing illegitimate as distinct from legitimate children. During the fourteenth century the convention was simply that younger sons and cadet branches of the family bore arms that were differenced from the main line in some way and this appears to have applied equally to recognised bastards. For example, John Lovel of Minster Lovell (d. 1314) bore *barry undy or and gules*. The arms of his illegitimate brother John Lovel of Snorscomb were differenced with *a label azure and a mullet argent*. The arms of the Montforts of Beaudesert were *bendy or and azure*. From evidence of their seals, it appears that the illegitimate sons of Peter de Montfort (d. 1370) differenced their arms with a *fess and a bordure* respectively. Sir Nicholas Stafford (1331–1394) bore the arms of his uncle, Ralph, 1ˢᵗ Earl of Stafford, differenced by an *azure chief*. At this time, bastards whose fathers had arranged for them to receive the bulk of their estates and become *de facto* heirs bore undifferenced arms in the same way as if they had legitimate eldest sons and heirs. William de Vescy of Kildare, the illegitimate son of William de Vescy (d. 1297) bore *or, a cross sable*, Baldwin de Bereford, the illegitimate son of Edmund Bereford (d. 1354) bore *argent, crusilly and three fleurs-de-lis sable*, whilst Thomas de Sackville, illegitimate son of Sir Andrew Sackville (*c.* 1369) bore *quarterly gules and or, a bend vair*.

During the fifteenth century a more standardised system evolved, whereby specific marks of cadency were used according to seniority: a label for the eldest son, a crescent for the second son, etc. From the end of the fourteenth century the arms of some bastards took the form of a plain or party field with their fathers' arms on a figure such as a *bend, fess, chief, chevron* or *quarter*. Sir Roger de Clarendon (*c.* 1350–1402), the illegitimate son of Edward, the Black Prince, bore *on a sable bend three ostrich feathers*. The choice of the mark of difference seems to have been left to individual taste. The term 'abatement' to refer to a mark of dishonour, such as in the case of illegitimacy, first appears in heraldic writings in the sixteenth century. It would therefore appear that there was a gradual transformation in the heraldic representation over the period from the late fourteenth century, which mirrored the evolution of coats of arms from a means of battlefield identification to a family status symbol.

On the subject of family status symbols, the 'eagle and child' crest of the Stanley family, Earls of Derby is worth a closer look. The crest originated with the Lathom family, whose heiress Isabel married Sir John Stanley by 1385. There are several versions of the legend, but the essence of the story is that an ageing member of the Lathom family, despairing of a male heir, found a child which an eagle had brought to her nest, and adopted it. Seacome, in his history of the House of Stanley suggests that this was a deliberate ruse to allow an illegitimate son to be brought into the family. Certainly that seems a more likely explanation if there is any truth in the legend at all, but is it is probably just a story. It does nonetheless seem an apt crest to have been adopted by the medieval Stanleys, who between them managed to produce quite a number of bastards, including two bishops (see Chapter Five). They were not unique in this. Sir John Savage (d. 1492), a neighbour and relation of the Stanleys had an illegitimate son George, who became parson of Davenham and had several illegitimate children of his own, including George Savage, chancellor of Chester, John Wilmslow, archdeacon of Middlesex and perhaps Edmund Bonner, Bishop of London.

Bastards and History

The history of illegitimacy has received greater attention in recent years, with the publication of a number of works dealing with historical aspects of bastardy, covering a range of periods and locations from ancient Greece to early modern France, colonial Spanish America and nineteenth-century Scotland. In respect of England, there is comparatively little literature specifically devoted to illegitimacy during the medieval period. Illegitimacy as a topic occurs mainly in the work of historical demographers and legal historians, though it is touched on also by social historians and, increasingly, by those working on gender and sexuality. Whilst there are studies of illegitimacy in the medieval period, they mostly concentrate on parts of continental Europe.

For medieval Europe as a whole, the traditional narrative follows the interpretation of Jacob Burckhardt's *The Civilisation of the Renaissance in Italy*, which identified a 'golden age' of bastards, one of increasing opportunity for bastards in the later Middle Ages that came to an end as a result of heightened moral concern stemming from either the Protestant Reformation or the Catholic Counter Reformation, according to location. According to this narrative, a weakening of moral constraints combined with the demands of war to provide opportunities for bastards from aristocratic families to come to the fore, and to be treated on a near equal basis with legitimate children. Burckhardt was much exercised by the apparent acceptance of bastards within the elites of Italian city states, particularly in the fifteenth century, and drew parallels between illegitimacy of power and illegitimacy of birth. He contrasted Burgundy and other more northerly states where he believed that well-born bastards were foisted upon the Church or provided for in other ways which kept them distinct from the main line of succession, with Italy, where bastards were not only tolerated, but could even be admitted to the succession in preference to legitimate minors. The most extreme example of bastard succession in Italy is probably that of the Este family of Ferrara, which was led by princes of illegitimate birth for a period of almost 150 years until 1471. Recognition of bastards provided a means by which aristocratic families could ensure a supply of male heirs, despite the prohibition on marriage for members of the military orders. More recently, Burckhard's view has been challenged by historians such as Julius Kirshner, Anthony Molho and Thomas Kuehn who have studied records in the Florentine archives to gain a more nuanced picture of provision for illegitimate children in medieval Italy, and Ludwig Schmugge who has worked on the archives of the papal penitentiary. Their findings will be discussed more fully in chapters four and five.

In considering contrasts between England and the Continent, it is important to understand that nobility can be a problematic concept to apply to medieval English society. On the Continent, nobility was a defined legal status, though there were some geographical variations in the requirements for nobility. Generally, nobility was deemed to be inherited from the father, but it was more strictly defined in Germany, where both parents needed to be noble. Whilst nobility had implications of lineage and noble connections, in France in the late-thirteenth century patents of ennoblement were introduced by which wealthy commoners could purchase the privileges of nobility, including freedom from tolls, certain tax exemptions and eligibility to be knighted and to wear high-status clothing. Similar patents were also introduced in parts of the Netherlands. Angus Mackay cites the fifteenth-century Spanish chronicler Diego de Valera, according to whom Spain had a particularly lax approach to nobility, even extending to bastards. He contrasted the situation in Spain, where even those engaged in low status occupations and bastards who had not been legitimated retained the status of a *hidalgo* (member of the lesser nobility) provided that they could prove their fathers and grandfathers were exempt from taxation, with Germany, where noble status lasted whilst the nobles were able to live 'honestly' without undertaking low status jobs, and Italy where all legitimate descendants of a noble retained noble status until they sank into poverty.

In England, by contrast, noble status was less concerned with bloodline than with landed wealth and the ability to support the necessary lifestyle. David Crouch's tongue-in-cheek suggestion that as far as medieval England was concerned, a nobleman was anyone capable of dressing and behaving like a nobleman without being laughed at has a certain degree of truth. The parliamentary peerage evolved during the course of the fourteenth and fifteenth centuries into a distinct group, identifiable as those receiving an individual summons to Parliament. Below that level, the knights, esquires and wealthy landowners who collectively formed the lesser nobility or gentry had no single defining characteristic, although they were, in general, those individuals who were likely to serve locally as sheriffs, justices or the peace, or representatives in Parliament. The precise nature of the gentry and the point at which they emerged as a distinct group continue to be the subject of much academic debate. By the sixteenth century, entitlement to a coat of arms had come to be regarded as an indicator of genteel status, but at the start of the period it was still associated with military activity rather than social position.

The one part of English landed society for which a comprehensive study of illegitimacy has already been undertaken is the royal family and so they will not be covered in any depth in this book. Chris Given-Wilson and Alice Curteis's 1984 survey of royal bastards, *The Royal Bastards of Medieval England* identified no fewer than forty-one royal bastards for the period 1066–1485, plus twelve for whom the evidence is less conclusive and 13 individuals who have sometimes been described as royal bastards, but about whom the attribution seems doubtful. The bastards of Edward IV and Richard III are also included by Beauclerk-Dewar and Powell in their 2008 survey of subsequent royal bastards. The only kings of England during the period from 1066 to 1485 for whom there was not even a doubtful rumour of having fathered a bastard were William I (who was of course himself a bastard), Henry III, Henry V and Henry VI, though William II, Edward I and Richard II had only one potential bastard of doubtful attribution each to their name. The suggestion that William Peverel of Nottingham was a bastard son of William I cannot be traced earlier than the Tudor period and is therefore probably a case of wishful thinking by Tudor genealogists. Even Edward II, whose sexual preferences are generally believed to have been in the other direction, fathered at least one bastard son. If the kings behaved in this way, a similar pattern of behaviour might be expected in their peers.

Researching Bastards

One of the challenges of researching illegitimacy in later medieval England is that there is no single source of reliable records of the kind that is available, for example, for some the Italian city states. It is no accident that the comprehensive study of bastardy in England begins with the sixteenth century and the introduction of parochial registration of births, marriages and deaths in 1538. Even then, the level of detail prior to 1850 is limited. Any attempt to establish the prevalence of illegitimacy in the period before parish registers are available is clearly even more problematic. Illegitimate children cannot be identified by their name alone. Bastards who were recognised by their fathers would very often take their father's name, though some were known by their mother's surname. It should be noted that a surname beginning 'Fitz-' simply means 'son of' and does not itself denote illegitimacy, although it became common for royal bastards to have names of this type, for example Henry FitzRoy, the son of Henry VIII (1509–47) and Elizabeth Blount, a lady-in-waiting to Katherine of Aragon.

However, some attempts have been made to do so at the level of peasant society by exploiting manorial court records, mainly in the context of wider studies of a particular peasant community. As in the Italian city states, it is the existence of financial records that makes this possible. In this case the records concerned are payments of fines. These were either *leyrwite*, a fine for single women and widows of unfree status who committed fornication, or *childwyte*, a fine for giving birth to an illegitimate child. These fines were exacted by the manorial court and tended to be mutually exclusive—any one manor would levy either *leyrwite* or *childwyte* but not both. Whilst members of the nobility and gentry would benefit from the receipt of these fines on their manors, they would not be subject to them themselves. Zvi Razi estimated, on the basis of recorded payments of *leyrwite*, that the frequency of illegitimate births on the manor of Halesowen in the West Midlands between 1270 and 1348 was high, with as many as one illegitimate birth for about every two marriages. However, this estimate was based on the assumption that all or most of the women of Halesowen who paid *leyrwite* actually conceived and gave birth out of wedlock, which seems unlikely. Other researchers working on different areas have suggested much lower rates, and the assumption that *leyrwite* payments were associated with the birth of illegitimate children may not be reliable. The birth of a bastard was of course not the only possible evidence of fornication. Razi himself noted that in most of the cases from Halesowen the court roll merely recorded the fact that a woman had lost her virginity: '*deflorata est*'. Only in a few cases was pregnancy specifically mentioned. On the manor of Winslow (Buckinghamshire), *leyrwite* was the name given to the offence, rather than the fine, but seems not to have been mentioned in association with pregnancy, though some women who committed *leyrwite* did have illegitimate children, who are mentioned elsewhere in the court books.

Whilst quantifying the rate of illegitimacy has proved problematic, studies of English peasant society have also looked at the practical consequences of illegitimacy, highlighting examples where customary law differed from both canon and common law in its treatment of bastards. For example, Barbara Hanawalt observed a tendency for the authorities, both lay and ecclesiastical, to take a lenient view of illegitimacy for the practical purpose of ensuring smooth succession to property. There was also an interesting side effect of illegitimacy. Since bastards had no right of inheritance, in theory they were free, as they could not inherit servile status. This interpretation was accepted into common law from the reign of Edward II and bastardy became the usual reply to a claim that one of the litigants was a villein. In practice, however, some bastards were able to inherit. For example, in Halesowen, Razi noted the cases of John Prick, a bond tenant nicknamed 'the bastard' who was able to take over the family holding, presumably because there was no other heir, and of Geoffrey Byrd from Ridgeacre, another bastard who inherited the family holding and apparently did so well that on his death in 1369, his son John was required to pay an entry fine of £5 for the half virgate holding. There was, however, a slight complication in the transfer of the property to John Byrd, as the son of a bastard was not supposed to be able to inherit a customary holding from his father. This difficulty was solved by declaring John to be the son of Felicity, Geoffrey Byrd's wife. In a 1285 case from Wakefield cited by J. S. Beckerman in an unpublished thesis, two brothers contested the right of admission to their father's land. The younger claimed that the elder should not be the heir as he was born before their parents' marriage was solemnized at the church door. The elder argued successfully that it was the local custom for the eldest son born after trothplight to be the heir. However, Beckerman's research into customary law at manorial courts suggests that where inheritance by bastards was permitted, they retained unfree status, and that when manorial custom came to accept the common law doctrine that bastards were free, they lost their ability to inherit. Manorial custom was not the only means by which bastards were able to succeed to lands. Hanawalt points out that the peasantry only resorted to customs and rules if the father had neglected to make arrangements before his death, and that peasants mostly manipulated the rules by making settlements during their lifetime or making arrangements in wills – a similar approach to that taken by the gentry and nobility. This suggests that the consequences of illegitimacy were not necessarily severe in economic terms. It would appear that the social consequences were not too severe either. Razi found that women who had given birth to illegitimate offspring often married subsequently, and not below their social level, while the children were not treated as outcasts. Alice, the co-heiress of a rich peasant from Oldbury, paid *leyrwite* in 1325, but three years later married another rich peasant, Roger Sweyn. The existing literature on English medieval peasant bastardy, while inconclusive as to illegitimacy rates, may suggest that where bastardy did occur, the consequences were not necessarily severe, as manorial customs and developing legal devices such as wills enabled the common law difficulties to be surmounted.

There are no such records for the landed classes. Relevant information can be found in wills, inquisitions post mortem, records of legal disputes, property transactions, ecclesiastical records and private correspondence, but all have weaknesses and can provide only part of the picture.

A number of medieval wills contain explicit mention of bastard offspring. Indeed, the frequency of such bequests caused Sir Nicholas Harris Nicolas to observe, in his preface to *Testamenta Vetusta* (1836), that 'the moral state of this Country is shewn in many instances by the numerous bequests to natural children, who are described in the most unequivocal manner; and if it be argued that in that sense society has not improved, still there is now a feeling of morality which prevents so bold an unblushing avowal of them'. This comment perhaps reveals more about the decline in the status of illegitimate children between the medieval period and the early-nineteenth century than the incidence of illegitimacy in the medieval period. However, the medieval willingness to acknowledge illegitimate children in so many words renders wills a promising source, since it is fairly certain that an individual explicitly identified as 'my bastard son/daughter' is indeed a bastard. Moreover, explicit references to bastards in wills provide positive identification of at least one of the parents. Comparison with bequests made to legitimate children or relatives provides an indication of the relative status of the bastard offspring, whilst wills that record bequests by family members other than the father provide evidence of the extent to which illegitimate children were integrated into the wider family.

However, they do have some disadvantages. There can be difficulties with terminology and interpretation. Some testators certainly made explicit reference to the illegitimacy of a beneficiary. For example, in 1413, Thomas Gippying, alias Lincoln, a London draper, left the residue of his goods to be divided equally between his bastard daughters, Juliana and Beatrice. There is also a bequest to Juliana Pleydon, who might perhaps be their mother. In 1428 John Pigot made a bequest of ten pounds to Matilda *'filiae meae bastard'* and in 1438 Sir John Conyers of Ormesby included Thomas *'filio meo bastardo'* as one of the children to share in the residue of his goods. But this was not always the case. Some testators were more circumspect and referred to a child who is identifiable as illegitimate only by implication or from other knowledge of the family context. For example, the Derbyshire knight Sir John Leek referred in his will of 1522 to his daughter Anne 'got by Jane my wife' and to three further daughters, Susan, Elizabeth and Dorothy, plus a further child as yet unborn 'got by Anne Menwaryng [Mainwaring]'. In this case it is fairly self-evident from the context that the latter three were illegitimate, even if they were not explicitly described as such. In some instances, the illegitimacy of a beneficiary described simply as 'my son' or 'my daughter' can only be inferred from the context, as with the will made by Sir Gerard Usflete in 1405, which referred to one of his sons simply as '*Johanni filio meo*', but then included a bequest to Anyn who, though not his wife, is described as the mother of this John. Poor Anyn was only to get her five pounds if she bothered to turn up for the funeral. The will of Sir Humphrey Stafford of Hooke (December 1442) contained a bequest to his brother John, Bishop of Bath and Wells (Somerset). The illegitimacy of this beneficiary can only be identified from external sources. Fortunately, in this case enough is known about the future Archbishop of Canterbury for this information to be easily obtained. It is less obvious in the case of the will of Sir William Sturmy (d. 1427), which referred to his illegitimate son John Sturmy simply as '*filio meo*'. Contextual information is needed in this case and, where it is missing, bastards may easily go unidentified.

Wills do not necessarily present a full picture of the provision made for the bastard's livelihood. Cash bequests, for example, for the marriage of an illegitimate daughter, or the education of an illegitimate son, will supply part of the story, but may not necessarily provide details of landed provision if this was done as part of an earlier settlement, for example on a marriage. Bequests of personal items or household goods can indicate the closeness of a family relationship, but not how the livelihood of the illegitimate child was to be ensured. However, wills were originally designed to deal with movable property only. Whilst many boroughs permitted bequest of landed property by will, it was only with the development of a legal device known as 'enfeoffment to use' that most landowners were able to dispose of their property by will and it took time for the possibilities to be fully understood by testators. Furthermore, wills are generally of little use for providing information about bastards who were unacknowledged or unprovided for, although there are some exceptions. The will of Sir Henry Pierrepont of Holme in Nottinghamshire, dated 23 October 1489, specifically excluded one Edmund, who claimed to be his bastard son, stating that Edmund was to have 'nether landes, ne tenements ne goodes that to me perteneth an belongith'. In contrast, Sir Henry's godson, Henry, was to receive lands which Sir Henry had purchased during his lifetime, together with a cash sum of twenty pounds, and Roger Pierrepont, a relative, was to receive lands in Mansfield and Pleasley (Derbyshire) with ten pounds. The bulk of the estate, including the lordship of Tibshelf (Derbyshire), which had lately been recovered from the executors of Ralph, Lord Cromwell, was to go to Sir Henry's right heirs. Wills are also unlikely to provide much information about bastards who predeceased their parents, although this is not necessarily the case if the bastards lived long enough to have children of their own. John Godyn, a London grocer who died in 1469, left a reversionary interest in certain tenements to George, John and Johanna Godyn, the children of his bastard son Thomas Godyn, in succession, with other tenements left to John. Wills therefore tend to underestimate the number of cases of illegitimacy. There are also some potential pitfalls in the language of wills. A bequest to 'my natural son' might easily be assumed to mean an illegitimate son, but this is not necessarily a safe assumption, since the term 'natural' could simply be used to distinguish between biological children and step–children.

Inquisitions post mortem are another useful source of information. These provide a supposedly impartial account of the rights of succession to property held in chief of the Crown, although the extent to which they were truly impartial has been open to debate. An inquisition was held when an individual who held land in chief of the Crown died, in order to determine what property they held in each county, how much it was worth, the identity of the next heir and whether they were of age. The purpose was to ascertain the value of the property that was taken into the king's hands, and whether there was an adult male heir to whom the property should be released, or whether there were opportunities for the Crown to benefit from feudal incidents (payments to, or rights of the lord on the death of the tenant, for example wardship of the heir if under age.) As the inquisitions dealt specifically with right of succession, these records not only identify the next heir, but contain details of property settlements, which affected the property and may explicitly state that particular individuals were illegitimate, especially if the deceased was a bastard without heirs of his body, whose property would therefore revert to the superior lord—a process known as escheat. Inquisitions post mortem are of particular use in identifying individuals who were themselves bastards. They do, however, have some weaknesses. One problem is that they were only held for individuals who were believed to hold land of the Crown in chief, although the juries would report on all the property the deceased held in the county in question, whether held directly of the Crown or not. Furthermore, their accuracy as a source has been questioned, particularly with regard to the valuations, and the possibility that the juries could be ill-informed or open to manipulation.

Inquisitions were taken in each county where the deceased was believed to have held land, and their findings did not always tally exactly. It was certainly not uncommon for juries in different counties to arrive at different conclusions regarding the identity of the next heir. For example, an inquisition held at Oxford in 1357 found that John Bereford, son of Edmund Bereford was a bastard who died without heir of his body, but that the property he held in the county had previously been settled with reversion after John's death to his brother Baldwin, whereas an inquisition held in Derby did not mention his illegitimacy and simply found that his brother Baldwin was his heir. A Warwick jury also omitted any mention of bastardy, but found that he died without heir of his body. Similarly, an inquisition held in Berkshire in 1349 following the death of William Hastings, an illegitimate son of Laurence Hastings, Earl of Pembroke, found that William held the manor of Benham Valence for life, together with certain other lands in Westbrook and Newbury, and that he had no heir because he was a bastard. A similar inquisition taken in Kent found that William held the manor of Cleyndon for life from the heir of Laurence Hastings, as a result of a gift by Laurence, but made no reference to his illegitimacy, whilst an inquisition taken in Surrey found erroneously that John de Hastings, the infant son of his kinsman Laurence de Hastings was his heir. After the death of the bastard William de Vescy of Kildare in 1314, the property he held should have reverted to the right heirs of William de Vescy, his father, by virtue of a previous settlement, but the various juries came to different conclusions. A Pickering jury was aware that the property should remain to William senior's right heir, but was unaware who this might have been, whilst a jury in York merely observed that he died without heir. A Northumberland jury found that the right heir was John, son of Arnald de Percy. A number of claimants came forward before Gilbert de Aton, a distant kinsman of William de Vescy senior, was eventually determined to be the heir.

In some cases, reference was made to the illegitimacy of a third party, such as William, the bastard son of Sir John de Cokeryngton, who held certain lands in Cokeryngton (Lincolnshire) of William de Vavasour, according to the 1370 inquisition on the latter. Similarly, the inquisition on the death of Joan Richmond in 1499 reveals that she was previously married to Thomas Herle, bastard son of Sir John Herle of Ilfracombe, who had conveyed certain tenements in Exeter to feoffees in order to provide for his illegitimate son.

Records of legal disputes over property may contain allegations of illegitimacy on the part of one or more of the parties to the dispute, or the ancestors on whom their claim depended. Where property was at stake, litigation was common, and a claim of illegitimacy on the part of a rival was a tactic that could be used if there was any room for doubt, as occurred in the Kerdiston case, which will be discussed in more detail in Chapter Four. The difficulties are that it is not always clear whether the allegations had any real basis in fact and relevant documents may be scattered or the records may be incomplete, inconclusive or inaccurate, as they rely on the litigants' reconstruction of family histories. The case of Mistress Swete, outlined in the introduction to *Kingsford's Stonor Letters and Papers 1290–1483*, illustrates the complexity medieval lawyers faced in disentangling the various relationships after the elapse of several generations amid potential claims of bastardy.

In 1836, the antiquary Sir Nicholas Harris Nicolas was inspired to publish a *Treatise on the Law of Adulterine Bastardy* in which he aimed to 'insert, in chronological order, and as nearly as possible in the words of the original, every authority and every case that in any way bears on the question'. His motivation for conducting an in-depth study of the origins of the English law of bastardy was the 1813 Banbury peerage case, which turned on the parentage of Nicholas Knollys alias Vaux, who had claimed the right to sit in the House of Lords as Earl of Banbury in 1661. Knollys was purportedly the second and surviving son of William Knollys, who had been created Earl of Banbury on 18 August 1626. The circumstances of Nicholas' birth were such that there were grounds for suspicion as to his actual biological parentage. At the time of Nicholas's birth in 1631, the Earl was over eighty. The Earl's wife Elizabeth, who was almost forty years his junior, gave birth to Nicholas at the home of a family friend, Lord Vaux of Harrowden, whom she subsequently married within five weeks of her husband's death in 1633. Nicholas Knollys alias Vaux was nonetheless the son of a married woman, and should have been presumed legitimate by English law. He sat in the Lords as Earl of Banbury in the Convention Parliament from June to November 1660, but having received no writ of summons to the next parliament in May 1661, petitioned the king. Despite the opinion of the Committee of Privileges on 1 July 1661 that 'Nicholas, Earl of Banbury, is a legitimate person', and a further statement on 19 July 1661 that he was in the eyes of the law the son of the late earl of Banbury, the matter was not resolved before Nicholas's death in 1674. His son Charles Knollys made several attempts to establish his own right to the Earldom without resolution, and after his death the matter seems to have been dropped until 1806, when his descendant William Knollys petitioned the Crown for a writ of summons, which led to the resolution of the House of Lords in 1813 that 'the Petitioner is not entitled to use the title etc. of Earl of Banbury', to which Nicolas took such exception. As will be seen, the Committee of Privileges in 1661 had in fact applied the law that developed during the late medieval period. Nicolas' *Treatise* provides an interesting narrative on the development of the law relating to this particular category of illegitimacy.

For information on how parents made some form of provision in land for their illegitimate children it is necessary to use records of property settlements such as feet of fines. Feet of fines are the court copies of agreements following disputes over property. In practice, these often relate to fictitious disputes as they were used in order to have the transfer of ownership of land recorded officially for conveyancing purposes. As there was no reason to identify bastards explicitly as such in these documents, rather the reverse, they seldom did so and are mainly of use in establishing details of provision for bastards whose existence has been identified from other records. One example, however, in which bastards were described explicitly is a 1425 fine in which John Chenduyt mentioned his bastard son and daughter. Illegitimacy may sometimes be inferred from the wording, as in the case of Sir John Arundell of Lanherne (d. 1435), who settled a reversionary interest in certain property to Emeline Wode to hold during the life of her daughter Agnes, with successive reversions to Edward Arundell, son of Agnes and then to his various siblings. The implication is that Edward and his brothers and sisters were the offpring of Sir John by Agnes Wode. Such records are of course reliable only as evidence of how the landowner intended to settle his property, and the eventual outcome might well be different. Sir John Arundell later resettled his property and the outcome of John Chenduyt's settlement was not a happy one for his surviving bastard daughter.

Dispensations granted to enable those of illegitimate birth to pursue a career in the Church are useful in that they relate to individuals whose illegitimacy was not in doubt. They generally also give some details of the context of the illegitimacy and, in some cases, even the identity or at least the rank of the individual's parents. Such dispensations are found in bishops' registers, papal letters and the papal penitentiary records and are primarily useful for identifying bastards for whom provision was made in the form of a church career. These records are useful in that they are likely to be accurate regarding the illegitimacy, but they do not necessarily provide full details of the parentage, only stating the type of illegitimacy involved. They are however a useful source of information on this aspect of illegitimacy, which is seldom available in secular records. Usually cases involve children of a single man and single woman '*de soluto et soluta*', but occasionally they involve children of clerics: '*de subdiaconus et soluta*' or, more rarely, '*de presbytero et soluta*'. Parents of high status were more likely to be mentioned explicitly in dispensations. The dispensation that permitted John Wensley to hold benefices with cure of souls identified him as son of the late Sir Thomas Wensley (d. 1403), and as the son of a married nobleman and an unmarried woman. Noble parentage was often mentioned even if the names of the actual parents were not given, as in the cases of Thomas Ludlow, Rector of Tawstock (Devon) who was described in a dispensation of 1435 as the son of an unmarried nobleman and an unmarried noblewoman. Thomas Fitzwilliam, Rector of Stock in the diocese of Bath and Wells, and later of Emley and Sprotborough (Yorkshire) as a member of the Fitzwilliam family of Emley and Sprotborough, was described as of 'noble race' in dispensations of 1429 and 1437. The dispensation granted in 1432 to Alice Burton, nun of the Augustinian priory of St Margaret, Bramhall, in the diocese of Salisbury, allowing her to hold any benefice wont to be held by nuns of her order, similarly described her as the daughter of an unmarried nobleman and an unmarried noblewoman. Dispensations of this type obviously include only those bastards who followed a church career, and probably not all of those. It is clear that some cases only came to light after the individuals concerned had received the first tonsure and so it is probable that there were others of illegitimate birth who never disclosed this fact. For example, Thomas de Mandeville of the diocese of Norwich managed to have himself promoted to holy orders and acquire two benefices before his illegitimacy came to light in 1402. Another possible example of this is the case of Sir Nicholas Stafford, son of Richard, Lord Stafford of Clifton (d. 1380). He was in receipt of a papal dispensation, but it was not for illegitimacy. In October 1349 he obtained a dispensation to enable him to hold a benefice with cure of souls, he being in his eighteenth year. Neither the original petition to the pope by his father nor the subsequent dispensation made any mention of illegitimate birth. It is clear the purpose of the dispensation sought was to address a deficiency of age rather than birth as the same petition had sought a similar dispensation for another son, John, aged 16, which was not granted. However, both boys must have been illegitimate, since their father did not marry until 1337 and Richard Stafford's heir was Sir Richard de Stafford the younger, who was born *c.* 1339, when Nicholas would already have been eight years old and John would have been six. In some cases, the full facts of the case were not disclosed initially, but came to light at a later date, requiring a further dispensation, which provided more details of the circumstances of the illegitimate birth. John de Saunford, a canon of London, received dispensations on account of illegitimacy in 1364 and 1367 and subsequent provisions of benefices and canonries of Wells and St John's, Beverley (Yorkshire), but when it subsequently came to light that he was an adulterine bastard, his mother having been married to someone other than his father at the time of his birth, some doubt was cast on the validity of the dispensation and the provision of benefices. Robert Dalton, a priest of York, who sought a dispensation as the son of an unmarried man and married woman, initially concealed the fact that his parents were related and had been living together. Further confirmation of his dispensations was required when this subsequently came to light in 1401. Dispensations are therefore likely to under-represent the true number of illegitimates in the Church.

Ecclesiastical records can also provide examples that arose from disputed or problematic marriages. In October 1319 William de Kirkebrunne, a subdeacon, obtained a dispensation to minister in the orders which he had received, to be promoted to higher orders, and to hold a benefice. This dispensation was required because his parents, who were related in the third and fourth degree, had intermarried without dispensation. Richard de Hale, who as rector of Bentley (Lichfield diocese) already held a dispensation for illegitimacy, claimed to have believed that the subsequent clandestine marriage of his parents had legitimized him when he resigned Bentley and accepted further benefices without having obtained a further dispensation. This proved not to be correct, and he needed to obtain a further dispensation in 1328 in order to retain his new benefices. When Richard FitzAlan, Earl of Arundel, had his marriage to Isabella Despenser annulled in 1344, their son Edmund, who was thereby effectively bastardised, appealed to the papal authorities.

Whilst private letters are insufficiently numerous for this period to permit their use as anything more than anecdotal evidence, they are of some help in throwing light on contemporary attitudes, though references are not always explicit. Examples of bastards occur in connection with all the main private letter collections that survive from the later Middle Ages—those of the Pastons, Plumptons, Stonors and Celys. The Pastons were a gentry family whose rapid rise to prominence in fifteenth-century England is documented in a substantial body of correspondence that has been much plundered by historians since it was rediscovered in the eighteenth century. A letter of Margaret Paston relates with some relish the interesting case of John Heydon's wife, one of the relatively few known examples of a bastard being born to a married woman and disowned by her husband. But as far as the family's own activities were concerned, the surviving letters are rather more circumspect. There are only hints of Paston bastard children in the letters. A letter of John Paston III to his mother Margaret, in which he asks her to see that his 'little man' is sent to school, may well refer to an illegitimate child. Edmond Paston fathered a child by a married woman known as 'Mistress Dixon'. Sir John Paston II had a bastard daughter, who does not appear to be mentioned in the surviving letters at all, yet she received a legacy of ten marks in her grandmother Margaret Paston's will in 1482. (A mark was a unit of accounting worth 13 shillings and fourpence, or two-thirds of a pound sterling.)

The Yorkshire knight Sir William Plumpton had two bastard sons: Robert, who was common clerk of the city of York between 1490 and 1507, and William. Sir William also had a legitimate son, another Robert, by his second marriage to Joan Wintringham. Since this clandestine marriage took place in the 1450s and was not made public until 1468, Sir William does not appear to have worried unduly about any consequences for his son of being presumed a bastard. The letters of the Stonor family from Oxfordshire refer to the complicated legal case in which a useful piece of documentary evidence had come to light, and that as a result their opponent 'most breff Margete, Suster to Th., bastard', whilst Thomas Stonor (d. 1474) is believed to have married an illegitimate daughter of William de la Pole, Duke of Suffolk. The Cely letters, which document the affairs of a family of London wool merchants, provide perhaps the most useful insight into attitudes, since they include a letter in which a young man confessed to his brother that he believed he had made a girl pregnant. Another letter collection, the Armburgh papers, relates to a disputed inheritance in which a rather implausible allegation of bastardy was made, though this was not the essence of the dispute. (See Chapter Three for further details.) Letter collections provide useful illustrations of what medieval gentry and burgesses thought about illegitimacy and the ways in which it affected them but, as with wills, additional contextual information about the families concerned is usually required.

The nature of the available evidence creates a crucial difference between the study of illegitimacy among the medieval nobility and gentry and that of illegitimacy at lower levels of society or during later periods. The manorial records on which studies of illegitimacy among the peasantry depend gave the names of the mothers, as they dealt with penalties and fines incurred by women for fornication or bastard-bearing. In the parish records of the sixteenth century and later, in which the intention was to record the birth of an illegitimate child and of the two parents, the mother was the one whose identity was not in doubt. Studies of illegitimacy in medieval peasant society and of illegitimacy more generally from the early modern period onwards thus tended to focus on the mothers. In contrast, records from which details of the bastard offspring of the nobility and gentry can be found tended to relate to financial provision made for the livelihood of the illegitimate offspring in a will or property settlement or to legal disputes over property. As a result they are more likely to be identified with the father than the mother, though in some cases the name of the mother might be mentioned as a form of identification. As explained further in the next chapter, children born to a married woman were generally deemed to be legitimate offspring of her husband (though there were some exceptions). For this reason there will by necessity be more emphasis on the fathers in this book, although mothers will be included wherever information is available. Similarly, bastard daughters tend to appear less frequently in the records than bastard sons, just as legitimate daughters appear less frequently than legitimate sons. Elsewhere in Europe the records are more helpful in identifying female bastards. In fifteenth-century Florence it was recognized that raising children, whether legitimate or not, involved a financial outlay and under the *castato* tax, introduced in 1427, bastards were tax-deductible as a personal expense and so more likely to be recorded. Records of the civic fund, the *Monte delle doti*, in which fathers invested to provide a future dowry for their daughters also provides information on provision for legitimate and illegitimate daughters.

For the reasons above, the nature of the surviving sources makes it very difficult to establish any accurate estimate of the prevalence of illegitimate births among the upper levels of late medieval English society. However, the three biographical volumes of *The History of Parliament* relating to the members of the House of Commons during the period 1386–1421 (also now available online) provide a sample of over 3,000 individuals living in the middle of the period under study, who were eligible to serve as knights of the shire or burgesses, and whose lives, property and family relationships have already been researched as thoroughly as possible within the surviving records. Of the 3,168 named individuals who served as MPs during this period, forty-three or 1.36 per cent can be shown to have definitely or probably fathered an illegitimate child and of these, thirty-four or 1.0 per cent of the total number of MPs are known to have done so. However, not all individuals named in the parliamentary returns are identifiable and very limited information has been discovered for others so a better measure is against the subset of 1453 MPs who can be identified as having definitely or probably fathered offspring. For the sample of MPs as a whole, legitimate sons outnumber legitimate daughters by 2,045 to 1,185. Since the actual proportion of sons would be expected to be nearer fifty per cent than sixty-three per cent, there is clearly under-representation of legitimate daughters in the surviving evidence, but the number of known legitimate daughters of the MPs with illegitimate children, forty-six, is higher than that of legitimate sons, thirty-four. This is most likely a reflection of the fact that both legitimate daughters and illegitimate children were of greater significance in the absence of a legitimate son and heir and are thus more likely to appear in the records. In the case of sixteen (38.1 per cent) of the forty-two known or probable begetters of bastards no legitimate children at all are recorded. It is a reasonable inference therefore that illegitimate children are significantly under-represented in the evidence.

What follows is not a scientific study of the prevalence of illegitimacy among the medieval English landed and mercantile classes, but a survey of the context within which they lived, and the opportunities that were open to them. Chapter One deals with the theory of bastardy and the complexities of the law relating to bastardy and landed property. Chapter Two is a detailed case study of illegitimacy in practice, looking at one particular noble family, the Warenne earls of Surrey, in context. Chapter Three is a more general survey of attitudes towards sexual misconduct and the procreation of bastards. In Chapter Four, provision for bastards, in the form of landed property or money is considered in more detail. The fifth chapter considers wider opportunities for bastards: in the Church, in military service and in public life.

Chapter 1

Bastardy in Theory: The Legal Context

*a proof might indeed be made in the court of Christianity, which in some cases is
contrary to the law and customs of England.*

(Bracton, IV)

In 1381 Sir John Ipstones (d. 1394) dispossessed Maud Swynnerton, the young granddaughter of Nicholas Beck, of the manors of Hopton and Tean (Staffordshire). In the subsequent court case, Sir John contended that he was the nephew and next heir of Nicholas Beck. His argument was that on Beck's death, his two daughters, Elizabeth and Margaret had entered as his heiresses, but that both had died without heirs of their bodies and that Maud was illegitimate. As Maud's mother, Elizabeth Beck, had married Robert Swynnerton, it is probable that Ipstone argued that the marriage was invalid because the couple were related within the prohibited degrees. The matter was eventually referred to the Bishop of Coventry and Lichfield and although the legal argument proved untenable, Ipstones managed to remain in possession for the next seven years. Maud was supported by her father-in-law, Sir Richard Peshale, who had a long-standing grudge against the Ipstones family. By the time Peshale died in 1388, Maud was already a widow, and Ipstones seized an opportunity. He and a group of armed men abducted Maud and forced her to marry his own son, William. Ipstones was a powerful, if not notorious, man in the locality and it proved difficult for Maud's relatives to take action against him. In December 1390 he managed to secure a papal dispensation absolving William Ipstones and Maud from the sentence of excommunication they would have incurred for both marrying in secret without the publication of banns and for being within the prohibited three degrees of kinship. The dispensation decreed that the couple were to be separated for a time and might then remarry, after which past and future children would be declared legitimate. Ipstones thus effected a *fait accompli* in which both claimants to the property were united in marriage and the legitimacy of their offspring was a matter of record. This case illustrates how both canon law and common law approaches to illegitimacy had an impact on the lives and estates of the landed classes: matters relating to marriage and legitimacy were reserved for the Church, but when it came to property, illegitimacy was simply one factor which could be used tactically in a dispute. Violence was of course another.

The word 'legitimate' derives from the Latin *lex*, *leg-* meaning 'law'. In order to understand the implications of illegitimacy in late medieval England it is therefore necessary to turn to the law. Illegitimacy was a complex issue, which impinged on the lives of the nobility and gentry in several ways. They might have had bastard children of their own, for whom they wished to provide. They might even have wished to favour the children of a second marriage over those of an annulled first marriage, as in the case of Richard FitzAlan, Earl of Arundel (d. 1376), who ensured that the son of his annulled first marriage was declared to be illegitimate so that he would have no right of inheritance. Illegitimacy might have been raised in a dispute over property rights, with bastardy alleged against the person or an ancestor of one or other party, or even both. Members of the landowning classes might have also had tenants who were illegitimate; a situation which could have positive or negative implications for the landowner, depending on the circumstances. Illegitimacy meant that an individual was technically *fillius nullius*, the child of no one, so legally had no relatives or heirs other than their own children. An illegitimate tenant who died without an heir of his/her body (legitimate child of his/her own) could therefore provide a windfall, as the property would then pass to the lord by the process known as escheat. On the other hand, a tenant of unfree status might claim freedom as a result of his or her illegitimacy, since they could not inherit unfree status.

A further cause of the legal complexity was that rather than a single law code dealing with illegitimacy and inheritance, there were two overlapping and sometimes conflicting law codes. As the events of the Council of Merton had made clear, church, or canon law, which determined the validity of marriage, and the English common law, which dealt with property rights, did not agree on certain crucial points. The result was a complex situation in which a child might be regarded as legitimate by the Church but not by the courts for the purpose of inheritance or vice versa. This provided opportunities for canny individuals to exploit the situation for their own benefit.

Canon Law

In order for the legitimacy or otherwise of the offspring of a marriage to have become a concern, there first needed to be a clear understanding of what constituted a valid marriage. Sara McDougall has recently shown that it was only after the requirements of a valid marriage were finally resolved in the early-thirteenth century that the concepts of legitimate and illegitimate children as we now understand them developed. Prior to that, legitimacy of offspring could be defined more by lineage than by marriage laws, with the status of the mother proving a significant factor.

During the twelfth century, the canon law view of marriage gradually evolved as it became accepted that Church courts had jurisdiction over the validity of marriage, and a body of case law developed as a consequence. The fundamental concern of the Church was with the spiritual nature of marriage and the salvation of souls. During the second half of the twelfth century, judgements on marriage cases by Pope Alexander III (1159–1181) stressed the need for the free consent of the bride and groom (and no one else) in order to make a valid marriage. A Christian couple who were free to marry could create a permanent lifelong bond simply by exchanging vows in the present tense, or by exchanging vows in the future tense and subsequently consummating the marriage. David d'Avray has pointed out that the western Christian marriage tradition which evolved over the 800 years from St Augustine of Hippo in the fifth century to the pontificate of Innocent III in the early-thirteenth century was unlike that of any other major civilization in that it combined indissolubility with monogamy. Other marriage systems either permitted polygamy or allowed for divorce.

Innocent III (1198–1216) sought to translate the notion of the indissolubility of marriage that had evolved over the course of the preceding centuries into one that could be applied in practice. Any rule-based system inevitably leaves room for creative interpretation and the discovery of loopholes. As the idea of the indissolubility of marriage gained ground, the elites continued to change marital partners making use of the legal loophole provided by the rules on forbidden degrees of relationship (consanguinity). Degrees of relationship were counted by the number of steps from the common ancestor, so that a brother and sister sharing a common parent would be related in the first degree, and first cousins, sharing a common grandparent, would be related in the second degree and so on. Until the early-thirteenth century, the number of forbidden degrees of relationship that would invalidate a marriage was seven. A couple related in the seventh degree shared a common great-great-great-great-great-grandparent—a level of connection which provided ample opportunity for the discovery of a hitherto unknown relationship with an unwanted spouse. The Fourth Lateran Council (1215) reduced the number of prohibited degrees of relationship that invalidated a marriage to a more practical number of four. It was rather more feasible to identify those sharing a common great-great-grandparent. The council also called for the public announcement of banns prior to marriage so that any potential impediments could be brought to light before the marriage took place. It stopped short, however, of declaring clandestine marriages invalid, as the doctrine that free consent was sufficient to make a marriage prevailed. In the absence of banns, there could be no presumption of good faith should an impediment subsequently come to light, but the inclusion of many of Alexander III's decisions in a compilation of case law issued in 1234 ensured that the doctrine of free consent remained legally binding throughout the medieval period and beyond.

From the thirteenth century therefore there was a body of canon law which explained what constituted a valid marriage. It also clarified what constituted an impediment to marriage which could be used as grounds for subsequent annulment. Consanguinity was not the only such impediment. Other impediments which caused a marriage to be annulled included those in which the consent given by the bride and groom was compromised in some way. This could be because one of them had previously formed a contract of marriage with a third party, or they were incapable of giving meaningful consent because they were under age or mentally incapable, or had only consented under duress. Children below the age of seven were not deemed capable of consenting to marriage. Those aged between seven and puberty (notionally twelve for girls and fourteen for boys) could give future consent which became binding if the parties had intercourse or gave present consent when they reached puberty. Until puberty they were not considered to have the physical capacity to contract a binding marriage. Another lack of physical capacity, impotence, could also be an impediment if the other party was unaware at the time of consenting to the marriage. These impediments also had implications for the subsequent status of any children of an annulled marriage.

Whilst the word 'bastard' was used indiscriminately, in England at least, and without any offensive intent, to describe anyone of illegitimate birth, different types of bastards had different rights under canon law. Canon lawyers classified children into four groups according to the marital status of the parents and whether or not the union of the parents was 'natural', that is, not subject to any impediment, such as being related within the prohibited degrees. Children who were born of a lawful marriage were both natural and legitimate; those born outside marriage to parents who were free to marry were merely natural and not legitimate; adopted children were legitimate only but not natural; whilst those who were born of a prohibited union, or whose paternity was unknown were neither legitimate nor natural, and were known as *spurii*. These distinctions had practical implications, particularly with regard to *spurii* who were regarded as inferior to natural illegitimate children and unlike them, could not be legitimated by the subsequent marriage of the parents.

In continental Europe, the legal system was generally based on the *ius commune*, a combination of canon law and Roman law, which incorporated the canon law distinction between different types of illegitimacy. *Naturales* had some limited rights of inheritance (one-twelfth of the father's property, by testament if there were legitimate heirs or on intestacy if there were no legitimate heirs), but *spurii* could neither inherit from their fathers nor even receive gifts during the father's lifetime. Whilst there were local variations, which will be covered in more detail in Chapter Five, the main principles of canon law relating to legitimacy were incorporated into civil law relating to inheritance. Legitimation of bastards was also possible in certain circumstances, though there were still distinctions in the forms of legitimation available to *naturales* and *spurii*. Such legitimation transformed the legal status of the bastard though, in those countries or cities where illegitimacy was regarded as a stigma or taint, a legitimated bastard might still be barred from political office or membership of a guild.

Common Law

English common law, however, took a somewhat different approach and, as noted in Pollock and Maitland's classic *History of English Law before the Time of Edward I:* 'in our English law bastardy cannot be called a status or condition'. Nevertheless, the thirteenth-century treatise on *The Laws and Customs of England*, known as Bracton borrowed from canon lawyers in describing the different types of children, subdivides natural and legitimate children according to whether they were heirs on the side of either or both parents, or not at all. For the author of Bracton, it was the distinction between children who were heirs and those who were not that was the crucial point, rather than that between different types of illegitimate children. The important issue was whether a child was eligible to inherit, which was a consequence of legitimacy, rather than the legitimacy itself. If a child was illegitimate, and therefore unable to inherit, reasons for illegitimacy were not so important.

Yet this did not necessarily mean that the circumstances of birth were completely irrelevant. They could be of crucial importance. The validity of a marriage, and hence the legitimacy of children, was held to be a matter for the Church courts. However, common law and canon law differed on a number of crucial issues. Canon law held that natural children were legitimated if parents subsequently married, but this was not the case in English common law. As a result, a different verdict on the illegitimacy or otherwise of an individual could be found depending on the court in which the case was heard. Thus, although the reasons for illegitimacy did not affect the status of a person once he or she had been proved to be illegitimate, the need to ensure that the determination of legitimacy was in accordance with common law meant that it was important that the reasons for an allegation of bastardy were clearly specified. There is plenty of evidence that mistakes could and did happen in practice, either by accident or design.

Although closely connected, legitimacy and the right of inheritance were slightly different issues. Common law inheritance followed the rules of male primogeniture and whilst a legitimate child was eligible to inherit, younger sons and daughters would not necessarily do so directly, although there was always the possibility that they or their descendants might eventually inherit as a result of a failure in the main line. This absence of any right to collateral inheritance was the main disadvantage that distinguished the bastard from legitimate younger children. The other, which did not disadvantage the bastard so much as their legitimate half-brothers and sisters, was that if they had been given a share of the family property and later died with no heirs of their bodies, or if their direct line of issue failed, there would be no common law right of inheritance for their legitimate siblings and their descendants. In a case from the reign of Edward II it was even noted that 'if the issue of a bastard die without heir of his body the bastard is said to die without heir; and this holds good down to the fifth degree, when one can make a resort without mentioning the bastard'. Prior to 1290, this did not matter too much in practical terms, as property would have been granted by means of subinfeudation. This meant that the property was granted so that the bastard would hold the property of the father and his heirs, and would therefore escheat or revert to them should he die without heir of his body. In simple terms, person A might grant land to person B, who would hold it of A. If B died without an heir of his body the land would escheat back to A. However, B might grant some of this land to person C, who would hold it of B. If C then died without heir of his body, it would escheat to B. Over time, the process of subinfeudation inevitably led to very complex landholding arrangements. In 1290 the statute *Quia Emptores* simplified matters so that any property granted was held directly of the superior lord from whom the grantor had held it and the grantor was removed from the chain. After *Quia Emptores*, if B granted the land to C, C would hold it directly of A and B and his heirs would no longer have any interest in the property. One effect of this was that any property granted to a bastard son would no longer escheat to the father and his right heirs if the bastard died without legitimate issue, but was alienated for good. As a result of *Quia Emptores*, from the late-thirteenth century onwards various legal devices evolved that would enable a donor greater control over the distribution of his property after his death.

Differences in Practice

From the above it can be seen that the Church was concerned with internal matters in terms of the intentions and good faith of the couple whereas the common law was more concerned with outward signs such as the formal marriage ceremony. For the Church, marriage was a sacrament, and good faith was important. The common law was concerned with the inheritance of real property and was therefore more interested in the evidence of marriage than the spiritual bond. The different priorities of canon law and common law informed their approaches to determining legitimacy. In general, the Church was more tolerant of bastards born outside lawful wedlock, provided that they were 'natural', whereas common law was more favourable to those born within wedlock, whether natural or not. Both codes had some difficulty in dealing with the children of marriages that were subsequently annulled.

Our understanding of both codes is derived from legal treatises, which are more theoretical in content, and the records of actual legal cases. For the English common law, as well as the formal record of cases, we also have less formal accounts in the form of the Year Books, notes made by law students observing the proceedings, which provide an insight into arguments actually made in court. The Year Book accounts are particularly helpful in showing how those involved actually understood the law, and how this understanding and practice evolved over time.

Accounts of legal cases demonstrate that individuals at all levels of society had some basic understanding of the requirements of a valid marriage and were likely to have been aware of issues relating to the legitimacy or otherwise of their children and the potential legal pitfalls and loopholes, but the complexity was such that there was plenty of work for the growing legal profession. The convoluted nature of the laws relating to bastardy meant that litigants often went to some lengths to avoid mentioning it in court at all, or tried to manipulate the discrepancy between the two legal codes by phrasing a plea in such a way as to avoid use of the word 'bastard', claiming instead that an individual was not 'not the son of' the supposed parent or that his father had not been married to his mother.

The approaches taken by the canon and common law in different sets of circumstances are described below.

Single man and single woman who were free to marry but did not do so
Children born of unmarried parents who were free to marry (those born *ex soluto et soluta*) were illegitimate by both canon and common law, being born outside wedlock. Such children were natural but not legitimate (*naturales tantum et non legitimi*) and might be the product of a casual liaison or of a more regular concubinage. Such children could not take holy orders without a dispensation and had no common law rights to inheritance, but were the category of

illegitimate children treated most leniently under canon law. According to canon law, such children could receive testamentary bequests from their father's estate and if there were no legitimate children, the father could leave his entire estate to his natural but illegitimate children.

Single man and single woman who married after the birth of the child

The subsequent marriage of the parents of a natural but illegitimate child led to a situation in which canon and common laws held different interpretations. Such children were regarded as legitimate by canon law. A decretal of Alexander III sent to the Bishop of Exeter in 1172 stated that the power of marriage was such that children born before marriage were held to be legitimate afterwards. This should be seen in the context of the efforts by the Church to define and promote marriage. Legitimation by subsequent marriage had not been part of classical Roman law. In the Roman Republic, illegitimate children acquired the civil status of their mother and the only means of formal legitimation was by adoption.

In medieval England, children born before marriage remained bastards according to common law. Under canon law a child could not be disinherited on the grounds of being born before marriage. However, the determination of cases involving inheritance was a matter for the secular courts. In the twelfth century when papal judge-delegates dared to adjudicate in an English inheritance case involving a claim through a mother who was challenged as illegitimate, Henry II objected in the strongest of terms to the infringement of his rights and Alexander III ordered that the case be returned to the royal courts, acknowledging in another decretal that the secular court had final jurisdiction over the ownership of the land, whilst reserving the right to canonical determination of legitimacy. This was a compromise that canonists tried hard to justify, but which, in reality, was based on nothing more substantial than expediency. The procedure developed that, where an allegation of bastardy arose, the secular courts would send a writ to the bishop to determine the legitimacy issue. The different views of the two legal systems regarding the legitimacy of prenuptial children therefore potentially posed a problem. In the late-twelfth century the ecclesiastical authorities had apparently co-operated with the secular authorities by pronouncing on the issue of whether or not an individual was born before or after marriage, as this is the procedure described in *The Treatise on the Laws and Customs of the Kingdom of England* compiled in the late 1180s and now commonly known as Glanvill after Henry II's justiciar Ranulf de Glanvill. Whilst the attribution to Glanvill is of later date and he was probably not the actual author, the treatise provides a useful guide to actual practice in the royal courts at the time:

> 'If there is a dispute as to whether he was born before or after the marriage, this is resolved, as was said, before an ecclesiastical judge, who is to inform the lord king or his justices of his judgment; so that the decision of the ecclesiastical court concerning the marriage, namely whether he who claims the inheritance was born before or after the marriage was contracted, shall be used by the lord king's court in awarding or denying him the disputed inheritance.'

The English ecclesiastical courts appear to have been slow to adopt the doctrine of legitimation by subsequent marriage, hence their apparent willingness to answer queries as to whether children were born before or after marriage even after the decretal of Alexander III. By the late 1220s, however, this process of dealing with cases involving a birth before espousals proved problematic, with the confusion as to how to handle such allegations being sufficient enough to delay or halt proceedings. Even so, it seems that the bishops were initially willing to tolerate accommodating the English courts. In 1234 an assembly of lords temporal and spiritual reached an agreement that such cases would be referred to the bishop to determine whether the individual concerned had been born before the marriage of his parents or after. Matters really only came to a head in the following year when the scholar and theologian Robert Grosseteste (c. 1170–1253) was appointed to the bishopric of Lincoln and found it quite impossible to reconcile such a process with his conscience. Having refused to respond to a question in that form he was cited on 21 October 1235 to appear before the king's court. He wrote at great length to William of Ralegh (d. 1250), the Chief Justice, to justify his view that the common law position was 'a wicked and unjust law, contrary to natural and divine law and also to canon and civil law' and that justices who persisted in disinheriting children born before matrimony were, in the words of the prophet Amos, 'turning judgment into wormwood and forsaking justice in the land'. Grosseteste also claimed that there was an English custom that if such children were placed under a pall or mantle at the subsequent marriage of their parents they were regarded 'as legitimate and entitled to inherit', a custom for which there is little supporting evidence. If the custom did exist, it may have been a form of adoption, but cannot be accepted as evidence that English law was once in accordance with the canon law, as Grosseteste claimed, for it is by no means clear that legitimation by subsequent marriage was part of canon law before the twelfth century. Grosseteste also sought guidance from the Archbishop of Canterbury as to how he was to deal with this matter of conscience. In 1236 the clergy accordingly raised the matter at the Merton Parliament, but, as noted above, the barons rejected their arguments with the response that they did not wish to change the laws of England. Thereafter cases of 'special bastardy' were not referred to the bishop but were heard in the secular courts.

The debate at Merton concerning legitimation by subsequent marriage requires further consideration as it demonstrates the nobility apparently stating a strongly held view on a matter relating to legitimacy. It might appear that their reluctance to agree to legitimation by subsequent marriage arose from concerns over its effect on inheritance of property. In practice, however, the barons were unlikely to be personally affected. Where marriage alliances and accompanying property settlements were arranged between landed families, cases of precontract or prior clandestine marriage involving one of the parties would be a more serious problem than a child of the couple being born before the marriage. It is probably best interpreted as an expression of the struggle concerning foreign influences which is related in the thirteenth-century chronicles of Matthew Paris and Roger of Wendover. From the late twelfth century the papacy had increasingly been asserting its right to taxation of the church and to appoint candidates to ecclesiastical office. This was deeply unpopular. In 1232 there had been a series of attacks on Italian clerics appointed to English livings. Similarly, politics at court had been characterised by disputes between English-born ministers such as Hubert de Burgh, earl of Kent (c. 1170–1243) and more recent arrivals such as Peter des Roches, bishop of Winchester (d. 1238). Viewed in this light, the barons' famous *nolumus* appears less a concern over legitimacy than a straightforward desire to resist the imposition of change to English practice from a foreign source. There was also one potential economic benefit for the landowning classes: by rejecting a proposal that could reduce the number of bastards, they avoided a potential reduction in their own opportunities to benefit from escheats. Self-interest thus coincided with principle.

This conflict between canon law and common law had serious implications for the inheritance of real property. In practical terms, legitimacy only really mattered in certain contexts, such as inheritance, taking orders or joining a guild. Cases involving alleged prenuptial children were common. Of ninety-two distinct bastardy cases for the reigns of the first three Edwards and Richard II, which have been printed in modern editions, seventeen, or almost one in five contain a specific allegation that one or other party was born before espousals. It is likely that some of the remaining cases may include further examples of pre-nuptial bastards, which were not brought out in the pleading.

Single man and single woman who could not lawfully have married
Children born of an unmarried couple who were unable to have a lawful
marriage owing to some impediment were deemed illegitimate by both canon
and common law and could not be legitimated as a valid marriage could not take
place. Such children were also known, according to Bracton and his canonist
sources, as *spurii*, although this is not a term that is frequently found in common
law texts. In Year Book accounts concerning legal proceedings the word 'bastard'
is used in the majority of cases, the only exception being the allegation that a
party was born before espousals, which needed to be handled differently for
the reasons outlined above. As far as the common law was concerned, there was
no difference between children born to an unmarried couple who could not
lawfully marry and those born to a couple who were free to marry. The crucial
point was the absence of a marriage between the parents.

Married man and unmarried woman
This is the classic archetype of adultery. The children were illegitimate by both
canon and common law and, as *spurii*, could not normally be legitimated by
canon law in the event of the man marrying the children's mother after the death
of his wife. However, there were cases in which such children were exceptionally
declared to be legitimate, as in the case of the Beauforts, the children of Edward
III's son John of Gaunt, duke of Lancaster (1340–1399) children by his mistress
Katherine Swynford (*c*. 1350–1403).

*Unmarried man and married (to a third party) woman/Man and woman
both married to other parties*
In this case the common law was more accommodating towards the bastard than
the canon law. From the point of view of canon law, such children would be
spurii and could not be legitimated. Common law, however, took a very different
view, based on the pragmatic difficulties of proving the biological parentage of
a child.

This was the issue that motivated Nicholas Harris Nicolas to write his *Treatise*
in 1836. Since the treatise was inspired by the legal issues arising from the
Banbury case, Nicolas reviewed the texts dealing with the position of children
born to a married woman involved in an adulterous relationship, starting with
the twelfth-century treatise known as Glanvill, and continuing via Bracton and
Britton (a late thirteenth-century treatise in French largely based on Bracton)
and subsequent cases reported in the Year Books.

In Glanvill's time, fornication by the mother did not affect a son's inheritance,
as a son was regarded as a lawful heir if born of a marriage: 'The general rule
that fornication does not take away the inheritance refers to fornication by the

mother; for a son is a lawful heir if born of a marriage'. The writers of thirteenth-century common law treatises continued to stress that children born within a legitimate marriage were to be regarded as legitimate heirs, unless there were unassailable grounds for believing that the child was not that of the husband, although it appears that it may have been possible for the husband to disown the child. Most of Bracton's comments on female adulterine bastardy derived ultimately from civil law, but the text is contradictory. It refers in places to the behaviour of the husband towards the child, stating that

> 'where a wife has had a child by someone other than her husband, and where ... the husband has taken the child into his house, avowed him and raised him as his son, or if he has not avowed him expressly has not turned him away; he will be adjudged legitimate and his father's heir, whether the husband does not know that the child is not his or knows or is in doubt, because he is born of the wife.'

Elsewhere it is clear that the presumption of legitimacy could only be rebutted if the husband was impotent or absent:

> 'if husband and wife live together and there is no impediment on either side to prevent conception and the wife conceives by someone other than her husband, the issue will be legitimate because of the presumption, because it is born of the wife, whether the husband avows it or disavows it, for this presumption admits of no proof to the contrary.'

Britton similarly holds that children resulting from an adulterous liaison on the part of the wife are to be regarded as legitimate, but also refers to the behaviour of the husband and whether he accepts and brings up the child:

> 'If any heir is begotten by another than the husband of his mother, that is to say, at a time when it may be presumed that the husband might have begotten the child in matrimony, we will not that the adultery of the mother be a bar to the inheritance of the child. So, where a child begotten by another and imposed upon the husband as his issue, is brought up by the husband and owned by him as his heir, we will that such children be admissible to the inheritance, if it may be presumed that the husband of the mother may have begotten them.'

Britton goes on to say that adulterine bastards who are immediately disowned by the husbands may not inherit, stressing that such children must be publicly disowned straight away, as once the husband had owned a child to be his, it could not later be disowned.

Cases from the Year Books, however, largely ignored the behaviour of the husband, relying instead on the specific tests of physical capacity and access. Even then, impotence was difficult to prove, and was not necessarily regarded as a permanent condition. In one case cited by Nicolas, it was decided that a man who had been divorced on the grounds of impotence and who had married a second wife who subsequently gave birth, was the father of the child, because a man might be impotent at one time and capable at another.

One form of temporary incapacity that could be proved was minority, and the child of a married woman whose husband was too young to be able to procreate would be regarded as a bastard. In a case from the reign of Richard II, one of the lawyers put the hypothetical case of a husband only five years of age at espousals and seven at the time of the child's birth, 'so that E. could not possibly be his son'. In the case of Machon v Holt from the first year of Henry VI's reign, the lawyer Strangways remarked that 'if an infant within the age of fourteen years take a wife and she is pregnant, the issue will be a bastard through this special matter, because it cannot be understood by any law that a child within such an age can procreate'.

In the absence of such a clear impediment, there was a very strong presumption that any child born of a married woman was the child of the husband, no matter how unlikely this might seem. However, in the case from Richard II mentioned above, Justice Skipwith observed that 'certainly our law and every law always presumed that one who is born and begotten within the espousals is legitimate and not a bastard; but due to some other special fact he could be a bastard. For instance, if a wife leaves her husband and lives with an adulterer and has a son begotten between them after the espousals, if such facts be found, he will be adjudged a bastard'. This does not however appear to have been a generally held opinion.

The case of Machon v Holt involved a woman who was already pregnant by another man at the time of her marriage, and who later eloped with her adulterer. It was maintained that 'the law of the land is that although she eloped from her husband and lives with her adulterer, still the issue is legitimate and able to inherit if there be no other special matter shown' and commented that the reason for this was that it was impossible to try actual paternity 'since it does not lie in the knowledge of anyone of the country nor of anyone else save God'.

The common law evolved a test for access that became essentially formulaic. According to Bracton, the rule was that a child could be regarded as illegitimate if it 'is not likely upon any grounds that he is the heir of the husband, as where the latter has been absent for a long time in the Holy Land, so that the truth may overcome the presumption'. However, distance was important. Bracton goes on to add that 'it will be otherwise, if the husband has been within the country or out of the country that he could have had access to his wife secretly'. In a case of Edward I's reign, Justice Hengham recalled an earlier occasion on which it had been found that after a claimant's parents had married, her father had gone overseas and remained there for three years, returning to find a daughter only about a month old in which the justices had awarded her the land 'for the privities of husband and wife are not to be known, and he might have come by night and engendered the plaintiff'. This test of access became known as doctrine of the Four Seas, as was later set out in Coke's First Institute:

> 'By the Common Law, if the husband be within the four seas, that is, within the jurisdiction of the King of England, if the wife hath issue, no proof is to be admitted to prove the child a bastard, (for in that case, *filiatio non potest probari*) unless the husband hath an apparent impossibility of procreation; as if the husband be but eight years old, or under the age of procreation, such issue is a bastard, albeit he be born within marriage.'

There was thus a strong presumption that the child of a married woman was legitimate. Common lawyers applied the maxim 'whoso bulleth my cow, the calf is mine'. This maxim was clearly widely known and understood for a version of it later appears in Shakespeare's *King John*:

> 'Sirrah, your brother is legitimate;
> Your father's wife did after wedlock bear him,
> And if she did play false the fault was hers;
> Which fault lies on the hazards of all husbands
> That marry wives.
> ...
> In sooth, good friend, your father might have kept
> This calf bred from his cow from all the world... .'
> (Act I, Scene 1)

The Church courts took a different view, as is shown by a case from 1366 in which a plea of general bastardy was referred to the bishop, who found that the party in question was a bastard, having been begotten when his mother eloped with an adulterer. Although the common law would have taken a different view, the bishop's findings were accepted, but in general such cases were retained for trial by the secular courts.

The letters of the Paston family in the fifteenth century provide an apparent example of a bastard born to a married woman being accepted as the son of her husband. Edmund Paston II had an affair with a woman known as 'Mistress Dixon'. When, in November 1479, Edmond was involved in negotiations to marry Katherine, widow of William Clippesby, it was suggested that he should try to obtain the wardship of John Clippesby, her son, as an incentive to the match. Edmond's brother John Paston III went on to argue that it would be only fair for the king to grant Edmund this wardship, as he had taken the wardship of Edmund's own son 'otherwyse callyd Dyxons, the childys fadyr being alive. Dyxson is ded, God have hys sowle'. The son of Mistress Dixon and Edmund Paston had evidently been regarded as the legitimate offspring of Dixon.

However, law and practice did not always coincide. Where on the facts of the case, bastardy was clear, there could be an attempt to ensure that the actual parentage, rather than the legal fiction, would prevail. William Beaumont deserted his wife Joanna, a daughter of Sir William Courtenay, two years before his death in 1453. They reputedly never saw one another again, yet during this period she gave birth to a son. The boy's presumed father was Sir Henry Bodrugan, whom she later married. After William Beaumont's death his brother Philip was found to be his heir, but the potential for a claim by the son, John Beaumont, who was the son of a married woman, seems to have been realised. In February 1467 letters patent were obtained to the effect that whereas it had been understood that Joan, wife of Henry Bodrugan and late the wife of William Beaumont, had a child John, the lawful son of the said William, it had been proved that John was a bastard, and that Philip Beaumont was William's brother and next heir. How this could have been 'proved' in a legally binding sense, when the married couple were living in the same country, if not the same county, remains unclear and this was not the last word on the matter. Philip remained in possession of the Beaumont estate, and after his death it passed firstly to his brother Thomas, and then to another brother, Hugh. After Hugh's death, there was a succession dispute between rival claimants, and John Beaumont took the opportunity to assert his own claim. It appears that the case went before parliament, which declined to change the law in order to make person born in wedlock into a bastard for legal purposes, although it did go so far as making a proclamation to the effect that John was not the actual descendant of William Beaumont. The estates were eventually divided between the rival claimants, and John Beaumont (described as 'son of Joan Bodrugan') received his share, including the manor of Gittisham (Devon) and other lands. It was not until the reign of Henry VIII that the bastardization by act of parliament of children born to an adulterous wife was contemplated.

Divorce or annulment

There were a number of diriment impediments that could lead to the annulment of a marriage: consanguinity, affinity, godsib (spiritual affinity arising from the relationship with a godparent), *quasi-affinitas* or *publica honestas*, pre-contract, pre-marital adultery, impotence and profession of either party in a religious order. Opinions as to the legitimacy of the children of putative marriages varied according to the reasons for the annulment, and the positions taken by canon and common law were again slightly different. Each of these impediments is considered in more detail below. It should be noted, however, that the children remained legitimate until the sentence of divorce had been pronounced by the Ecclesiastical court. Under canon law, the legitimacy of children depended on various factors, including the good faith of the parents. If at least one of the parents was ignorant of the impediment, the children were legitimate. Good faith was of course difficult to prove, but the actual test applied under canon law was whether the marriage had been contracted openly in church, with banns having been read. The common law position was slightly different and these cases were therefore not referred to the bishop.

Consanguinity

The Fourth Lateran Council (1215) had determined that marriages between persons related in the fourth degree according to the canonical method of calculation were invalid. The means of calculation was to count the steps down from the common ancestor. Where the number of steps between the parties and the common ancestor varied, the longer line would be measured.

The position taken by the English courts regarding children of annulled marriages for reasons of consanguinity evolved over time. In 1300, the jury of the *inquisition post mortem* concerning Hubert de Multon (a younger son of Thomas de Multon of Gilsland) held at Carlisle found that Hubert had been married to Ada le Brun, with whom he had had a son, William, aged 14. After Hubert and Ada had cohabited for a period of four years, they were divorced on the grounds of consanguinity, of which it was proven that Hubert had known prior to their espousal. Hubert subsequently remarried. With his second wife Margaret de Boys, he had a son, John, aged seven at the time of the inquest. A Norfolk jury gave a similar account of the facts of the case, but stated explicitly that John was the son and heir. Seven years later, when William le Brun came of age, he attempted to claim as heir. As a result of a petition by Margaret, the king ordered that no livery of the estates should be granted unless by his order and William le Brun ultimately lost his case. John de Multon proved his age and received livery of his estates in 1314.

During the reign of Edward II, the royal courts were apparently willing to accept determination by the Church courts in cases of bastardy arising from the parents' divorce for consanguinity. In the case of Stafford v Stafford (1317), the plaintiff intended to base his claim on the assertion that the tenant was a bastard by virtue of his parents' divorce for consanguinity, but the case was initially dismissed as he made the error of describing the tenant as 'son of' in Latin. When the case was tried again, a writ was issued to the Bishop of Coventry and Lichfield, who confirmed that the tenant was illegitimate.

During the reign of Edward III, the courts appeared to take the view that divorce on account of consanguinity did not bastardise the children. This was not quite the same as the canon law position which stressed the need for good faith on the part of the parents, or one of them, at least. Richard Helmholz suggested that the reason for the divergence was that 'English law required a simpler rule, one easier to state, less difficult to prove, and not so open to fraud'. Nevertheless, the canon law position that good faith was demonstrated by a public marriage in church, thus providing an opportunity for anyone knowing of an impediment to object to the marriage, was straightforward and easy to prove. Canon law was very clear on the point that if the marriage had been contracted publicly, the children should not suffer as a result of a subsequent divorce and should be held to be no less legitimate as a result. Where a marriage had been contracted publicly in church, the fact of an impediment was not sufficient to make the children illegitimate. The question of fraud would be more likely to arise in the case of clandestine marriages, than in those for which banns had been read.

Affinity

Affinity was, in effect, a special type of consanguinity, based on the Church's view that sexual intercourse made a man and a woman one flesh. After a consummated marriage the husband was accordingly related to his wife's kin by the same number of degrees as she was. Thus he would be related to her sister in the first degree. The connection was created by the act of sexual intercourse rather than the solemnization of a marriage, so affinity could also be created as a result of adultery or fornication.

Divorce for affinity was very similar to divorce for consanguinity and seems to have been treated in the same way. In an anonymous case from 1339, it was stated that the child of a marriage could not be his father's heir because of the existence of a child of an earlier marriage 'notwithstanding the divorce ... by reason of affinity, since no divorce for that cause makes any one a bastard who was born after the marriage and before the divorce'.

Quasi-affinity

Since affinity was created by the act of sexual intercourse, a betrothal or unconsummated marriage was insufficient to create full affinity. However, if one of the parties to a marriage had previously contracted to marry a blood relative of the other, it was considered a diriment impediment to their marriage, even if there had been no actual previous marriage or sexual relationship. This impediment of quasi-affinity was also known as public honesty (*publica honestas*) because such cases were regarded as scandalous. A decretal of Celestine III (1191–98) stated that children of such a marriage were illegitimate: 'Children born of marriage, contracted against justice of the public honour, are illegitimate, and excluded from the parents' inheritance.'

Godsib

Godsib was a special case of affinity arising from the bond of spiritual kinship created between a child and their godparent. Whilst it created an impediment to marriage in the same number of degrees as actual kinship, divorces involving this form of affinity were rare. Richard Helmholz found a case from the reign of Edward IV which involved a divorce for this reason, but in that case the reason for the divorce was less of an issue for the courts than the fact that it was posthumous. An over-zealous official, having discovered that a man's father had been the godfather of his wife's cousin and that no dispensation had been obtained for their marriage, decided to celebrate a divorce between them, even though both were dead. When the man was subsequently involved in litigation over his inheritance, bastardy was alleged against him as a result of this 'divorce'. The court was unsympathetic to this argument.

Pre-contract

Common law took a harder line on divorce for pre-contract than for consanguinity or affinity. Divorce for this reason would automatically bastardise the issue. This was the point that had been an issue in the Anstey case in the twelfth century, a case that is well known to legal historians because one of the litigants, Richard of Anstey, kept a careful note of the considerable expenses he incurred in pursuing the case, which has survived, thus providing insight into how the legal process worked in practice. William de Sackville had contracted a second marriage following his betrothal to Albreda of Tregoze, but the papal legate pronounced the first betrothal binding and the second marriage was declared null at a synod in London. Richard of Anstey, the son of Sackville's sister, Agnes, therefore claimed his estates as heir, on the basis that Mabel, the child of this second, annulled, marriage was illegitimate. The question of Mabel's legitimacy took some time to resolve, and was referred to Pope Alexander III before Mabel was eventually declared illegitimate. Mabel's illegitimacy having been established, consideration of the property issue resumed in the secular courts and Richard of Anstey eventually won his case.

There is some logic to the distinction between divorce for consanguinity and affinity and divorce for pre-contract. As Helmholz points out 'one may more easily believe that a person has ignored the extent of his kinship than that he has forgotten contracting marriage'. Pre-contract was the basis for Richard III's claim that Edward IV's children were illegitimate. The story (of which several versions exist) was that Edward's marriage to Elizabeth Woodville was invalid as he was already contracted to marry another lady, variously named as Eleanor Butler or Elizabeth Lucy. However, even if true, this would not have been sufficient to render the children of his marriage to Elizabeth Woodville illegitimate, until such time as the marriage had formally been annulled.

Impotence
Impotence was a ground for divorce, since it would prevent the consummation of the marriage. In order to prove impotence, the ecclesiastical court would ask a jury of matrons to perform a physical examination and attempt to stimulate the alleged impotent man in order to confirm whether the erectile dysfunction was genuine. Once the impotence of the husband had been proved by this method, any children borne by the wife would presumably not have been regarded by the royal courts as legitimate offspring of the husband, this being one of the few exceptions to the presumption that children born to a married woman were the legitimate offspring of her husband. However, cases of divorce for impotence were rare, it being a sensitive matter. One case is that of Elizabeth Shore, the mistress of Edward IV, who secured an annulment of her marriage to the London mercer William Shore in 1476 on the grounds of his impotence. Husbands defended themselves vigorously against such allegations as can be seen from the Cantilupe case. In 1368 Nicholas Cantilupe reacted to his wife Katherine's attempts to have her marriage annulled on the grounds of his impotence by abducting her from her father's manor, and threatening to keep her in chains in Greasley Castle if she did not publicly swear to his sexual prowess. Within a few days of the solemnization of her marriage Katherine had told a confidante that Nicholas was unable to consummate the relationship as he had no testicles. Initially, the problem was put down to her inexperience, but eventually her family accepted her account. When the case came to court, there were several witnesses who were able to swear to rumours about Nicholas' impotence. The lengths to which Nicholas went in order to avoid undergoing a physical examination, including violent threats, and an appeal to the papal *curia*, suggest that Katherine's claims were true.

Minority
Minority was in effect a particular type of impotence. Since a child under the age of fourteen (males) and twelve (females) could not validly consent to a

marriage, the marriage was invalid unless the parties gave consent on reaching the appropriate age. Furthermore, a male under the age of fourteen was deemed incapable of procreation. This is another instance in which children born of a married woman were not automatically deemed to be legitimate children of the husband, as was the case in Machon v Holt mentioned above.

Religious profession
Profession of monastic vows would lead to the annulment of a marriage, but as this was an event which took place after the marriage, the children would remain legitimate and the wife would retain her rights to dower.

By the end of Edward III's reign, the courts appear to have settled on the firmer line that divorce for any reason other than profession would bastardise the issue.

Children of priest and any woman
Children of priests were illegitimate by both laws. The Church was particularly opposed to clerical bastards, in order to avoid the emergence of a hereditary priesthood, and they therefore occupied the lowest position in the canon law hierarchy of bastards, although by the twelfth century attitudes had relaxed from the harsh position taken by a seventh-century Spanish canon, according to which such bastards were slaves of the Church. In practice, there are plentiful examples of dispensations to enter the priesthood. The prejudice against clerical bastards can perhaps be seen in the tendency to note the circumstances of birth in the dispensations, but it was certainly not unknown for the sons of those in orders to obtain dispensations.

In some cases it might not be entirely clear whether a child was a clerical bastard or not. In the late-eleventh century the rules on clerical marriage were not as clearly defined as they later became. This can be seen in a case from 1227 between two sons of Andrew le Guiz. The younger son, also named Andrew, as plaintiff, claimed that the father had been a cleric in possession of several benefices and had had a mistress, named Amice, who was the mother of the elder son John. According to his version, when Geoffrey Ridel, Bishop of Ely, heard about Andrew senior's domestic arrangements, he summoned the pair, who swore that they were not married. After that time, the pair ceased to cohabit. Some time later, Andrew senior resigned his benefices and married Felicia, who was the mother of the younger Andrew. John's version was that Andrew senior married Amice and that both John and Andrew junior were born after the marriage. According to the plaintiff's argument, a cleric in possession of benefices could not contract a valid marriage, whilst according to the defendant, he could have a legitimate heir. In the event, the case seems to have been settled by a compromise.

In the reign of Edward I, the implications of illegitimacy being tried in the Church courts whilst inheritance was handled by the royal courts were still being worked out in practice. Litigants could find themselves in difficulties if they approached the wrong court. William de Valence and his wife Joan, daughter of Warin de Montchenesy, discovered this when they tried to pursue Joan's claim to the inheritance of William de Montchenesy. William and Joan had obtained a bull requiring the archbishop of Canterbury to hold a hearing into whether a certain Denise was the daughter and heiress of William de Montchenesy. William and Joan petitioned the king in the parliament of 1290 seeking the appointment of a guardian *ad litem* to represent Denise before the archbishop and the judges named in the bull. Their petition was rejected on the grounds that the purpose was to determine the right of hereditary succession, which was a matter specifically for the king's court and as such, the inquiry was contrary to previous custom. Furthermore, the king had recently decreed that appeals should not be made or cases begun in the ecclesiastical courts about matters which were referred to them by the royal courts. William and Joan were attempting to overturn a previous decision of the bishop of Worcester, who had already found Denise to be legitimate. As Denise was a royal ward, it was in the king's interest for her to be the heiress. The response to William and Joan's petition also referred to in the precedent of the recent case of Simon of Ludgate, who had acquired a certain bull in similar circumstances and been sent to prison as a result, although his case had been less prejudicial to the Crown. Ludgate had been attempting to defend his son Laurence St.Maur, whose sisters were seeking to have him declared a bastard and to deprive him of his inheritance.

Valence tried again with another petition to permit him to pursue an appeal to the archbishop of Canterbury against the unjust decision of the bishop of Worcester, claiming that he had been advised that the decision would have permanent force unless the appeal which he had lodged was prosecuted within a year. Since this was patently still an attempt to use the Church courts to obtain determination of entitlement to the Montchenesey inheritance, this petition was also refused.

Legitimation and its opposite

Neither legitimacy nor illegitimacy was necessarily a permanent state. It was possible for a child to be apparently legitimate at birth and subsequently bastardised, for example as a result of the annulment of the parents' marriage.

An example of the issue of a marriage being bastardised by a subsequent annulment is provided by the case of Richard FitzAlan, Earl of Arundel. Richard had been married to Isabella Despenser in 1321 when they were both children. In 1344, he petitioned the pope for an annulment on the grounds that the couple had never consented to the marriage, but had been forced into it by their relations. The wording of the petition made it clear that the marriage had been contracted when the couple were minors, at the ages of seven and eight respectively; that they had not freely consented, but had been forced to contract espousals through fear of their relatives; and that despite renouncing the marriage when they reached puberty, had been 'forced by blows' to cohabit, neatly explaining the existence of their son, who might otherwise have presented something of an impediment to their case. This petition thus carefully addressed all the points which were necessary in order to show that the marriage was invalid: there had been no consent; the parties had been minors and they had expressly renounced the arrangement when they reached puberty.

The annulment was duly received, and FitzAlan subsequently married Eleanor Beaumont at Ditton on 5 February 1345, in the king's presence. Yet this marriage was also not without its technical problems. Since Eleanor was related to his first wife, a dispensation for affinity was needed. Interestingly, this fact was not 'discovered' until after the marriage had taken place. Dispensations were duly obtained, the couple agreeing in return to found three chaplaincies of ten marks each in the church of Arundel.

The fact that Richard FitzAlan had had a son by Isabella Despenser appears not to have been an insuperable obstacle to his divorce. Nonetheless, as the marriage was annulled, the son was rendered illegitimate. Edmund, the son in question, did not give up without protest. He petitioned the pope on the matter, and a commission was issued to William, Cardinal of St Stephen's to cite Richard, Isabella and Eleanor. An appeal against the citation by Richard and Isabella was unsuccessful, but Richard appears to have triumphed in the end.

Forms of Legitimation

Illegitimacy was not necessarily permanent. There were ways by which bastards could be legitimated either in a formal legal sense or for practical purposes. Again, common law and canon law had slightly different rules.

Formal Legitimation
Formal legitimation was possible on the Continent by civil/papal authority, although it was subject to complex rules, *naturales* being viewed more favourably than *spurii*. In continental Europe, the blend of canon law and Roman law known as *ius commune* allowed for the legitimation of *naturales* by the subsequent marriage of the parents, *per curie oblationem* or by testament. Legitimation *per curie oblationem* involved the father taking his natural son to the papal court to

be legitimated as his heir. Legitimation by testament occurred when a father who had no legitimate children named his natural children as full heirs in his testament. A further form of legitimation, by rescript, which originated from Innocent III's decretal *Per venerabilem*, was intended for cases in which marriage was impossible, for example when the mother had died, and could be used for *spurii* as well as *naturales*. The authority to grant such legitimation came from the Holy Roman Emperor, although it could be, and was, delegated to counts palatine (nobles who held sovereign power in their own lands). Whilst it was possible, the success of formal legitimation was not necessarily guaranteed. Thomas Kuehn has shown that the mere act of legitimation was not necessarily sufficient for legal purposes— 'the fate of legitimated bastards lay in the hands of jurists whose judgments could seem unfathomable to others'.

Formal legitimation was not, however, usual in England, the one exception being the legitimation of the Beauforts. John, Henry, Thomas and Joan Beaufort were the children of John of Gaunt, Duke of Lancaster, and his mistress and later wife, Katherine Swynford. These children were born during the 1370s, when Gaunt was married to his second wife, Constanza of Castile. Following her death in 1394, Gaunt and Katherine married. The couple sought and obtained from the pope on rather dubious grounds a ratification and confirmation of their marriage, with declaration of the legitimacy of their offspring as far as the Church was concerned ('lest grave scandals arise'). Then on 4 February 1397 Richard II 'as undoubted emperor in our realm of England' declared in parliament the Beauforts 'by the plenitude of our royal power, and with the assent of parliament' to be fully legitimate in the eyes of the law, and to be capable of inheriting 'whatsoever honours, dignities, pre-eminencies, status, ranks and offices, public and private, perpetual and temporal, feudal and noble there may be ... as fully, freely and lawfully as if you had been born in lawful wedlock ...' The Beauforts thus became the only English medieval bastards to be legitimated by secular authority according to English law.

The wording is worth noting. The reference to Richard as 'emperor' may perhaps have been deliberately intended to emphasise his right though 'imperial' authority to grant legitimation by rescript, since this was, as far as England was concerned, a new procedure. It should perhaps be viewed, however, in the context of the more exalted vocabulary of address that had developed in the second half of Richard's reign.

Whilst the Beauforts were the only bastards legitimated in parliament in the medieval period, they were not, however, the only bastards to be legitimated by a king of England. In January 1408, Leonard de Barde, the son of a Bordeaux merchant, was legitimated by Henry IV (1399–1413) acting in his capacity as Duke of Aquitaine, following continental practice. The next time that bastards were legitimated in parliament was not until 1547 and the circumstances were rather different. Sir Ralph Sadler married Ellen Mitchell in about 1534, believing her to be a widow, her first husband, Matthew Barre, having disappeared some years previously and all attempts to trace him having failed. After the couple had been 'married' for a number of years, and had three sons and four daughters, Barre reappeared. Sadler successfully obtained an act allowing his children with Ellen to be legitimate, on the grounds that the marriage had been entered into in good faith.

Legitimation by subsequent marriage

As already noted, under canon law, the children of a couple who were free to marry without impediment were legitimated by their parents' marriage, but legitimation by subsequent marriage was most definitely not recognised by the common law, as the barons indicated at Merton in 1236. The nearest common law came to recognising this principle was the case of the prenuptial bastard who took possession after his father's death and held it peacefully until his own death, after which bastardy could no longer be cited in any subsequent lawsuit over the property. However, this was really an expression of the common law reluctance to bastardise the dead. It was also possible that in some such cases the supposed bastard might have been the issue of a clandestine marriage, whose legitimacy was not challenged during his lifetime as there was a good chance that he would be able to bring proof of the marriage. Supposed bastards who later turned out to be the products of a clandestine marriage were a hazard for landed families contracting marriage alliances, as the Sotehills and Rocliffes were to discover shortly after arranging marriages to the two granddaughters and supposed co-heiresses of Sir William Plumpton, children of his son William who had been killed at the battle of Towton in 1461. In January 1464 Sir William had received £400 for the marriage of the elder girl, Margaret, to Brian Rocliffe and £333 for the marriage of Henry Sotehill to her younger sister, Elizabeth. In 1468 it was revealed that Sir William's younger son Robert was not illegitimate as had previously been believed when Sir William proved that he had contracted a clandestine marriage with Robert's mother, Joan Wintringham, in the 1450s.

Pseudo legitimation by collusive lawsuit

In general, once a decision had been taken by the secular court to refer a question of bastardy in a property dispute to the bishop, the response of the bishop was accepted and judgement given on that basis. This judgement then became part of the legal record, to which reference could be made in subsequent lawsuits, including those involving different parties, as in the case of Bayeux v Beryhale (1309), in which the demandant, having been accused of bastardy, produced a certificate that he was legitimate which had been obtained in an earlier case.

There is evidence that litigants were anxious to ensure that certificates were entered on the record as proof of legitimacy. It is clear that judgement had to be given on a case and the certificate entered on the record for it to be acceptable as evidence, though specific judgement on the legitimacy issue did not have to be given. In one case from 1337, the judge reassured a litigant that even though judgement had been given by default as the other party did not appear in court, it would still be entered on the record that he was legitimate.

It was clearly in the interests of a pre-nuptial bastard to try to ensure that the issue of bastardy was referred to the bishop, who would find that the bastard was 'mulier' (legitimate), rather than for the issue to be tried by a jury under the special bastardy procedure. However, errors in pleading were not infrequent. The rules concerning which cases were and were not referred to the ecclesiastical court were complex, and there was a tendency for the courts to focus on technical aspects of pleading rather than the substantive legal issue. There was particular confusion regarding possessory writs and writs of right. Possessory writs were used to obtain possession of property from someone who had entered it unlawfully and continued in possession, but did not deal with the actual right to the property, whereas writs of right were intended to restore property to the rightful owner. By the end of the thirteenth century it had become an established principle that bastardy cases were only referred to the bishop in the case of writs of right.

This concentration on the forms of pleading led to a situation in which how questions of bastardy were raised became more important than the alleged reasons. In consequence, it was sometimes assumed that because bastardy could only be referred to the bishop in cases involving writs of right, that it must be referred to the bishop in such cases, irrespective of the circumstances. This happened in the case of Le Fevre v Sleght (1313) when the lawyer for the demandant argued that general bastardy had to be alleged as it was a writ of right. In Chamber v Chamber (1312), it appears that a prenuptial bastard tried to exploit this confusion by choosing to sue under a writ of right in the first instance, rather than under a possessory writ. On this occasion Chief Justice Bereford was alert to the ploy: 'and if of your own accord you have waived your possessionary writ and gone to your writ of right, has the tenant thereby lost his answer?' But even justices succumbed to confusion on occasion. In the case of Surrey v Colet (1313), the judge, Sir William Inge, put certain facts to the jury, but was unwilling to ask the jury whether the defendant was born before his parents' marriage or not as this question was so close to bastardy that he was reluctant to encroach on the province of the Church. Because this was the very issue which was supposed to have been determined by the king's courts since the Statute of Merton, it was fortunate that the jury 'said gratuitously ... that the defendant and his elder brother were born out of wedlock'.

De Facto legitimation by adoption

Adoption, as such, seems not to have been a widely accepted practice in medieval England, but there are a few cases which seem to have involved a form of adoption. For example, in a case from the second year of Edward II's reign, a plaintiff brought a possessory writ against a certain Thomas on the death of a man named Hervey. However, despite allegations that Thomas was in fact the son of William of Rusting and Margery la Dayne, who was never lawfully married to Hervey, the plaintiff was unsuccessful as Thomas had been recognised by Hervey as his son and heir and had entered the property as such. Note that this was not necessarily a case of the son of an adulterous wife being accepted as the legitimate heir of her husband, since the lady in the case was claimed never to have been married to Hervey. The point was that Thomas had been accepted by Hervey as his 'son' and was therefore in possession as heir. During discussion of the case, one of the judges referred to the 'ancient case' of 'Sir Henry of Berkeley' who had had only one wife, but she never conceived a child. He did, however, have six sons, the eldest of whom entered after his death and retained the inheritance, because he was acknowledged as Sir Henry's son in his lifetime.

De Facto legitimation by dying seised

Cases in which bastardy was alleged against a deceased person were determined by the common law courts and not by the bishop. Bastardy could only be tried in the court Christian if the person against whom bastardy was alleged was a party to the proceedings, which they could not be after death. The common law was, in general, reluctant to bastardise the dead and it was a principle that if a prenuptial bastard entered upon his father's death and held the land peacefully and died seised (in possession), his illegitimacy could not be used in subsequent actions against his children by his father's right heir. This principle can be seen in operation in cases stretching back to the last quarter of the thirteenth century. The bastard had to have been seised of the property and to have entered by hereditary succession rather than purchase. It was not necessary for the bastard to take possession directly; an entry by the lord or by the widow of the deceased before the bastard took possession would not affect the claim that he had entered as heir, as Justice Bereford declared in the case of Sagor v Atte Welle (1311). However, the bastard must have been in continuous possession without challenge during their lifetime.

If the bastard alienated the property during his lifetime then the case would be regarded differently.

In 1317, Peter of Lymesey claimed twenty-eight acres of wood and twenty marks of rent in Great Amwell (Hertfordshire) against the abbot of Westminster, who had purchased it from Peter's uncle, Ralph de Lymesey. Ralph was apparently the elder of two brothers. Peter, who was the son of the younger brother, Richard, argued that Ralph was a bastard. The allegation of bastardy was countered with the objection that bastardy had not been alleged during Ralph's lifetime. However, the objection was not upheld because Ralph had not died in possession.

De Facto legitimation by transmission of property as if to heir

Whilst formal legitimation of children was not part of English law, there were circumstances in which a bastard child might be legitimated in a *de facto* sense so that an illegitimate son could continue the family in the absence of a legitimate son (for example by transmitting property to illegitimate offspring by ways other than simple inheritance). As the main disadvantage of illegitimacy was an inability to inherit at common law, the use of legal devices to circumvent the normal rules of inheritance resulted in individuals who were technically illegitimate, but in practice enjoyed the lands and trappings of their father's rank.

According to Glanvill, a man could give part of his inherited land to any stranger, including his bastard son, but he could not give part of his inherited land to one of his younger sons without the permission of his eldest son and heir because 'if this were allowed, the disinheritance of eldest sons would often occur, because of the greater affection which fathers tend to have for younger sons'. From this point of view a bastard son was, theoretically at least, in a better position than a legitimate younger son. However, a gift during the donor's lifetime reduced his own landed income.

There were additional legal pitfalls of which landowners needed to be aware in making provision for a bastard. As a bastard was legally the son of no one, if he died without heir of his body, the property would escheat to the lord rather than reverting to his father's next heir. In the first decade of the fourteenth century Thomas Corbet of Morton Corbet (Shropshire) enfeoffed a bastard, John L'Estrange, in a third part of his manor of Houghton (Leicestershire). In 1311, after Thomas Corbet's death, his widow, Amice, sued the chief lord, William de Bois, for dower in Houghton. By this time John L'Estrange had also died without heir of his body. William's response to the suit was that Amice was entitled to dower in respect of two-thirds of the manor only, since he held the third part as of right by escheat, as a result of the death of a bastard.

Where property was settled on a bastard and the heirs of his body it was vital to include a reversion to the main family line in order to prevent permanent alienation of the property in the event of the failure of the bastard line, since there was no common law right of collateral inheritance.

Whilst such a gift could provide a bastard with a means of support, it was originally more difficult for a landowner to make provision for a bastard to receive a share of the inheritance after his own death. The gradual evolution of the legal devices such as the entail and the enfeoffment to use provided landowners with more control over the descent of their estates, including the ability to transmit them to illegitimate children.

Legal Devices

The entail

An entail was a conditional grant in which in the event of the death of the original recipient without heirs of his body, the property would not be inherited by his collateral heirs but revert to the donor, or remain to a specified third party. Grants of land in fee tail appeared with increasing frequency from the late-twelfth century until they had become a common form of grant by the third decade of the thirteenth century. At the same time, marriage settlements began to include words of entail. Early entails were more limited in their duration. The statute *De Donis* (1285) provided a milestone in the evolution of the entail, but interpretations of the duration of an entail were to gradually evolve over the following century and a half until it came to be understood that the effects were perpetual. It is important to note that there were two aspects of the entail: the conditional remainders and reversions and the restraint on alienation, and that understanding of the duration of the entail for the two different purposes developed along different timescales. In the years after *De Donis*, a fee tail was understood to last until the entry of the third heir for the purposes of reversion, but the first issue of the donee was able to alienate. By 1309, the restriction on alienation was considered to include the first heir of the original donee, and during the next twenty years, this extended to the second heir, so that entry of the third heir became the limit on the duration of entails for both succession and alienation. However, this phase of uniformity did not last, as the period 1330–1420 saw the entail become perpetual for the purpose of succession, whilst the restriction on alienation lasted only until the entry of the fourth heir. It was only after 1420 that the entail was seen as a permanent restraint on alienation. Twenty years later, the procedure known as common recovery made an appearance as a means of barring entails.

The enfeoffment to use

Land held under feudal tenure could not be devised by will, but had to descend by the rules of male primogeniture. A father could only make provision for younger (or bastard) children during his own lifetime, and then only if they were of age. However, it would appear that attempts to circumvent the rules were already being made by the second half of the thirteenth century, for the 1267 Statute of Marlborough specifically forbade fraudulent enfeoffments designed to deprive lords of their rights. At the same time, the idea of an individual being seised of property to the use (*ad opus*) of another as a form of trusteeship evolved. J. M. W. Bean considered that there was no doubt that at the end of the thirteenth century 'lawyers and landowners in English were well aware of the possibility of transactions in which lands were granted to one person to the use of another' although the enfeoffment to use was not yet in its final form. It was only after the statute of *Quia Emptores* in 1290 which abolished subinfeudation and thereby simplified the tenurial arrangments for feoffees so that the full potential of the enfeoffment to use could be appreciated. The increase in use was also assisted by the more relaxed attitude demonstrated by the Crown towards the issue of licences to alienate lands held in chief from 1294 onwards. On the basis of a study of surviving inquisitions post mortem, Bean was able to demonstrate that the employment of uses grew steadily during the reign of Edward III, the practice spreading from lesser landowners to barons and earls. He also noted that by this stage they were frequently being used with the specific intention of making arrangements for the post-mortem distribution of estates. The enfeoffment to use was employed extensively from the mid-fourteenth century onwards, and it was only at the end of the fifteenth century that the Crown attempted to control the practice.

The use was frequently combined with the entail for the purposes of estate planning, resulting in what Joseph Biancalana has described as a 'powerful combination of legal devices for disinheritance'. Legitimate common law heirs could be disinherited in favour of illegitimate children. However, as one of the cases cited by Biancalana demonstrates, this flexibility could work both ways. In 1407 William Waite was able to use this means to disinherit his 'son' by his first wife, who had been pregnant by another man when she married him, in favour of the offspring of a second marriage. The son, John, would otherwise have been regarded as his heir by the common law principle that a child born within wedlock was legitimate.

Escheats

For the landed classes, bastardy was not just important in terms of their own inheritance rights. A bastard who died without an heir of his body died without any heir, resulting in escheat to his lord. Even if the bastard had issue, once the direct line of heirs of his body failed, there could be no recourse to collateral heirs. Landowners were keen to claim escheats on the death of bastard tenants. In the Suffolk Eyre of 1240, Hamon Mundy and his wife Matilda claimed from William the son of Ralph a messuage, seventeen acres of land and five shillings of rent in Whissonsett which Emma the daughter of William held from them as their escheat because Emma was a bastard who died without heirs of her body. Consistency was, however, necessary. In a case from 1285, a landowner lost a case because whilst he had taken part of the tenant's inheritance as an escheat because he was a bastard, he had accepted his homage for another part of his lands. The court found that the landowner could not simultaneously allege that the tenant was his father's heir for part of the property and not the rest. The value of rights of escheat in bastardy cases may also be demonstrated by the determination of the Crown to exert its own rights to escheat on the death of bastards in the City of London from the end of the thirteenth century. In 1386, Henry Colas, a wealthy taverner and one-time Member of Parliament from Guildford found himself in difficulties after the death of his son, Walter, in 1383. It was found by an inquisition in 1386 that Walter was illegitimate and that Henry therefore had no right to any of the rents and profits of Walter's property that he had been taking since his death.

The approach taken by the English courts to the determination of cases involving illegitimacy was still developing during the first half of the fourteenth century, but thereafter the situation became much clearer. However, differences in canon law and common law approaches to illegitimacy remained, providing opportunities for manipulation by those who were able to exploit them. Despite this, the English courts retained the practice, largely abandoned on the Continent, of referring some bastardy cases to the ecclesiastical courts. The uncertainties of the outcome of any case in which illegitimacy was raised provided further incentives for title to be secured by means of settlements rather than relying on the common law inheritance rules.

Chapter 2

A Case Study of Bastardy in Practice:
The Warenne Family and After

Having considered how the law dealt with illegitimacy, it is time to turn to what actually happened in practice. The history of the earldom of Surrey from the Norman Conquest to the end of the fourteenth century provides a case study from the highest level of the nobility, which demonstrates provisions for illegitimate children through marriage, estate settlement and careers in the Church, as well as a royal mistress and bastard.

The Warenne family name comes from the hamlet of Varenne in Normandy, where they originated. In 1066 William, a younger son of Rodulf de Warenne, accompanied Duke William of Normandy on his invasion of England, and was ultimately rewarded with lands in thirteen counties, including Conisbrough in Yorkshire, Castle Acre in Norfolk and most of the rape of Lewes in Sussex, where he later founded Lewes Priory. In the spring of 1088 this William de Warenne was created Earl of Surrey by King William Rufus as a reward for his loyalty against rebels led by the Count of Mortain and Bishop of Bayeux.

William was succeeded by his eldest son and heir, William (II). As there are a lot of Williams in this story, I will number them from now on in order to avoid confusion. At this point, a royal bastard might well have been added to the family tree, for King Henry I at one point planned to marry William (II) to one of his many illegitimate daughters, but the Archbishop of Canterbury, Anselm, objected to the match on grounds of affinity. Instead, William (II) married Isabel, widow of Robert de Beaumont, Count of Meulan and Earl of Leicester. After his death in 1138, William (II) was succeeded by his son and heir William (III). William (III) was killed on crusade in 1147, leaving his daughter Isabel as heiress. She was married firstly to William de Blois, a younger son of King Stephen, but he died in 1159, leaving no children, and Isabel was subsequently married in 1164 to Hamelin, an illegitimate son of Count Geoffrey of Anjou and half-brother of King Henry II. Hamelin was responsible for rebuilding work at Conisbrough Castle, the Warenne family's principal residence in Yorkshire, including the distinctive circular keep. He died in 1202, leaving a son and heir, William (IV), as well as a daughter who was one of King John's mistresses, and mother of his bastard son, known as Richard de Dover or Richard de Chilham. William (IV)'s second wife was Maud, widow of Hugh Bigod, Earl of Norfolk and one of the heiresses of William Marshal, Earl of Pembroke, adding considerable Welsh property to the Warenne estate. William (IV) died in 1240, and was succeeded by his only son and heir by his second wife, John (I).

John (I) de Warenne (d. 1304), the sixth earl, was a feisty character who is reputed to have brandished a rusty sword during Edward I's *Quo Warranto* hearings to demonstrate his right as the descendant of one of the Conqueror's companions. Whether he did so in actual fact or not, and he seems to have been the sort of individual who might well have relished making a dramatic gesture before leaving his lawyers to pursue his case by more usual means, such a claim conveniently overlooked the fact that his descent from the first earl was through the female line.

After the death of his wife Alice in 1256, the sixth earl went on to father two bastard sons, John and William, both of whom followed similar careers in the Church, and were presented to churches controlled by the Warenne family. Some authorities have included them among the numerous bastards of the seventh earl, but this is clearly impossible, as he was not born until 1286 and would thus have been far too young to have been the father of this John and William. From the evidence provided in their dispensations, it would appear that John and William were probably born in the late 1260s or early 1270s.

The first mention of the two illegitimate sons of the sixth earl in connection with their future church careers is found on 23 December 1291. Richard de Swinefield, Bishop of Hereford, granted a dispensation for illegitimacy for John, and another for William. Despite their illegitimacy, the brothers were able to benefit from the support of friends in high places. John was presented to the church of Dewsbury (Yorkshire) by the prior and convent of Lewes (a Warenne foundation) in 1293. William de Rouleby was to represent him until the next ordination in Lent. He was a canon of York Minster by 1296, when William de Suretoft acknowledged a debt to him of 120 marks, and remained so at least until 1342, when he was one of the canons summoned for occupying the archiepiscopal palace after the death of the Archbishop of York, William de Melton, and refusing to allow those appointed by the king to receive the temporalities to enter.

On 22 February 1303, the archbishop of Canterbury, Robert Winchelsea, wrote to Pope Boniface VIII (1295–1303) on behalf of John and William de Warenne, Masters of Arts, illegitimate sons of Earl John de Warenne. The brothers had already been given a dispensation to take orders and hold benefices with cure of souls. The archbishop asked for further favours on account of their learning and virtuous lives. By 1306, when he was granted three years' leave of absence, John had also acquired the churches of Dorking (Surrey) and Fishlake (Yorkshire). In the same year he received a dispensation from Pope Clement V (1305–14) for having been ordained as a priest before his twenty-fourth year and holding without a dispensation the church of Dewsbury first, and afterwards a canonry and prebend in the church of York and the churches of Dorking and Fishlake. He received a further licence for three years' study leave on 3 October 1309, but his pursuits do not appear to have been entirely scholarly; in 1313 he was fined £20 for fornication with Matilda Malbuche and Alicia Benet—his life was no longer quite so virtuous. Perhaps in order to remove him from temptation, he was granted a further period of study leave. His frequent absences seem to have become a matter of some concern, as officials attempted to fine him for non-residence. In 1318 he may have been forced to resign Fishlake, which he held as a pluralist without dispensation. He also appears to have had some financial difficulties during the 1320s. He resigned Dorking by 1322 and Dewsbury by January 1326, when Richard de Mosely replaced him.

His brother William was rector of Nafferton (Yorkshire) by 1300, but he resigned on 1 January 1303, when he was presumably studying at Oxford, as his letter of resignation was dated in Oxford and bore the university seal. In 1306 he received a dispensation for having been ordained priest under age, and held the churches of Hatfield (Yorkshire) and Northrepps (Norfolk), with a dispensation to retain the same and a licence to accept an additional benefice.

The example of these brothers demonstrates the strength of their family connections. Not only were the brothers, who must have been close in age, provided with family churches in the Warenne heartlands of South Yorkshire, Norfolk and Surrey, they appear to have remained close. Dispensations for the brothers were obtained at the same time in 1291 and 1303 and William was granted study leave along with his brother in 1306 and 1314. Yet it is perhaps worth noting that neither of the brothers managed to rise to great heights within the Church hierarchy.

The career of John (II), the seventh and last earl Warenne (1286–1347) put the activities of his ancestors with regard to fathering bastards in the shade. He was the father of at least eight bastards, no fewer than six of whom, among them three sons, appear to have survived him. He had no recorded legitimate issue and made numerous resettlements of his estates, yet on his death his estates were divided between his nephew Richard FitzAlan, Earl of Arundel, the son of his sister Alice, and the Crown.

His father, William (V), had been killed whilst participating in a tournament at Croydon in 1286 and so on the death of his grandfather, John (I) the sixth earl, in 1304, he inherited the earldom of Surrey and a large estates spread across Surrey, Sussex, Wales, Norfolk and Yorkshire. As he was a royal ward, his marriage was arranged by the king. On 15 May 1305, it was proposed that he should be married to Edward I's granddaughter Joan, the daughter of Henry, Count of Bar and it is said that he 'willingly accepted' the marriage. Joan was still in France at this time and on 18 October the bishop of Coventry and Lichfield was granted powers to make arrangements for her to travel to England. John (II) was granted seisin of his inheritance on 7 April 1306, though he was not yet 21. The marriage took place on 25 May 1306. Joan, aged ten, was only half the new earl's age, and the marriage was not a success.

Warenne's marital difficulties became notorious. By 1311 he was living openly with a mistress, Maud Nerford. On 22 November of that year, the Archbishop of Canterbury, Robert Winchelsea, wrote to the bishop of Salisbury with a mandate to excommunicate the earl for his failure to appear before the archbishop in the matter of his adultery with Maud. The scandal continued for the next few years. On 21 May 1313 the king tried to postpone the publication of Winchelsea's sentence of excommunication of Warenne until he himself had returned to England as Warenne had been charged with the preservation of the peace whilst the king was overseas.

Maud was probably the daughter of Sir William Nerford and his wife Petronilla, daughter of Sir John Vaux, a neighbour of Warenne's estates in Norfolk. Her own marital status is not entirely clear. In Winchelsea's letter of November 1311 and in a later citation of Warenne she was said to be the wife of a Simon de Driby. Driby, who can possibly be identified with the king's yeoman and steward of the household of that name, whilst Winchelsea was archbishop, had apparently secured a divorce from Maud on the grounds of her notorious conduct. He seems to have been able to remarry. He died in 1322, without surviving issue, and his inquisition post mortem and several other royal records refer to a wife named Margery, although Maud was still living at this time. Driby witnessed a charter of Warenne's in 1316, at the height of Warenne's divorce proceedings, so if this was the same individual he apparently bore no grudge about the matter. Maud is recorded as the mother of two of Warenne's bastard sons, and was almost certainly the mother of at least one more, but was not necessarily the only woman to bear Warenne a bastard.

The key to understanding Warenne's behaviour is that Maud was not simply a mistress or concubine. As Winchelsea's letter of 1311 reveals, Warenne was behaving as if Maud was his lawful wife, '*ac si esset eius uxor legitima*'. He wanted to marry her and went to extraordinary lengths in his attempts to divorce Joan in order to do so. His first attempt was made before the Archbishop of York, William Greenfield. His case was that, when as a minor and a ward of the late king, he had been forced to marry Joan, even though he was related to her in the third and fourth degrees. The archbishop duly served a citation to the countess to appear before him at York on 2 October 1314. William de Rothwell, rector of Normanton and professor of civil law, and Henry de Wylton, rector of Corney, were appointed to hear the case. Presumably as a result of Joan's response,

Greenfield then asked the bishop of Durham to ask Maud Nerford to attend before him in order to answer certain articles concerning the weal of her soul. The bishop dutifully delivered the citation to the manor of the abbot of Byland at Clifton, where Maud was supposed to be staying, though he was unable to see Maud in person, being prevented from doing so by members of Warenne's household.

Warren's petition mentions three factors that could have invalidated the marriage: minority, absence of freely given consent and consanguinity of which he had been ignorant at the time. In fact, at 19, Warenne would have been considered of age for marriage, even if 10-year-old Joan was still too young and he is recorded as having 'willingly accepted' his suggested bride. As far as consanguinity was concerned, Warenne's claim to have been unaware of the relationship was undermined by the existence of a dispensation for intermarriage within the fourth degree of kindred which had been obtained from Pope Clement V at the time of the marriage.

The York attempt having failed, a further effort was made before the archdeacon of Norfolk. This time Maud herself brought the case on the grounds of pre-contract. On 8 March 1315 Robert, chaplain of Yaxley, who was deputy to the archdeacon's official, delivered notice to Joan de Bar that she was cited to appear before the archdeacon, Thomas Gerdeston, or his commissary to answer in a case of matrimony and divorce between Maud and John de Warenne. However, the citation was served on the countess when she was in attendance with the queen. For this breach of protocol the archdeacon's official was committed to the Tower, and the archdeacon was ordered to appear before the next parliament. The problem at this point seems to have been the tactlessness of the archdeacon's official. The following year, Warenne and Maud tried again, this time in London, and initially it looked as if all was going well. On 20 February 1316 the king granted protection for Maud and her advocates and witnesses in the cause of pre-contract between her and John de Warenne, Earl of Surrey, and also offered similar protection for Warenne and his men, advocates, proctors and witnesses in the cause of divorce between him and Joan de Bar. On 23 February Warenne undertook that he would be bound to the king for the £200 yearly, for the maintenance of Joan de Bar while the plea of divorce was pending in the Church courts. On 24 February the earl was granted licence to bring his suit for divorce in the court Christian before Masters Gilbert de Middleton and William de Bray, canons of St Paul's, London, and the prior of Holy Trinity, Aldgate. The same licence also permitted Maud to recommence proceedings for pre-contract before the same judges or others, on withdrawing the suit which she had brought before the official of the archdeacon of Norfolk. It seems that both the king and Warenne expected that the divorce would be granted for Warenne agreed to enfeoff Joan of 740 marks a year of land within a quarter of a year after the pronouncement of the divorce.

Meanwhile, Warenne set out to resettle his estates in anticipation that the divorce would be obtained and he would be able to marry Maud. On 24 June 1316 he granted his Yorkshire, Surrey, Sussex and Welsh estates, together with the towns of Grantham and Stamford (Lincolnshire) to the king. The king took possession on 1 July 1316 and on 6 July regranted the estates to Warenne for life only. Yet, a month later, on 4 August 1316, the king granted Warenne fresh charters regranting to him the surrendered estates (excepting the manor of Kennington, Surrey, which he retained, and the towns of Stamford and Grantham, which were regranted to Warenne for life only, with reversion to the Crown). This settlement aimed to provide for the couple's children. The Surrey, Sussex and Welsh estates were granted with remainders to 'John de Warenne son of Matilda de Neirford, and the heirs male of his body, and failing such issue to Thomas de Warenne son of the said Matilda, and the heirs male of his body, with final remainder failing such issue to the heirs of the body of the said earl'. The Yorkshire estates were granted with remainders to Matilda, for her life, with successive remainders to John de Warenne and Thomas de Warenne, sons of the said Matilda and to the heirs of the body of the earl.

Warenne thus successfully managed to resettle his estates in such a way as to endow his two bastard sons by Maud Nerford. There was a substantial inducement for the king to agree to the settlement, in the shape of the manor of Kennington and the reversion of the two wealthy Lincolnshire towns of Grantham and Stamford. Warenne's aim was to divorce his wife and marry the mother of the bastard sons. It is not clear how old the boys were at this stage, though they cannot have been much beyond their early teens. Presumably, at this time these were his only sons by Maud. If he had been able to marry Maud as planned any further offspring born after the marriage would have been covered by the reversion to heirs of the body of the earl. Where the plan failed was that, contrary to expectations, the divorce was not obtained and so the marriage could not take place. Warenne's subsequent hostility towards Thomas, Earl of Lancaster suggests that he felt that Lancaster was in some way to blame.

It appears that relations between Warenne and Maud broke down following the failure of their final attempt to secure his divorce. In 1320, Warenne petitioned the king to suspend a commission sitting against some of his retainers by the procurement of 'Lady de Nerford' as the plaintiff was her son John and all the justices were her men, saying that they were doing harm to him since he had 'ouste de sa companye Maud de Nerforde'. The original commission was dated 1 December 1319 and had been reissued in the same terms on 8 July 1320.

It was alleged that John Sprygi, Simon Plesent, Robert de Reppes and John Caunceler had broken John de Nerford's close at Wesenham, Norfolk and carried away his goods. The John de Nerford mentioned was probably Maud's brother rather than her son John. The 'Lady de Nerford' is more likely to be Petronilla, the mother of Maud and her brothers, John, Thomas and Edmund. Quite when this split between Warenne and the Nerfords occurred is not clear. However, on 12 February 1323 the king granted protection to Warenne and those accompanying him on the king's business in the north of England including one Thomas de Nerford. This Thomas was more likely to have been Maud's brother, Sir Thomas Nerford (d. 1375), than the younger of the two bastard sons mentioned above.

Meanwhile, in 1317 Warenne, possibly seeking revenge, embarked on what amounted to a private war with Thomas of Lancaster, during the course of which his men carried off the countess of Lancaster, Alice de Lacy, who may not have been an entirely unwilling victim. Warenne's men abducted the countess from her manor of Canford in Dorset. One of them, named Richard St Martin, claimed to have contracted marriage to Alice before she married the earl, but there is no evidence to support this. Alice never returned to her husband, and after his attainder and death following the battle of Boroughbridge, she married Ebulo Lestrange of Knockin, a minor baron of the Welsh marches.

Initially, Lancaster gained the upper hand in the struggle with Warenne, and there was an exchange of lands to Warenne's detriment, with Lancaster taking control of his castles and estates in Wales and Yorkshire. These then fell into the king's hands following Lancaster's attainder in 1322. The Surrey and Sussex estates remained under the settlement of 1316. Maud Nerford also lost property as a result of the conflict, and although she was able to petition the king in 1323 for the restoration of tenements that she had purchased in Wakefield, of which she had been dispossessed by Lancaster, her situation did not improve. In 1326 Warenne resettled what remained of his estates, taking the opportunity to deprive Maud and her sons of succession, and settled the remainder of his Surrey, Sussex and Welsh estates on his sister, Alice, wife of Edmund, Earl of Arundel, and her son, leaving Maud with an interest only in the manor of Hatfield, not far from Warenne's castle of Conisbrough. Meanwhile, the two boys had been admitted to the Order of St John of Jerusalem in London. The Yorkshire estates which had been forfeited by Lancaster were regranted to Warenne for life, with reversion to the king. Ensuring the survival of the family name through the transfer of estates to an illegitimate son was clearly not a priority at this stage. It was only to be expected that Maud would be less than happy with this arrangement. Edmund, Earl of Arundel, undertook on behalf of himself and his heirs to recompense the king for the value of any of the Yorkshire lands that Maud might temporarily recover until the time they reverted to the king or his heirs.

Warenne's relations with his wife Joan appears to have improved slightly by the early 1330s— perhaps because the relationship with Maud Nerford was over. On 31 May 1331 he issued a charter confirming grants to Lewes Priory 'for his own soul and that of the countess, Joan de Bar, his consort', which was witnessed by Joan herself and her chaplain, among others, including 'Sir William de Warenna', another of Warenne's illegitimate sons. This charter marks a contrast with one from 1316 when Warenne confirmed his and his ancestors' donations to the Priory of Thetford. Then it had been Maud Nerford and their children, rather than his wife, whose souls he had been concerned about: '*ac etiam pro salute animae Matildis de Nereford et antecessorum suorum, et puerorum nostrorum*'.

In the mid–1330s Warenne still regarded his Arundel relations as his preferred heirs. On 6 June 1335 he released to the king his castle and manor of Castle Acre, Norfolk and the following day the estate was regranted to him and his heirs, with the remainder to Richard, Earl of Arundel, the son of Warenne's sister, Alice, and her husband, Edmund, Earl of Arundel. The improved relationship with Joan did not last, however. By 1344 the earl's marriage was once again in question. In February of that year Pope Clement VI (1342–52) wrote, at the request of the queens of France and England, to the bishop of Winchester asking him to 'warn and compel John, Earl of Warenne, to receive and treat with marital affection his wife, Joan de Barre, whom he married by virtue of a dispensation granted by Clement V (they being related in the fourth degree), and having lived together for 32 years; notwithstanding his pretence that the said dispensation was surreptitious, inasmuch as they are related respectively in the third and fourth degrees from a common stock'.

At about the same time as the queens of France and England appealed to the pope on Joan's behalf, the earl petitioned the pope for plenary indulgence at the hour of death for himself, his wife Joan, one of his bastard sons, Sir William de Warenne and Margaret his wife and for Robert de Lynne, his chaplain, a monk of Castle Acre. This was granted by Clement VI just a month after his letter to the bishop of Winchester. Why Warenne included his estranged wife along with his chaplain, his illegitimate son and the latter's wife is something of a mystery. Perhaps it was for appearance's sake, but Warenne does not appear to have been too concerned about such matters, as subsequent events show.

Warenne then made yet another attempt to get a divorce. He had apparently taken legal advice on the dispensation for consanguinity obtained at the time of his marriage, which had earlier proved a stumbling block. He challenged its validity on the grounds that the dispensation was for persons related in the fourth degree, whereas Joan was related to the common stock in the third degree, and Warenne in the fourth. Despite the opinion of 'divers doctors' on this technicality, however, in June 1344 Clement VI ruled that the dispensation was valid. This declaration not only put an end to Warenne's hopes, but set a new legal precedent, for some ten years later, Innocent VI (1352–62) provided confirmation to Sir Richard de Baskerville and Isabella, his wife, of Clement VI's ruling in the case of Warenne and Joan de Bar, that a dispensation for 'the marriage of persons related in the fourth degree of kindred shall hold good if they are related in the third and fourth degrees'. In 1358 Innocent again confirmed the ruling, this time at the request of Sir Robert de Bures.

Meanwhile, Warenne became ever more desperate in his attempts to gain a divorce. Whilst challenging the validity of the dispensation, he came up with an entirely new story, stating that there had been intimate relations between himself and his relative, his wife's aunt, the Princess Mary (a daughter of Edward I) before he was married. Mary was a nun of Amesbury Abbey (Wiltshire), but had died in 1332 and was therefore unavailable to answer to the truth or otherwise of this claim. The matter was put before Clement VI who issued a mandate to the bishop of St Asaph to absolve John de Warenne from excommunication, which he incurred by intermarrying with Joan de Bar, whose mother's sister Mary, he had carnally known. A penance was to be enjoined; and as to the marriage, 'canonical action is to be taken'. It is not clear what form this canonical action was to take, but it appears that this was not quite the end of the matter, for shortly afterwards the pope had to write to the archbishop of Canterbury and his official to stop them from pursing Joan de Bar in the archbishop's court on this matter. Warenne's failure to obtain a divorce in 1344 can be contrasted with the success of his nephew Richard FitzAlan, despite the fact that FitzAlan's marriage, unlike Warenne's, had produced offspring. However, FitzAlan's petition was on the basis of minority, lack of consent and coercion rather than consanguinity or precontract.

By this time Maud Nerford was no longer in the picture. On 22 November 1345 Warenne was granted licence to grant the advowson of Hatfield to the abbot and convent of Roche. Hatfield had been regranted to Warenne for life with successive remainders to Maud and her two sons, but Maud was now dead and John and Thomas had both taken religious habits in the Order of the Brethren of the Hospital of St John of Jerusalem at Clerkenwell. Warenne's renewed determination to obtain a divorce from Joan in the 1340s arose as a result of his relationship with another woman, Isabel Holland, the daughter of Sir Robert Holland. In the early part of 1346 Warenne attempted to resettle his estates in Surrey, Sussex and Wales, which had in 1326 been settled with reversion to his sister and her husband, Edmund FitzAlan, Earl of Arundel.

The document, as recorded by the seventeenth-century antiquarian William Dugdale, states that

> 'and if God should please to send him an heir by Isabel de Holand then his wife, should the same heir be male or female, it should be joined in marriage to some one of blood royal, whom the King should think fittest; so that the whole inheritance of this earl, with the name and arms of Warenne, should be preserved by the blood royal in the blood of him, the said earl. And, in case he should depart this life without any such issue, begotten on the body of the said Isabel, that then all his castles, manors, lands and tenements in Surrey, Sussex and Wales, should after his decease remain to the King, to be bestowed upon some one of his own sons, on whom he should think fit; on condition that in the person of such son and his heirs, the name, honour and arms of Warenne should forever be maintained and kept.'

In referring to Isabel as his wife, Warenne may merely have been anticipating his divorce and remarriage, but it is worth noting that in his will he described Isabel as 'ma compaigne', a term usually used to refer to a wife. It seems that, whilst he wanted to settle his estates on any issue of his liaison with Isabel and to ensure the survival of the name and arms of Warenne, he was also concerned about legitimacy, or at least the appearance of legitimacy. He clearly regarded his relationships with Maud Nerford and Isabel Holland as a form of marriage in all but legal terms. Once again, there was a substantial inducement to the king to acquiesce in this arrangement, since one of his own offspring would benefit, whether Warenne had issue with Isabel or not.

Unfortunately for Warenne, and for the king, Richard, Earl of Arundel, the son of Edmund and Alice, was not prepared to allow himself to be disinherited so easily. He visited King Edward III whilst he was near Yarmouth, Isle of Wight, on his way to Calais, and drew his attention to the earlier settlement agreed by Edward II. In November 1346 Edward III ordered execution of the feoffment to be stayed pending further deliberation, and ultimately decided that 'in consideration of the service of the petitioner in the war of France' it should not be put into effect. In December 1346, he revoked the arrangement on the grounds that he had not been 'fully instructed of the grant of his late father'. Richard was not only in his prime and needed for the war in France, he was also extremely wealthy and a useful source of loans. Warenne, however, was so infirm by this time that he had in October 1346 been excused from personal attendance at parliaments and councils. No doubt the Warenne estates in Surrey, Sussex and Wales would have been useful to provide for Edward's large family, but he already had the reversion of the Yorkshire estates and the price of antagonising Earl Richard was not one he was prepared to pay.

Warenne died on his sixty-first birthday, 30 June 1347, at his castle of Conisbrough in Yorkshire. Under the terms of the 1326 settlement, the Yorkshire estates reverted to the Crown, and on 6 August the castles, manors, towns, lands and tenements held by Warenne north of the Trent were granted to the king's son Edmund of Langley. The Surrey, Sussex and Welsh lands passed to Warenne's nephew Richard, Earl of Arundel.

The last Warenne, earl of Surrey thus died without legitimate issue. He had not, however, died without surviving illegitimate issue. Warenne's will left bequests to the following of his children:

> Sir William de Warenne: 100 marks and a hure of silver gilt for Stratherne with its band or wreath of silver gilt, two tags and the lace of silver gilt for the mantling and all his armour for jousting. (The hure was a kind of hat worn over the helmet, also known to modern writers on heraldry as a cap or chapeau of dignity. The earl had been granted Strathearn by Edward Bailiol in 1332, and thereafter used the title 'Earl of Surrey and Strathearn')
>
> Sir William's wife (not named in the will, but described as 'my daughter his wife' (*ma fille sa compaigne*)): a '*nouche d'or*', or jewelled clasp
>
> Edward de Warenne: £20
>
> Joanne de Basing: a silver cup
>
> Katherine: 10 marks
>
> Isabel (a nun of Sempringham): £20
>
> William de Warenne (prior of Castle Acre): a bible in French

Warenne thus had six illegitimate children who survived him, in addition to John and Thomas, the sons by Maud Nerford already mentioned. There was another possible bastard of the last earl of Warenne, not mentioned in the will. A petition, probably of 1334, by Sir Ralph Botiller refers to a 'Ravlyn fitz al Count de Garrein' who was alleged to be one of a gang that attacked one of Botiller's manors on Warenne's orders, doing £200 worth of damage. There are no other extant references to this Ravlyn or Rawlin. Possibly he predeceased his father.

It is not clear who the mothers of all these children were. If they were, as tradition has it, all children of the earl and Maud Nerford, they must all have been conceived before the split, which occurred by 1320. However, whilst Sir William was certainly born before August 1310, when he received a grant of the manor of Beeston (Norfolk), there is nothing to connect him with Maud Nerford, unlike Sir Edward, and he may therefore have a different mother. Sir Edward would appear to have been Maud Nerford's son, but if he had been born before 1316, it is strange that he was not mentioned in the settlement of that date and it is therefore probable that he was born between 1316 and 1320. Prior William was born at Conisbrough, so must have been born before January 1318, by which time this castle was in the hands of Thomas of Lancaster, and he was, in any case, old enough to be prior of Monks Horton in 1337. If he was intended for the Church there would have been no need to include him in the settlement of 1316. Some or all of the girls may also have been born earlier as they would not necessarily have been included in the settlement. Why did Warenne never try to settle his some of his estates on one or more of his other sons? Sir William in particular would seem to have been a potential candidate to continue the name and honour of Warenne.

It has been shown that his intention in 1316 had been for John or Thomas to inherit a large part of his estates, although he later changed this arrangement. On the eve of his death he does not appear to have made any attempts to enable his other illegitimate children to inherit. Why did he treat the other bastards differently? It seems that Warenne was concerned with legitimacy. In 1316, when his sons by Maud Nerford were included in the settlement, he expected to be free to marry Maud. If they had married, their two sons would not be legitimate by common law—hence the need to name them explicitly in the settlement—but it was possible that he believed the marriage could at least legitimate them according to canon law. When it became clear that he would be unable to marry Maud and the relationship broke down, he resettled his estates on his heir general, his sister Alice, wife of Edmund, Earl of Arundel. His omission of the future Sir William from the settlement is thus explicable if he were not the son of Maud, as he could not be 'legitimated' by Warenne's marriage to Maud. He might bear the Warenne name and arms, but the earl seems to have had scruples about making an undeniable bastard his heir. His final attempt at resettlement of his estates was made in the belief that he would be able to marry Isabel Holland. She is referred to as 'then his wife' in the charter, and it is clear that he intended the arrangement to refer to legitimate issue. The letter patent of Edward III revoking the arrangement states that the estates were to have been regranted to 'the said earl and to *the heirs of his body lawfully begotten*'. Bastard sons were regarded as part of the family and needed to be provided for, but arranging for a bastard son to 'inherit' part of the estate and continue the family name seems not to have occurred to Warenne, although he would probably been aware of the arrangement made by the last Vescy, Lord of Alnwick in 1297 who did just that. It is interesting that although Warenne was apparently not prepared to go to the lengths of settling his estates on one of his surviving bastard sons, the proposed resettlement of 1346 allowed for the continuation of the name, honour and arms of Warenne in the person of one of the king's sons, implying that he considered the name and honour of Warenne to be more important than the true (if illegitimate) bloodline. Although he bequeathed valuable armour to his bastard son Sir William, the hure bore the arms of Strathearn, not Warenne. Possibly the knowledge that there was already a bastard in the Warenne lineage, albeit one with royal connections, affected his thinking on this point. It is also worth noting that none of the bastard children mentioned in the will are explicitly described as illegitimate in the document.

It was not a case of estrangement and deathbed reconciliation. His son Sir William was provided with a sufficient livelihood to enable him to live as a knight, and he pursued a military career. In 1332 he was a witness to letters patent of his father granting twenty acres of land in fee to his serjeant or esquire, Henry de Kelsterne. In 1333 he received a pardon for acquiring the manor of Beeston for life, from John de Warenne, Earl of Surrey, without a licence and licence to remain. In 1340 he received a grant in fee of 122 acres of waste in Warenne's manor of Hatfield at a rent of ten shillings. Sir William was one of three commanders of the thirty men–at–arms and forty archers supplied by Warenne for the French war in 1339 and he was with Edward III in Brittany in 1342, when he was sent with Sir Walter Mauny and Sir John Stirling to reconnoitre the city of Vannes. He seems to have borne a version of the Warenne arms, *checky or and azure,* differenced with *a chief argent.* He was married by 1344, when Earl Warenne petitioned the pope for plenary indulgence at the hour of death for his son and the latter's wife Margaret. He witnessed a charter by his father, granting pasture rights in Wakefield to a tenant in June 1345. After his father's death he continued to serve on commissions and was granted a life annuity of forty marks at the Exchequer in 1364 as a reward for long service.

Edward de Warenne is a more shadowy figure, but he appears to have been the ancestor of the Warren family of Poynton (Cheshire). It seems probable that Edward was a son of Maud Nerford, since the Warren family possessed a manor formerly in the hands of the Nerfords, and their coat of arms included both the *lion rampant ermine* of Nerford and the *checky* of Warenne. In 1346, Earl Warenne petitioned the king to suggest that since his sons Edward and William de Warenne were ready to attend the king abroad, Edward might be excused from the demand to provide a man-at-arms from his lands in Norfolk, since he held no others there. He held rights of advowson over a third part of the church of St Mary, Iteringham (Norfolk) in 1349.

The career of Prior William de Warenne demonstrates that patronage was needed not only to achieve a position in life, but to retain it. William was destined for the monastic life and was duly enrolled in the Cluniac priory of Lewes, a Warenne family foundation. By August 1337 he was prior of the daughter house of Monks Horton in Kent, and was granted a respite for the payment of 27 marks 6s 8d to the Treasury for custody, following the intervention of his father the earl. The relationship between the earl and prior was explicitly stated. A further respite was granted in May 1338, again at the request of Earl Warenne. Meanwhile, William endeavoured to prove that his house should not be subject to the penalties applied to alien priories during the war with France. By February 1339 an inquisition had found in his favour, accepting that the prior of Horton was an Englishman, the son of the earl of Surrey, born at Conisburgh Castle, and all the monks were Englishmen, and that neither he nor his predecessors had made any apportion, tax or service to a religious house overseas. Despite this, in July 1340 Prior William was still having some difficulties in this respect and the earl once again had to intervene on his behalf. A respite on the annual farm of forty marks required of Prior William as an alien was granted 'in consideration of John de Warenne, Earl of Surrey, the prior's father, and at the earl's request'. Despite his illegitimate birth, his relationship with the earl was clearly important.

Prior William's career continued to flourish, and by October 1342 he had been promoted to the larger house of Castle Acre in Norfolk, when he acknowledged a debt of £300 on behalf of the convent. However, there was a hitch, since William's dispensation for illegitimacy granted by Pope John XXII (1316–34) and renewed by order of Benedict XII (1335–42), applied only to a non-conventual priory, such as Monks Horton, and not to a conventual house such as Castle Acre. The earl therefore sought a further papal dispensation to enable William to take on the role of prior. The dispensation, along with a mandate to make provision of Castle Acre was granted by Clement VI (1342–52) on 16 January 1344.

Prior William's fortunes took a significant turn for the worse shortly after his father's death in 1347. Whilst he had apparently coped perfectly well at Monks Horton, he ran into difficulties at the larger Castle Acre priory and was not able to rely on his cousin Richard, Earl of Arundel, the new patron of the priory, for support. He was evidently forced to resign as prior. On 25 October 1348 Walter Picot, a fellow monk who had been ordained acolyte on the same date as Warenne in March 1325 and now named as prior, obtained a writ of *de apostate capiendo*, that is a writ against a person who has left a religious order, requiring them to be arrested and returned to the abbot or prior, for the apprehension of William de Warenne and one Robert de Neketon.

In 1349 Cluniac visitors reported that Prior William had fled, having alienated the priory's temporal and spiritual possessions, and endangered the priory's future, and ordered the prior of Lewes to apprehend and punish him. Their detailed report lays a number of charges at William's door: standards were lax, with customs and statutes of the order not being correctly observed and the psalms not being said at the accustomed times; the church and other buildings were falling into ruin and the infirm were not being cared for. William was said to have squandered the priory's resources and alienated property. William had not given up his appointment without a fight. After being forced to resign he travelled to the papal court at Avignon, resigned the priory over to the hands of pope Clement VI, not mentioning that he had already resigned. He then received it back as a papal provision, binding the priory to the payment of a large sum as first fruits in the process. The attempts of the papacy to recover this sum from the priory were to prove a bone of contention for many years.

In 1363 Urban V (1362–70) sought payment of the sum of £480 19s 7d as the fruits of one year's voidance of the priory reserved to the papal camera from William de Warenne, prior of Castleacre, who had been appointed by Clement VI. Reports from the papal collectors Hugh Pelegrini, John de Cabrespino and Arnold Garnieri concerning their failed attempts to recover this sum reveal some of the story. John de Cabrespino reported in 1370 that the papal provision was not valid because the priory was under lay patronage and Warenne was immediately excluded because he was a bastard who squandered the assets of the priory. The monks, in their efforts to rid themselves of a profligate and unpopular prior, had evidently decided to include William's defect of birth in their account of the grounds for dismissal, despite his papal dispensations. As for the validity of the other charges, even leaving aside the question of the first fruits, William certainly seems to have lived in some style. The luxuriously appointed prior's lodging at Castle Acre is still standing today, and the Warenne arms on the fourteenth century additions suggest where the priory income may have been spent. Meanwhile, the dispute over the first fruits dragged on until the papal collectors eventually lost patience and excommunicated the monks and sequestrated the fruits of the priory, whereupon in 1385 the next earl of Arundel intervened on the priory's behalf. In response to the earl's petition, the king ordered the papal collector was ordered to cease his demands. The earl's petition stated that William had never lawfully been in possession of the priory as a result of the papal provision. The version of events contained in the petition was that William had resigned the priory to the prior of Lewes, who then appointed another prior, who remained in peaceable possession for the duration of his life. Meanwhile, William made another resignation of the priory to the pope, omitting to mention his first resignation and obtained a papal provision, binding the prior for payment of the sum of £ 484 9s 9d as annates. William's position as prior had evidently owed much to the patronage of his father.

Prior William's brother and namesake, Sir William de Warenne, had a similar experience with enemies who would not have dared to take action against him during his father's lifetime. In August 1338, ostensibly acting by authority of a commission issued to his father, he had arrested the Sussex knight Sir John Waleys and imprisoned him for eight weeks at Lewes. Some nine years later, after the earl's death, Sir John brought an action of trespass. Although the action included other Warenne retainers such as Sir John Bigod and Sir John de St Pier, Warenne's was the only case which went to a jury; Sir John Bigod obtained a royal pardon and was released and Sir John de St Pier was also eventually pardoned. Warenne was found guilty and fined £40. It seems fairly clear that Waleys would not have dared bring this action during the earl's lifetime.

The experience of the Warenne brothers demonstrates how much bastards relied on the patronage of parents or other relatives. In their case, the death of their father left them without a powerful patron; their cousin, Richard FitzAlan, was not prepared to step into the breach. Family loyalty was perhaps not Richard FitzAlan's strong suit. His lack of support for illegitimate children was not restricted to his nephews by marriage, but reached closer to home. Richard succeeded, as his father Edmund had not, in surviving the vicissitudes of fourteenth-century politics and dying an extremely wealthy man. He had profited from the lack of legitimate heirs of his uncle, John, Earl of Warenne, acquiring a major part of the Warenne inheritance on his uncle's death, having frustrated the latter's final scheme for the resettlement of his estates in order to retain the family name. FitzAlan had no need to resort to complex settlements in order to continue his own family name—he had three sons to continue it: Richard, John and Thomas. But these sons were legitimate only because in 1344 FitzAlan had sought and obtained the annulment of his first marriage, leaving him free to marry his mistress, Eleanor Beaumont. In so doing, he had rendered his first-born son Edmund, the child of that marriage, a bastard. Edmund was by this time married to Sibyl, a daughter of William Montagu, Earl of Salisbury and the timing of the annulment shortly after Montagu's death in January 1344 is probably not a coincidence. FitzAlan's will did not include any bequest to Edmund or his children.

The Arundel case clearly led to bad feeling between Edmund and his half-siblings, which continued into the next generation. Edmund and Sibyl had three daughters: Elizabeth, Philippa and Katherine. Elizabeth married Sir John Meryett of Somerset, whilst Philippa married the Cornish knight Richard Cergeaux. In May 1382 both couples, together with Robert d'Eyncourt, Katherine's son, brought an action against against Richard, Earl of Arundel (the son of Richard FitzAlan senior and Eleanor Beaumont) claiming that they had been dispossessed of a tenement in Singleton (Sussex). The earl's attorney argued that the earl was the legitimate son and heir, and that since Edmund, through whom the plaintiffs made their claim, was a bastard, it was entirely lawful for the earl to have ejected them from the property concerned. A jury then swore that Edmund was indeed a bastard. The plaintiffs did not give up, however, and alleged that the members of the jury had lied on oath. A second jury of twenty-four knights agreed with the first that Edmund had been a bastard. It was accordingly ruled that not only should the plaintiffs take nothing, but that they should be arrested for bringing a false prosecution. Whilst the jurors were technically correct, the case suggests a continuation of bad feelings between the two branches of the family. Needless to say, the earl did not remember his half-nieces in his will. There was, however, some evidence of family links. One of Sir Richard Cergaux's executors was his wife's half-uncle, Thomas Arundel, Archbishop of York.

Earl Warenne in context: his contemporaries

Warenne's behaviour, though perhaps extreme in terms of the number of bastards he fathered and the number of times he changed his mind about the disposition of his estates, was not very different from that of his contemporaries. Aymer de Valence, Earl of Pembroke, also had no legitimate male heirs of his body, but had an illegitimate son, Henry. There is no apparent evidence that the earl made any attempt to settle his estate in his son's favour. It is true that Henry predeceased his father by a couple of years, but had the earl been minded to settle his estates upon his illegitimate son he might have been expected to have put arrangements in hand at least when the latter reached adulthood or married. In the absence of any other arrangement, on the earl's death his lands were divided between the heirs of his two sisters. Whilst he had not been regarded as a substitute for a legitimate heir, Henry de Valence was a knight and member of his father's retinue. He accompanied the earl on his mission to the papal court at Avignon in 1317 and was captured along with his father by Jean de Lamouilly and held prisoner in the County of Bar. The motive for the capture of the earl is not known, but one theory is that the Count of Bar was seeking to punish Edward II for the treatment of his sister Joan (Earl Warenne's estranged wife.) Henry remained as a hostage whilst his father set about raising the huge ransom. He had earlier married Margery, widow of Theobald de Gayton. The position of Henry de Valence is comparable with that of Sir William de Warenne, the illegitimate son of his father's contemporary. Both were illegitimate sons of earls who were knighted and served in their fathers' retinues but were not regarded as potential substitutes for a legitimate heir.

Thomas of Lancaster, Warenne's great rival, also lacked a legitimate male heir of his body and had little chance of securing one, given his marital difficulties with Alice de Lacy. He had two bastard sons, Thomas and John.

Again, there is no evidence of an attempt to transfer part of the estate to either of them in place of the earl's brother and right heir, Henry. Given the various land transactions in which Lancaster was involved as a result of his private war with Warenne, he could surely have managed to settle at least a reversionary interest in a part of the estate on a bastard son had he been so determined. After all, Warenne had managed something similar in 1316. There is, however, little evidence of any strong connection between Lancaster and his bastard sons. One of them, Thomas, became a knight, but unlike William de Warenne and Henry de Valence, he does not appear to have been particularly associated with his father. It is possible that he was still quite young at the time of the latter's death. Lancaster's sons seem at least to have received some support from his relatives. Thomas became a knight after spending some time at a university, and subsequently served as one of Edward III's chamberlains, participating in an attack on Sens. By 1354 he had tired of military life and sought to join the order of Friars Minor. The other son, John, entered the Church, obtaining the degrees of Master of Arts and Bachelor of Theology. He obtained benefices in Uttoxeter (Staffordshire) and Charing (Kent), but efforts on the part of his kinsmen Edward III and Henry of Lancaster in the 1350s to secure him a canonry and prebend at Lincoln or Salisbury were to prove more problematic, owing to the length of the waiting lists.

During the reign of Edward II there were thus three earls who all lacked legitimate male heirs of the body but who had at least one illegitimate son, yet none of them arranged for their estates to be settled on their bastards. It might be that their rank caused the difficulty. What was possible for a baron or knight might not be acceptable for an earl, either from the point of view of the king, whose consent would be required, or in the view of the earls themselves, or the barons. David Crouch has stressed the importance of the dignity and 'level of bearing and greatness', which sets apart those of comital rank. There was likely a price to be paid for royal consent. In Warenne's case, the Crown retained the manor of Kennington, Surrey and the reversion of the towns of Stamford and Grantham. Furthermore, whilst Warenne obtained royal consent to settle his estates with reversion to two bastard sons, this occurred at a time when both Warenne and the king expected his divorce and remarriage to take place. Had the precontract case been successful and Warenne married Maud Nerford, any irregularities with regard to the birth of their first two sons would no doubt have been glossed over. Had he been so inclined, Thomas of Lancaster could no doubt have tried to settle property on one of his illegitimate sons at a time when he was in the political ascendant. A dispensation for illegitimacy granted to one of his sons, John, in 1350 described him as the son of a married man and a spinster related in the third degree of kindred, so it is unlikely to be a result of concerns about the low status of the mother. Aymer de Valence made no apparent attempt to settle the reversion of his estates on his adult illegitimate son, though he lacked a legitimate son. However, none of these cases is clear cut, and it may be unwise to read too much into them in view of the differing circumstances in each case.

Despite the well-known doubts about his sexual preferences, Piers Gaveston, Earl of Cornwall, another of Warenne's contemporaries, had a daughter, Joan, by his wife, Margaret de Clare. J. S. Hamilton has suggested that there are grounds for believing that the 'Amie de Gaveston' who served as a damsel of the Queen's Chamber in the 1330s was another daughter, but illegitimate. This argument is based on the generosity of the king in celebrating the birth in 1312 of Gaveston's daughter by Margaret, which suggests that the birth of another daughter to the couple would not have gone unrecorded. After Gaveston's death, careful provision was made for his widow (who was the king's niece) and legitimate daughter. Joan was raised in the convent at Amesbury (a popular home for royal nieces) and a marriage to Thomas de Multon, Lord Egremont, was proposed, though she died whilst still a minor. The arrangements for Amie were of a lesser order. She married John de Driby, a king's yeoman, an individual whom Hamilton considers 'a suitable marriage for a damsel of the chamber endowed with a modest income provided through the queen's patronage, but by no means a suitable marriage for the legitimate daughter of an earl'.

Some support for the theory that there was a reluctance to raise a bastard to an exalted rank may be found in the history of royal bastards. Given-Wilson and Curteis point to a change in attitudes to bastardy at the turn of the thirteenth century that affected the treatment of English royal bastards for at least three hundred years. William Longspée, a bastard son of Henry II, was the last royal bastard to be raised to the peerage until Arthur Plantagenet, an illegitimate son of Edward IV, was created Viscount Lisle in 1523. There were, however, ten other identifiable male royal bastards born during this period, although most of these were born before the fourteenth century. Whilst this change in attitudes evidently did not prevent bastards of noble rather than royal origins from joining the ranks of the wider aristocracy, it may have been reflected in the reluctance of the earls to settle their estates on a bastard. The English earls were an elite group within the wider nobility. If such a change in attitudes did exist, it does not appear to have extended to Scotland, where, in about 1330, Alexander de Bruce, illegitimate son of Edward, Earl of Carrick (d. 1318), was created Earl of Carrick.

Chapter 3

Sexual Misconduct: Marriage and Adultery; Bastard-bearers and their Social Status

In the 1420s, Alice Wodehouse was at the centre of a scandal. The daughter of John Wodehouse of Roydon, near Castle Rising in Norfolk, an influential member of the East Anglian gentry, she had been married to her father's ward, Thomas Tuddenham, in about 1418. By 1425, the couple had separated amid Alice's public claims that the marriage was unconsummated and that the real father of her child was Richard Stapleton, her father's chamberlain. She received little sympathy from her father. In the later divorce proceedings, a witness, Robert Holley, gave evidence that Tuddenham, on hearing that Alice was publicly asserting that the child was not his and that there had never been any sexual relations between them, had sent him to inform her father of her claims. John Wodehouse told Holley to inform Alice that if she wished to have her father's blessing and avoid his anger she should abstain from saying such things that reflected on the honour of her husband and herself. Despite this intervention, the marriage could not be saved and in 1429 Alice was duly despatched to a nunnery, where she remained until her death in 1475. This tale of East Anglian gentlefolk might suggest that a dim view was taken of adultery and women who had illegitimate children, but the overall picture is more nuanced.

Marriage

Before looking in more detail at the procreation of illegitimate children, it is worth considering medieval marriage in more detail. For the nobility and gentry, marriage might sometimes have been viewed as a business transaction, aimed at securing estates, but, as seen in Chapter One, the view of marriage developed by the medieval Church was based on the doctrine that consent of the partners was sufficient enough to form an unbreakable marriage bond. This remained the case in England until the Marriage Act of 1753. Whilst the publication of banns and marriage in public was strongly encouraged, it nevertheless remained possible to contract a binding marriage through the exchange of vows in the present tense, even in the absence of witnesses. Provided that both parties remained committed to the marriage and there was no impediment, there was nothing that could be done to overturn the marriage however hard the families of the couple might try.

The Paston family discovered this to their cost when their daughter Margery married the family's bailiff, Richard Calle, in 1469. The family's reaction to the couple's request for permission to marry had been one of outrage, not because they disliked Calle, who was a reliable and competent servant, but because of his lower social status. The Pastons were not yet entirely secure in their rise through the social ranks, and looked to marriage to secure their status among the gentry. Margery's brother, John Paston III, wrote that he had told Calle that he would never have his goodwill to make Margery 'sell candle and mustard in Framlingham'. Unsurprisingly, the couple took matters into their own hands and married in secret. The Pastons were furious. The couple were separated from one another and put under immense pressure to change their story. A letter written by Margery's mother, Margaret, described the couple's subsequent examination on 8 September by the bishop of Norwich, Walter Lyhert, during which Margery told the bishop the form of words she had used to contract the marriage, adding that if those words did not make it sure, that she would make it sure before she went. Examined separately, Calle's account of the date and time of the marriage and the words used accorded with Margery's. Whilst the bishop, sympathetic to the family's position, delayed giving a final pronouncement for a month in case any other impediment should come to light, there was ultimately nothing the Pastons could do to overturn the marriage.

Nevertheless, proving the existence or absence of a marriage later might be more difficult if it had been conducted without banns, as studies of cases in the Church courts have shown. Cases claiming pre-contract are one of the most commonly found types among later-medieval English ecclesiastical court records, though the frequency declined over the course of the later Middle Ages. In some cases, a collusive claim of pre-contract could used as a fraudulent means of dissolving a marriage in order to marry someone else. This required credible witnesses prepared to perjure themselves to say that they had been present when an earlier marriage to the now-intended spouse had taken place. No doubt this did happen on occasion, though Shannon McSheffrey has argued that in fifteenth-century London it was commonplace for marriages to take place through the exchange of vows before witnesses in private homes and so witness statements should not necessarily be assumed to be collusive. There are also many cases of a marriage being challenged by a third party who claimed to have contracted a prior marriage with one of the parties. Equally, it was possible for rumours to circulate that a couple were married when they had in fact not exchanged the necessary vows, leading to problems if one of them actually did marry someone else later.

Given the room for doubt about whether a valid marriage had taken place or not, a couple might try to forestall trouble by obtaining documentation to confirm the validity of their marriage. David d'Avray has noted that there was increasing concern about the validity of marriages during the last three medieval centuries, and that individuals were prepared to go to great lengths in order to authenticate their marriage and thus ensure that the legitimacy of their children was not in any doubt. He notes that the effort taken to authenticate a marriage was proportionate to the social status of the couple, citing the lengths to which King Henry III was prepared to go in order to establish that his 'marriage' to Joan de Ponthieu (conducted by proxy and without a prior dispensation for the fact that they were related within the forbidden degrees) was invalid when he decided to marry Eleanor of Provence instead. It took eighteen years before Henry was finally satisfied by a papal bull issued on 20 May 1254, which put the matter beyond doubt. Establishing the validity of a royal marriage beyond reasonable doubt was of course a sensible precaution, as is demonstrated by the allegations which were bandied around in the course of the political upheaval of the late-fifteenth century. Following the death of Edward IV, his brother Richard (III) claimed the throne on the basis that Edward's marriage to Elizabeth Woodville was invalid on grounds of pre-contract. The identity of the lady concerned is uncertain: *Titulus Regis*, the Act by which Richard formally claimed the throne, cited Eleanor Butler, but other accounts name Edward's mistress Elizabeth Lucy, and the Italian scholar Dominic Mancini mentioned a marriage contracted by proxy on the continent by the earl of Warwick, who had certainly been actively pressing for an alliance with the French king's sister-in-law, Bona of Savoy, shortly before the Woodville marriage was made public. The fact that the Woodville marriage had been conducted secretly did not help, but the validity of the marriage was not questioned during Edward's lifetime.

An earlier secret marriage was that of Henry V's young widow, Catherine of Valois. In around the year 1425 rumours began to circulate that she had formed an amorous attachment to Edmund Beaufort, the nineteen-year-old nephew of the chancellor, Henry Beaufort. The royal council seem to have been concerned about this relationship, particularly since, in the words of one contemporary source, she was said to be unable 'to curb fully her carnal passions.' In the parliament of October 1427 to March 1428 a statute was enacted which forbade marriage to a queen without royal consent on pain of forfeiture of lands for life. Despite this precaution, sometime between 1428 and 1432 Catherine entered into a marriage with a Welsh squire called Owen Tudor. The marriage was known within court circles by May 1432 when Owen Tudor was given the rights of an Englishman, but it was not common knowledge until after Catherine's death in 1437. The origins of her relationship with Tudor are unknown. There has been speculation that the marriage was designed to protect Edmund Beaufort from the effect of the 1428 statute, Owen Tudor having rather less to lose, and even that the couple's first son, Edmund Tudor, might in fact have been Beaufort's son, but there is no real evidence of this.

Queen Catherine was not the only sexually active widow among the social elite. Another example is Constance (*c.* 1375–1416), daughter of Edmund of Langley, 1st Duke of York, and widow of Thomas Despenser, who had been executed for treason as a result of his part in the 'Epiphany Rising' of 1400 against Henry IV. After her husband's death, Constance began a relationship with Edmund Holland, 7th Earl of Kent (1383–1408). Holland was unmarried, and in January 1405 as a minor in the king's custody, was granted licence to marry whoever he pleased of the king's lieges. Unfortunately, Constance engaged in an active conspiracy against the Crown. In February 1405 she was intercepted at Cheltenham on her way to Cardiff where she was presumably intending to join with the Welsh rebel, Owain Glyn Dŵr. She was imprisoned for a while at Kenilworth Castle and her estates were temporarily confiscated. Holland went on to marry Lucia Visconti in 1407 instead. In the meantime, Constance had borne him a daughter, Eleanor, who later married James Tuchet, Lord Audley. Eleanor later tried unsuccessfully to prove that Constance and Edmund had actually married and that she was Edmund's heir. In 1431, Holland's heirs petitioned parliament to prevent Eleanor and Audley from obtaining 'proof' of her legitimacy by means of a collusive lawsuit aimed at obtaining a certification of her legitimacy from a bishop, which could then be used to pursue a claim on the estate.

Whilst younger noblewomen were more protected, they did occasionally manage to subvert planned marriages by making their own choices. John of Gaunt's daughter Elizabeth Lancaster was espoused in 1380 to John Hastings, the eight-year old heir to the earldom of Pembroke, but after being sent to the royal court to learn the ways of courtly society, she began a relationship with Sir John Holland, a younger brother of the Earl of Kent, by whom she became pregnant. The earlier betrothal was repudiated and she married Holland with her father's approval in June 1386. The couple subsequently joined Gaunt on his expedition to claim the crown of Castile, showing that there was no ill-will. Holland prospered through his connections first with Gaunt and later with Richard II and was created Earl of Huntingdon on 2 June 1388, and Duke of Exeter in September 1397. When his brother-in-law Bolingbroke invaded in 1399, Holland remained loyal to Richard II, and was executed in January 1400 for plotting against Henry. Elizabeth subsequently married John Cornwall, later Lord Fanhope (d. 1443).

Some relationships, whilst not marriages in the eyes of the authorities were perhaps viewed that way by the individuals concerned. Earl Warenne's relationship with Maud Nerford, discussed in the previous chapter, clearly falls into this category, as does his later relationship with Isabel Holland (an aunt of Sir John Holland). Eve, daughter of John FitzRobert, Lord Clavering, who married Thomas Audley is a case in point. After Thomas Audley's death she married Thomas Ufford (d. 1314), then entered into a relationship with James Audley (d. 1334) of Stratton Audley, a cousin of her first husband. They never married, perhaps because they were unable to obtain the necessary dispensation.

Adultery

The procreation of illegitimate children could be seen as the end result of sexual misbehaviour and although a distinction needs to be drawn between the parents who have conducted the illicit liaison and the children who are themselves innocent, it is worth considering medieval attitudes to sexual misbehaviour in general. This is an area of research which has received a certain amount of attention in recent years, particularly from historians of gender, though they have tended to use records of local courts and therefore deal more with 'middling folk' than the gentry and nobility. There is some evidence that concern about sexual misconduct varied over time, with a peak in the years around 1300, after which it dropped before starting to rise again towards the end of the fourteenth century.

At the parliament of May 1413, Commons submitted a petition complaining about the behaviour of the ecclesiastical authorities. One of their grievances was that those found guilty of adultery or lechery were punished with fines of forty shillings or more. The Commons' complaint was twofold and somewhat self-contradictory. This practice meant that 'your lieges of your same kingdom are greatly impoverished', and yet did it not act as an effective deterrent: 'while such sins are further encouraged and committed; whereas by the law of God it ought to be the case that such sinners are chastised by corporal punishment, so that these sins might be more swiftly eradicated from amongst the people'. How much can really be read into this petition is doubtful, but it suggests that adultery was both sufficiently widespread enough for fines to be common and potentially lucrative, and yet still regarded as reprehensible, perhaps in the same way that exceeding the speed limit is viewed today.

Feminist studies of sexual misconduct in the Middle Ages have tended to detect a double standard in which men's adultery was condoned or indulged, whilst adulteresses were treated more harshly, at least in theory. Ruth Karras has argued that because women's honour and virtue were defined by their domestic and sexual role, any wrongdoing reflected badly on their family, whereas men's reputations were not so dependent on domestic morality as they could gain honour on the battlefield or through other public activity. Perhaps more significantly, female adultery cast doubt on the actual paternity of children who would legally be assumed to be the children and heirs of the woman's husband.

Not all women accused of adultery were found guilty. Christine, wife of Nicholas Meinill (d. 1299), was charged in 1290 with attempting to poison her husband and of committing adultery with a William de Greenfield (perhaps the future Archbishop of York) and Walter de Hamerton. Following proceedings in the ecclesiastical court it was found that she was in fact blameless. John Le Romeyn, Archbishop of York, reported to the king in 1293 that rather than deserting her husband in favour of a sinful life, she had been driven from the marital home by her husband, who refused to maintain her. His cruelty, rather than her immoral behaviour, was the reason for the marital breakdown.

Adulteresses

There is some evidence that female adultery at the higher levels of society was a cause of concern for the Church, but that the authorities struggled to deal effectively with culprits. From 1285 it was possible for a wife who voluntarily left her husband to live with an adulterer to forfeit her claim to dower as a result of c.34 of the Statute of Westminster II. However, the developments in the form of estate settlements, including the replacement of the traditional dower rights with marriage settlements in jointure and greater freedom from the post-mortem disposition of estates following the widespread introduction of the enfeoffment to use, meant that any effects were relatively short-lived. Adulteresses who were also heiresses were, in any case, a different matter. At the turn of the fourteenth century, the heiress Lucy Thweng, daughter of Robert Thweng of Kilton, seems to have managed to have a colourful life without suffering particularly serious consequences, despite the best efforts of ecclesiastical authorities. Married in August 1294 at the age of fifteen to William, son of Sir William Latimer, Lucy may already have been sexually active. According to one account, a child was born in December of the same year, rather too soon after the wedding, and within a year of her marriage she had left her husband and was living at Kilton as the mistress of her cousin, Marmaduke Thweng. It was said that her father-in-law persuaded the king to give him a life grant of the lordship and forest of Danby in compensation. Whilst the original source of this story which appears in l'Anson's 'Kilton Castle' is unclear, there is certainly evidence that she had willingly left her husband in 1303 and Marmaduke Thweng appears to have been implicated in this so-called 'abduction'. It was not uncommon in the Middle Ages for women who wished to leave marriages to collude with an 'abductor' such as a lover or sometimes a family member in order to facilitate their escape. On 16 February 1304 the Sheriff of York was ordered to find Lucy, wife of William Latimer the younger, and return her to his manor of Brunne. It appears that she had left of her own free will and had applied to Archbishop Corbridge (d. 22 Sept 1304) for a divorce on the grounds of consanguinity in the fourth degree. Lucy also petitioned the king to recall his writ to the Sheriff. The Dean and Chapter of York therefore petitioned the king on 9 June 1305 claiming that it would be a breach of Church liberties to make her return to her husband whilst the matter was still pending in their court. Lucy also claimed that Latimer had treated her with cruelty, and that she would be in peril if forced to return. On 2 November 1305 William Latimer was excommunicated by the Dean and Chapter at Lucy's instance.

She later returned to Latimer, only to become the mistress of Nicholas Meinill of Whorlton, and shortly afterwards began proceedings to obtain a divorce from Latimer, again, on the grounds of consanguinity. In March 1307, Latimer was excommunicated for failing to pay the legal costs, whilst both Lucy and Meinill were cited for adultery. In 1309 Lucy was ordered to undertake penance in Watton Priory. However, she appears to have escaped remarkably lightly. She eventually agreed to separate from Meinill and to pay a fine of £40. She subsequently obtained her divorce from Latimer and went on to marry, not her former lover, Nicholas Meinill, with whom she had had a child, but Robert de Everingham. Meinill seems to have been reluctant to give her up: in January 1313 Robert de Everingham complained that Nicholas Meinill and others came by night to Everingham and abducted his wife, Lucy. She appears to have returned to her husband this time. In May 1313 she and Robert Everingham had licence to enfeoff Henry de Bretteville of their manor of Yarm, and regrant it to them and the heirs of their bodies with remainder to Nicholas, son of Lucy and his heirs. After Everingham's death, Lucy married again, her third and final husband being Bartholemew de Fanacourt. William, the son born during Lucy's marriage to William Latimer, was held to be Latimer's legitimate heir despite Lucy's behaviour providing ample reason for doubt as to his biological parentage. On the death of William Latimer senior in February 1327, the son duly succeeded him, taking livery of his estates in April 1327. He was summoned to parliament in August 1327. There does seem to have been some doubt about his position, however. There was a further inquiry in 1328, but this found that William Latimer was the lawful son of Sir William Latimer by Lucy Thweng. Lucy's son by Nicholas Meinill, whilst not legitimate, still acquired the bulk of the Meinill estate. Lucy herself seems to have escaped serious censure—her eventual punishment being the £40 fine rather than any form of public humiliation.

The penance required of another notorious adulteress, Ela, wife of Robert, Lord FitzPayne, was perhaps more draconian. Ela, the widow of John

Le Mareschal, had married Robert FitzPayne as his second wife in 1319. According to a letter sent by Archbishop Mepham in 1332 to the bishops of neighbouring dioceses to which he feared she would flee, Ela had been found guilty of adultery with both married and single partners, including clerics in holy orders, though John de Ford, rector of Okeford Fitzpayne, was the only one of Ela's conquests named. Her penance was to abstain from eating meat on Mondays and Wednesdays, except on medical advice, and to perform a penance on a Sunday between Michaelmas and the feast of St Luke every year for seven years, offering a lighted candle of four pounds of wax at the altar of the cathedral church in Salisbury, and proceeding barefoot from the west door. She was to offer alms of forty shillings to the Friars Preacher and same sum to the Friars Minor, and twenty shillings to other poor persons and beggars. In addition, she was required to give alms to the poor and beggars in each of the FitzPayne manors. Furthermore, for the period of seven years, in order to avoid the temptations of vanity, she was forbidden to adorn her head with gold, silver or precious stones or to paint her face or colour her eyebrows as was the habit of fashionable ladies. Despite her conduct, Ela was not repudiated by her husband, whom she survived.

There are several other early-fourteenth-century cases of sexual misconduct and it appears that the ecclesiastical authorities had difficulties in controlling such activities. We know the names of three different women who were involved at various times with Peter de Mauley of Mulgrave (d. 1348). In April 1313 he was absolved by the Archbishop of York in return for a payment of 100 marks towards the fabric of York Minster for having a sexual relationship with Aline, daughter of Thomas Furnival, the sister of his wife Eleanor. Ten years later he was fined for committing adultery with Alice Deyvil, and in 1328 he was again in trouble, this time for adultery with Sara de London. Anastasia de Fauconberg, the daughter of Ralph Neville of Raby, was excommunicated for adultery with John de Lilford. Her punishment was later changed to the penance of standing in the Galilee Chapel of Durham Cathedral on six Sundays wearing just her underclothes, with a veil over her head and holding a lighted candle, and fasting on bread and water once a week for a year. In 1313 there had been accusations of incest between her and her father. Isabella de Merley was accused of adultery with her brother-in-law John de Amundeville. Isabella's punishment, later suspended, was to be whipped around the marketplaces of Durham and Bishop Auckland, but her behaviour did not improve. Lucy, the wife of Sir John Barton of Fryton (Yorkshire) ran off with one of the monks of St Mary's York. Whilst this might suggest that extra-marital sex was rife in the northern province in the early-fourteenth century, and the case of Ralph Nevill and Anastasia Fauconberg seems particularly worrying, these citations cannot necessarily all be taken at face value. The king wrote to the archbishop of York in 1318 as a result of complaints that some individuals were maliciously obtaining citations of their enemies for adultery or fornication.

According to Thomas Tropenell, Constance, the inappropriately named wife of Sir Henry Percy of Great Chalfield, committed adultery with Robert Wyvill, Bishop of Salisbury (d. 1375), and bore him an illegitimate son. Her 'naughty lyf' with the bishop and others apparently drove her husband to embark on a pilgrimage to Jerusalem, from which he did not return, dying en route at Cologne. Wyvill was, it seems, neither as learned as his predecessors, nor particularly handsome, and contemporary chroniclers observed that the pope would never have appointed him had he actually seen him. Presumably he had hidden attractions. Constance's notorious history does not appear to have dented her marriage prospects, as she married three more times. After her husband's death she married John Percy (apparently no relation) of Little Chalfield. In 1361 Constance, who had managed to retain possession of Great Chalfield despite the claims of Sir Henry Percy's daughter from his first marriage, together with her third husband Sir Philip FitzWaryn, a younger son of Fulk, Lord Fitzwaryn, resettled the manor on themselves and their legitimate issue, with remainder to Robert, son of Constance, her illegitimate son. In 1385 Constance married for the fourth time. Her last husband was Sir Henry de la Ryvere (d. *c.* 1400) of Tormarton (Gloucestershire) Constance's family origins are unclear, but in a document of 1413 she is identified as sister and heiress of Robert Stokes.

Despite the obvious concern of the ecclesiastical authorities, it would seem that at the elite levels of lay society during the fourteenth century, adultery was not so shocking, although it is possible that heiresses such as Lucy Thweng had more freedom in this respect than other women of her class. Earl Warenne's mistress, Maud Nerford, seems to have fared rather less well: being divorced by her first husband, failing to marry Warenne and then losing her estates as a result of Warenne's private war with Lancaster.

It was several decades later that Thomas Tuddenham's wife Alice was claiming publicly that Tuddenham was not the father of her child, which suggests that any public disgrace resulting from being a known adulteress was not that great; it was at least preferable to marriage to Tuddenham. Tuddenham never remarried, although he did father an illegitimate child, Henry. Unlike some of the notorious ladies of the previous century, Alice remained in the nunnery, but that may have been her choice.

Sir Thomas Tuddenham was one of the enemies of the Paston family. Another of their adversaries, John Heydon, also seems to have had marital difficulties. A letter of Margaret Paston from 1444 mentions that Heydon's wife had recently given birth and she had heard it said that Heydon would have nothing to do with her or her child and that if she came into his presence he would cut off her nose so that she would be publicly shamed and that if the child came into his presence he would kill it. Margaret's report of this example of an adulteress who was repudiated by her husband after giving birth to an illegitimate child is non-judgemental, but the Pastons' continuing feud with Heydon meant she was hardly a disinterested observer. The lady in question was Eleanor Winter, daughter of Edmund Winter, with whom the Pastons had been engaged in an acrimonious dispute over the manor of East Beckham, and so a certain amount of *schadenfreude* on Margaret's part might be expected. Her account of Heydon's marital woe was, however, included only at the end of the letter. It was not headline news. In this case it appears that the woman was blamed, but her family's relationship with her husband was not permanently damaged. Her father remained on good terms with his son-in-law, making him supervisor of his will, and bequeathing him a book of chronicles. Heydon did not attempt to divorce his adulterous wife, he merely separated from her and took a mistress of his own.

There was little trace of any significant change in attitudes towards sexual misconduct in the higher echelons of society in the fifteenth century. Barbara Harris found that the attitude of the Yorkist and early Tudor aristocracy towards adulteresses was not particularly censorious. Whilst they might face a loss of property, they did not suffer social ruin and exclusion from aristocratic society. Sex was still essentially a private matter. As Colin Richmond observed, 'Once the Englishman's home was his castle, where he might have sex with security, whereas now sex is just as much a public business as is real estate. In the fifteenth century that was not the case.'

One adulteress of the early Tudor period, Elizabeth, Lady Scrope of Upshall and Masham, appears to have been particularly unrepentant. One of the five daughters and coheiresses of John Nevill, Marquess of Montagu, she was married to Thomas, Lord Scrope of Masham by 1477, with whom she had a daughter, Alice. After Scrope's death in 1493, she married Sir Henry Wentworth (d. 1500). She also had an affair with Thomas Grey, Marquess of Dorset. In her will dated 7 March 1518 she left a bequest to 'Mary, daughter in base unto Thomas Grey, Marquess of Dorset, my bed that my lord Marquess was wont to lie in', together with all the apparel of the same chamber.

Examples of well-born mothers who had illegitimate children as a result of their own adultery are particularly hard to find, principally because of the reluctance to regard any child born to a married woman as a bastard. The relatively few exceptions where a married woman of noble or gentle birth is known to have had a child as a result of an adulterous relationship show this clearly. The career of Lucy Thweng is a case in point. Her child with Nicholas Meinill was born whilst she was married to Sir William Latimer. The child was clearly recognised as a bastard, rather than the legitimate son of Latimer, but at the time Lucy was not only estranged from her husband, but going through divorce proceedings. The actual birth date of Lucy's son Nicholas is not recorded, though he was under age in 1322. Lucy had petitioned for divorce in 1305, and was not cited for adultery with Nicholas Meinill until 1307. Lucy's earlier child, William Latimer, born c.1301, was, however, regarded as the legitimate child of Sir William, despite apparent doubts about her conduct, even then. He succeeded to Sir William's estates in 1327, and although there may have been some rumours, resulting in an inquiry in 1328, he was found to be the son and heir of Sir William by Lucy Thweng.

A century and a half later, Johanna, wife of Sir William Beaumont, had an affair with Sir Henry Bodrugan, whilst estranged and separated from her husband. Although there was no doubt that Bodrugan was the father, the fact that John Beaumont had been born to a married woman meant that he eventually gained a share of the Beaumont inheritance, because of the reluctance to bastardise a child born within wedlock. Edmund Paston's child with 'Mistress Dixon' was likewise regarded as the legitimate child of her husband.

Proceedings in parliament in the mid–sixteenth century, noted by Nicolas in his *Treatise*, suggest that attitudes towards adulteresses and their bastard children were beginning to change. As previously discussed, during the medieval period there had been a reluctance to make a bastard of any child born to a married woman, and parliament had stopped short of an act to bastardise Joan Beaumont's son despite acknowledging him to be the son of Henry Bodrugan rather than her husband. In 1542, Anne Bourchier, heiress of Henry Bourchier, Earl of Essex, and the wife of William Parr (brother-in-law of Henry VIII) eloped from her husband with and refused to return, saying that she would live as she lusted. She subsequently gave birth to the child of one of her lovers. On 17 April 1543 Parr managed to obtain an act of parliament stating that as the child was 'notoriously begotten in adultery' but capable of inheriting under the law, it and any further children would be bastardised and incapable of inheriting the estates of either of them. At around the same time, Thomas Lord Burgh obtained a similar act in relation to the three children born to Lady Elizabeth Burgh during her marriage to his deceased son Sir Thomas. The act states that she had confessed that the children were the result of adultery and declared them to be illegitimate. The House of Lords subsequently attempted to legislate control over the behavior of adulteresses, with a bill proposing that women found guilty of adultery would lose their dower, goods, lands and possessions, but this was seemingly going too far and did not pass.

Adulterers

Men of high status do not seem to have been harshly judged. Michael Hicks points to the absence of social disgrace for noblemen involved in sexual misconduct, suggesting that adultery and the procreation of illegitimate children were even expected. However, Shannon McSheffrey and Derek G. Neal have suggested that male adultery could be frowned upon, less for purely moral reasons than for demonstrating a lack of control and acting contrary to the interests of others. McSheffery emphasised that good governance was important for both genders, but in different ways. Women were expected to be governed by male authority, but men were expected to govern themselves and failure to do so damaged their reputations. As Neal put it, 'the adulterer risked his vital connections, his credit' since failure to attend to his own interests cast doubt on his ability to take proper care of those of a patron or master. The association of adultery with lack of control and attention to business can be seen in Thomas Tropenell's comments about William Rous's carelessness with his inheritance and rights:

> 'And so for lak of sute made therfor ayene by the seid Will. Rous he afterward lost hit. For he was alwey occupied in lechery and avowtry, and toke none hede to sew therfor, but only for to devowre and selle away all his wodes and his tylestones, tymbre and his houses.' (Tropenell Cartulary)

This view of adultery can be seen in the measures taken by some towns in the late medieval period. In London, the mayor and aldermen declared in 1439 that fornicators and adulterers acted both to the displeasure of Almighty God and against the laws of the city. There is evidence that the civic authorities were prepared to enter domestic properties where they suspected that illicit sexual activity was taking place. In one case in 1386, a London beadle defended himself against an accusation of trespass by arguing that it was customary for officials to search a house where they had reason to believe that adultery or fornication was being committed. Similarly, in Coventry, various ordinances aimed at controlling public morality were issued by the civic authorities. Whilst many cases involved individuals of lower status, concern was not limited to the behaviour of the lower classes. An ordinance of 1492 specifically refers to the behaviour of members of the civic elite, or men 'of worship within this Citie' who, if found guilty of adultery, fornication or usury, having previously been warned to amend their behaviour, were to lose all honour and opportunities for further advancement and to be estranged from good company. The inclusion of usury shows that it was behaviour that could affect the interests of other citizens that was the crux of the matter.

The Cely letters provide a rare insight into the reactions of a putative bastard-begetter from the merchant elite of London. On 25 May 1482, Richard Cely the younger wrote, in something of a panic, to his brother George, who was at the time on the Continent, for advice on a problem that was worrying him. He was concerned that a girl he called 'Em' was with child and that he might be the father. At this time, Richard was seriously considering marriage. In March he had been 'spoken to for a wife in two places' and just three days before the date of the letter cited above, he had been encouraged to see 'Rawson's daughter'. His lapse could therefore have had serious implications for his future, though he seems to have been fortunate in this instance. The identity of 'Em' is unknown, though she may possibly have been one of his mother's servants, and there is no further reference in the correspondence to this affair. Richard did subsequently marry Rawson's daughter, Anne, so his marital prospects do not seem to have been seriously affected. Perhaps his brother George was indeed able to help Richard to resolve the situation. George had some experience in such matters as he was at the time sowing his own wild oats in France, where he had an illegitimate child with a Calais cook. This case does, however, show that fathering an illegitimate child could be regarded as a serious matter in some circumstances.

On the other hand, sometimes begetting a bastard might be regarded as a less serious offence. Karen Jones relates the case of William Brice of Kent who was accused in 1506 of 'suspiciously' keeping a young woman whom he claimed to be his illegitimate daughter. The city jury in Canterbury apparently accepted this argument, but fined him for keeping her as his harlot anyway, whilst the official of the archdeacon's court was less convinced, and referred to her as his 'pretended' daughter. Brice evidently considered that having fathered an illegitimate child in the past was a more acceptable misdemeanour to which to admit than living with a 'harlot' in the present.

Richard Helmholz identified a definite shift in the attitude of the ecclesiastical courts towards the procreation of illegitimate children in the sixteenth century. His study of act books of the English Church courts between 1370 and 1600 found that there was definite concern about sexual misconduct in the medieval period. He found cases indicating concern about 'harbouring', or knowingly permitting illicit sexual activity to take place under one's roof, in virtually all act books during the period of his study. However, from the latter part of Elizabeth's reign prosecutions relating to the harbouring of pregnant women began to appear in the act books. This was partly related to the effects of the Elizabethan Poor Law and a concern to ensure that an illegitimate child did not become a charge on the parish. However, there were also cases where prosecution took place even when the child was dead and the mother had fled, indicating that the concern was not simply financial, and that the prosecutors, at least, considered it morally wrong to permit an illegitimate birth on one's property. Whilst illicit sexual activity was frowned upon by the ecclesiastical courts of later medieval England, there was no singling out for especial censure of those who had illegitimate children as a result.

Attitudes to bastard children

If bastard-begetters were regarded as morally reprehensible, it was still possible for bastard children to be viewed as innocent victims. The rumours which surrounded the Percies' acquisition of Alnwick from the Bishop of Durham, Antony Bek [see pp. 72-4], at the turn of the fourteenth century may well have been groundless, but they do provide some insight into fourteenth-century attitudes. The story as related in Dugdale's *Baronage* is as follows:

> '[Bek], being irritated by some slanderous words which he had heard that the Bastard spoke of him, by his Deed, bearing date 19 Nov An. 1309 sold the Castle and Honor of Alnwicke to Henry de Percy (a great Man in the North) from whom the Earls of Northumberland, still possessors thereof, are descended.'

This is obviously of little value as evidence of the nature of the transaction between Vescy and Bek. Dugdale cited his source for the Bek story as Leland's excerpts from the *Scalachronica* of Thomas Gray. Gray, a Northumberland knight born *c.* 1310, wrote his chronicle more than forty years after these events took place and is unlikely to have had direct knowledge of the events he described. Another late source, *The Chronicle of Alnwick Abbey*, did not contain the same allegation; however, since the Percies had been *in situ* as lords of Alnwick and patrons of the abbey for over sixty years by the time of writing, this omission may not be significant. An account written closer to events can be found in the chronicle attributed to Robert Graystanes, a monk of Durham, who wrote that Bek was entrusted with it to the use of Vescy's young son, but sold it to Henry Percy.

As a monk at Durham, the author was well-placed to know about events, but the poor relationship between the bishop and priory at the time means that he cannot be regarded as an unbiased observer. What the chronicle evidence does show is that rumours circulating among those who were not particularly well-disposed towards the bishop cast him in a bad light by claiming that he had betrayed Vescy's trust by depriving the innocent young bastard son of his inheritance. William Vescy of Kildare is portrayed as the victim. The point of the anecdote was the supposed venality of the bishop in betraying his trust for personal gain rather than the action of William de Vescy in trying to provide for his bastard son.

Some individuals showed a remarkable lack of concern for public opinion about illegitimacy. This in itself may suggest that bastardy was not such a great social stigma—perhaps less of an embarrassment than the humble origins that the Pastons were at such pains to conceal. The most striking example of this is Sir William Plumpton. His son Robert was the product of a second, clandestine marriage to Joan Wintringham. Since the marriage reportedly took place in the 1450s and was not made public until 1468, Sir William does not appear to have been unduly worried about any consequences for his son of being presumed a bastard. In the meantime, his subterfuge had ensured good marriages for the granddaughters who were presumed to be his heiresses. In January 1464 Sir William had received £400 from Brian Rocliffe for the marriage of Margaret Plumpton, the elder, to his son John, and £333 from Henry Sotehill for the marriage of his son John to her younger sister Elizabeth. The problems later experienced by Robert Plumpton arose not from perceptions of illegitimacy as such, but from the actions of the aggrieved husbands of Margaret and Elizabeth, once his legitimacy had been certified and Sir William had disposed of his estates in Robert's favour. It is worth noting, however, that the clandestine marriage only became public because Sir William had been summoned to appear before the official of the civil court at York to account for his behaviour in harbouring Joan Wintringham in his house 'to the great peril of his soul and grievous scandal of the faithful' and it was only after the official, William Poteman, had certified the validity of the marriage in 1472 that Robert was recognised as his father's heir. In 1475 Sir William resettled his estates on himself with remainder to Robert Plumpton junior, son of Sir William and Joan his wife. Sir William also had bastard sons whom he provided with a life interest in certain lands in the manor of Ockbrook (Derbyshire).

Where bastardy had definite negative connotations was in connection with legal disputes. As discussed in Chapter One, bastardy was a bar to inheritance and allegations could therefore be made in the context of legal proceedings, sometimes vexatiously. An interesting example of this can be found in the Tropenell Cartulary, where John Lyngever of Kingston Deverill (Wiltshire) stated that William King and John Leveden tried to force him to sell a life interest in land in Chicklade (Wiltshire), by threatening to make efforts to prove that he was either a bastard or a bondman so that he would be unable to enjoy secure possession. Similar allegations were made against the Hody family in the 1470s. There is no evidence that Lyngever actually was either a bastard or a bondman, and the inclusion of both in the threat strongly suggests that this was purely vexatious, but the complications of proving that he was neither would be sufficient enough to prevent him or his children having quiet possession of the land. It was this that formed the essence of the threat.

Some further light is shed on medieval attitudes to illegitimacy by the dispute over the Brokholes inheritance, which is the subject of a collection of fifteenth-century correspondence edited by Christine Carpenter. If the startling allegations of one party to the dispute are to be believed, bastards were used to substitute for legitimate children who had inconveniently died, not as replacement heirs, but as actual substitutes. The dispute followed the death in 1419 of Ellen, wife of Geoffrey Brokholes, whose two daughters, Joan and Margery, became the heiresses of the Roos, Brokhole and Mancetter inheritances. Margery had married John Sumpter by whom she had had a son, also called John, and had died. John Sumpter junior was therefore the heir to Margery's share of the inheritance. He, too, died, in July 1420, before the division of the estates was finally settled. His inquisition post mortem was not held until October 1426, when it was found that his sisters, Ellen and Christine, aged fourteen and fifteen, were his heirs, and would thus be entitled to shares in the inheritance. According to Joan Brokholes, who was by this time married to Robert Armburgh, the girls were not the legitimate daughters of John Sumpter and Margery, but bastard daughters of John Sumpter. Joan's case was not only that the girls were illegitimate, but that they had been substituted for the real Christine and Ellen, who were also dead. It was claimed that John Sumpter had secretly buried the real Christine and Ellen and sent two bastard daughters of his own, as Christine and Ellen, away to friends of his with whom they stayed for five or six years, after which time he successfully produced them at the inquisition as the genuine heirs. This claim seems remarkably far-fetched, and suggests desperation on the part of Joan and her husband (who seems not to have had property of his own) rather than a genuine plot on the part of Sumpter, who would have needed to conveniently have had two bastard daughters of approximately the right age who would not be missed. If the claim was true, then Sumpter had found a most ingenious way of providing for two bastard daughters. If, however, as is far more likely, it was a fabrication, then Joan and her supporters must have felt that the allegation of bastardy added a further dimension to the case than simply claiming the girls to be imposters. If Sumpter was widely believed to have committed adultery, the claim that the girls were bastards may have added verisimilitude to their case, and also provided an excuse to drag Sumpter's personal morals into the matter and, thus, the suggestion that he was badly governed and untrustworthy. An anonymous account of the dispute states that 'John holde divers women by side his wyf which ... is openly known'. This same account of the case also provides a definition of bastardy as understood by the writer: 'for a child that is got[en] in suche maner women schuld be called *filiuis populi* that is for to say … peple and may clayme no manne to theyre fader'. Joan's efforts appear to have been to little avail. The Sumpter moiety of the manor of Brockholes was retained by Ellen, and passed to the Holt family as a result of her second marriage to Ralph Holt *c*. 1439. Joan's moiety eventually passed also to Ellen as Joan's heir.

An intriguing approach to the rights of illegitimate children can be found in the case of Sir Robert Brackenbury (d. 1485). Brackenbury was a retainer of Richard Duke of Gloucester, and flourished in royal service following Gloucester's assumption of the throne in 1483. He was killed fighting for Richard at Bosworth, and attainted in Henry VII's first parliament. He had two legitimate daughters, Anne and Elizabeth, and a bastard son. In 1489 Anne successfully petitioned parliament for the reversal of her father's attainder, on behalf of herself and her sister Elizabeth. The reversal specifically excluded Brackenbury's bastard children, but stipulated that in the event of Anne and Elizabeth dying without heirs of their body 'that then the bastard sonne of the seid Sir Robert be next heire unto the seid Anne and Elizabeth, and enherite all the landes and tenementes wherunto the same Anne and Elizabeth, by vertue of this acte, bee enabled and restored'. In this case, parliament was explicitly confirming the rights of a bastard child to be considered an heir, albeit one with lower priority than that of legitimate daughters.

The view that a male adulterer showed a disrespect for the interests of others (the husband, father or guardian of the woman with whom he misbehaved and the family of his own wife) that could reflect poorly on his trustworthiness to serve the interests of a master or patron is one that would be expected to have particular resonance for the landed classes where more was potentially at stake. This raises the question of attitudes to the products of sexual misdemeanours among the wider family group. It might be expected that those whose interests were affected by the existence of illegitimate offspring would demonstrate hostility, but it was not necessarily the case. Action taken by other family members in relation to bastards demonstrates the extent to which they were accepted as members of the wider family grouping.

It is worth noting that the official antagonism of the Church towards illegitimate children did not prevent actual family ties from being recognised. Papal letters and dispensations concerning illegitimacy demonstrate both that family members made representations on behalf of illegitimate kin, and that the papal authorities recognised these family bonds in practice. In 1347 Sir John de Willoughby and his wife successfully petitioned for a dispensation for their illegitimate kinsman, Thomas de Strubby, to enable him to hold one benefice with cure of souls and one without, and in 1364 Sir John Beauchamp, a kinsman of the earl of Warwick, was successful in obtaining a dispensation for his illegitimate kinsman, another John Beauchamp, to be ordained and hold a benefice and dignities short of the episcopal. In 1350 Edward III petitioned Clement VI on behalf of his kinsman, John de Lancaster, an illegitimate son of Thomas of Lancaster, for the grant of a canonry and prebend. The career of Robert Flemming, the humanist scholar, and probable illegitimate son of Robert Fleming (d. 1459) esquire of Wath (Yorkshire) owed much to family connections. With the bishop of Lincoln for an uncle and an aunt whose husband, Robert Waterton, was closely associated with Henry IV, he was, in addition to dean of Lincoln, a chaplain to Henry VI and royal proctor at the papal curia.

Such acceptance by the wider family was important for bastards, as they had more need than those of legitimate birth to rely on the goodwill of relatives. In general it seems that whilst there was some disapproval of fornication and adultery on moral grounds, it was widely accepted as a fact of life, and the children who resulted from illicit relations were generally accepted as part of the family. The arrangements that were made for them will be explored in the following chapters.

Chapter 4

The Inheritance of Bastards

Bastards and Estates

In the spring of 1383, the prior of Wymondley in Hertfordshire was travelling to Halesworth in Suffolk to conduct the funeral of the priory's patron, Sir John Argentine, when he was attacked on Newmarket Heath by 'certain evildoers'. He was held captive until he sent for certain documents which Sir John had deposited with him for safekeeping and handed them over to Sir John's illegitimate son, William. The same evildoers also disrupted the funeral. Or at least, this is the version of events given by Sir John's legitimate heirs. Was William a villainous bastard after the model of Shakepeare's Edmund? Not necessarily. He might have been a little heavy-handed, but he was only securing his own rights. The deeds in question related to Sir John's settlement of the bulk of his estates on William and his wife, Isabel, to the detriment of his legitimate heirs: his three legitimate daughters and their offspring.

By the late-fourteenth century, legal devices such as the entail and the enfeoffment to use had evolved, providing landowners an opportunity to control the descent of their property after death. This gave greater flexibility to provide for younger children and for illegitimate children. It also meant that an illegitimate son could be favoured over legitimate daughters and their heirs. This was precisely what Sir John Argentine had done, but his action was far from unprecedented. A look at his family connections provides other examples.

The story begins with a lawyer, and an eminent one at that: Sir John Argentine's grandfather, the Chief Justice Sir William Bereford. His legal training meant that Bereford had practical experience of the development of legal devices to control the descent of property in general and to illegitimate children in particular, as they were worked out in the courts during the early-fourteenth century. He also had direct personal experience. When he was a mere serjeant-at-law he had been involved in an arrangement to enable his brother Osbert, a cleric, to make provision for an illegitimate son. In the Easter law term of 1288, Osbert entered into an agreement with William, by which he granted all his lands in the Warwickshire villages of Wishaw, Langley, Sutton Coldfield, Curdworth, Minworth, Middleton and Bickenhill and the Leicestershire village of Stapleton to William to hold in fee tail to him and the heirs of his body, in return for a rent of ten pounds a year payable to Osbert's son Simon, until such time as the brother had settled lands of equivalent value in Warwickshire or Leicestershire on Simon. The grant included successive remainders to Simon and the heirs of his body, to James de la Launde and his wife Alice and the heirs of her body and to William's right heirs. Alice was presumably a sister of Osbert and William. In September 1288 William sued Osbert for dispossessing him of a landholding. William won the case which appears to have been a collusive suit intended to establish for the record that William had been given possession under the agreement. The transaction seems to have been an attempt to make provision for Osbert's illegitimate son, whilst securing the reversion to Osbert's (and William's) right heirs.

Sir William Bereford's daughter Agnes married John Argentine. When John died by October 1318, leaving Agnes a widow with a baby son, also called John, the custody of the bulk of the Argentine estate was granted to Sir William, who died in 1326. At this point more illegitimate children enter the story. Sir William's son and heir, Edmund, who had no legitimate children, settled his own property on his illegitimate son John Bereford, with reversion to another illegitimate son, Baldwin. John died in Gascony in 1356, just a couple of years after his father. Baldwin then successfully took possession of the estates under the terms of the Edmund's settlement. It was only after Baldwin's death in 1405, when the entail had expired, that the descendants of his three sisters (of whom Agnes, wife of Sir John Argentine was one) won their claim to the manor of Clopton, which Baldwin had sold. Baldwin, like his brother, was a soldier, serving as a knight in Gascony under the Black Prince and suffered no apparent disadvantage from his illegitimacy.

Meanwhile, Agnes and John Argentine's son John had married Margaret Darcy, with whom he had three daughters: Joan, who married Bartholomew de Naunton; Maud, who married Ivo Fitz Waryn; and Elizabeth, who married Baldwin St George. This younger John Argentine later had an illegitimate son, William. In 1381, William married Isabel Kerdiston, bringing another bastard connection into the story.

Isabel was the daughter of William Kerdiston, who was the illegitimate son of Sir William de Kerdiston of Kerdiston, Norfolk, having been born prior to his father's second marriage to Alice de Norwich. Sir William's heir was John de Burghersh, the son of his legitimate daughter, Maud. In 1341/2, before the birth of his grandson, Sir William had made a settlement of his estates on himself and his third wife, with remainders to his son Roger and his male issue and to William, brother of Roger. He later made another settlement, from which John de Burghersh was excluded on the grounds that he had a sufficient estate. When Sir William died in 1361, Maud was already dead and her son John was still a minor. The Norfolk inquisition found that the heir to the Kerdiston estate was William Kerdiston, son of the deceased, whereas the York and Suffolk inquisitions found the heir to be John de Burghersh, son of Maud, daughter of the deceased, although the Suffolk inquisition also found that William had taken possession. The Lincoln inquisition found that William was heir, except for a part of the estate to which John de Burghersh was heir. In view of the conflicting returns, a further enquiry was held, during which the settlement of 1341/2 was produced and it was found that William the elder, his wife and son Roger having died, William the younger had taken possession. In 1370–71 Sir John de Burghersh was involved in a legal dispute over the property, during which he asserted that William was a bastard. The parties came to an agreement in November 1371 in which William's right prevailed. Sir John de Burghersh received Skendleby (Lincolnshire) and Stratford (Suffolk), but relinquished his claim to the Kerdiston manors in Norfolk, along with Hunmanby (Yorkshire) and Bulkamp and Heenham (Suffolk). It may have taken ten years, but the illegitimate son prevailed.

William de Kerdiston's practical experience in asserting and defending his rights may have proved useful to his son-in-law, William Argentine. In May 1381, at the time of William Argentine's marriage to Isabel Kerdiston, his father, Sir John, obtained a royal licence to entail Great Wymondley and the advowson of the priory and chapel there on William and his wife. In the same year he also made entails of lands in Little Melton (Norfolk), and the manor of Melbourn (Cambridgeshire), and gave William and his wife immediate possession of the manors of Chalgrove (Oxfordshire), Fordham (Essex), Weston (Hertforshire) and Newmarket (Suffolk). He also arranged that Halesworth, his main residence in Suffolk, should pass to William after the death of his own wife. It was clearly his intention that William should be recognised as his heir.

Sir John died on 25 November 1382 and his legitimate heirs were found to be his daughter Maud, who was the wife of Sir Ivo Fitzwaryn of Caundle Haddon, Dorset, and his grandchildren Margaret Naunton (daughter of Sir John's daughter Joan) and Baldwin St George (son of Sir John's daughter Elizabeth and a minor at the time). They were not prepared to allow themselves to be disinherited without a struggle. However, William was of age and well able to look after his own interests and immediately took steps to secure the documents that proved his rights to the property. In March 1383, Ivo Fitzwaryn and his wife responded by obtaining a commission of *oyer* and *terminer* to investigate their allegations concerning the supposed assault on the prior of Wymondley, as a result of which he was forced to hand over the deeds that had been entrusted to him by Sir John to William Argentine. How much truth there was in this version of events is not clear as court records such as this often used a standard formula. Whatever the truth of the matter, William was certainly able to prove his right to the property in question without undue difficulty and had therefore presumably secured documentary proof of his claims. In January 1383 a Hertfordshire inquisition had found that Sir John had held Great and Little Wymondley in chief by serjeanty and that his heirs were Margaret Naunton, Baldwin St George and Maud Fitzwaryn. But on 8 April, the escheator was ordered to investigate William Argentine's case, and a further inquisition in May confirmed that the property had been enfeoffed with reversion to William as he claimed. Similarly, on 23 February, a Norfolk inquisition had found that Sir John held Ketteringham and that his heirs were Margaret Naunton, Baldwin St George and Maud Fitzwaryn, but on further investigation it was found that he had also previously held messuages in Little Melton which he had granted to feoffees who had granted them back to him for life, with remainder to William his son and Isabel de Kerdiston. The Suffolk inquisition in February had found that Sir John held Halesworth jointly with his wife, with remainder to his son William and Isabel de Kerdiston, and in March the Cambridge inquisition had found that William had the reversion of Melbourn.

Sir John's widow, Margaret, died in September 1383, less than a year after her husband, which may have simplified the situation. An inquisition post mortem held in Suffolk confirmed that she had had a life interest in Halesworth, with reversion to William Argentine and his wife Isabel. On 1 November, William was granted custody of Wymondley, Melbourn and the property at Little Melton, pending judgment in the royal courts as to whether they lawfully belonged to him or the heirs of Sir John, and in January 1384 he obtained possession of Halesworth under similar conditions. In May 1384 he won his case and obtained livery of all the entailed properties, almost eighteen months to the day after his father's death. He suffered no further serious challenge to his possession, except a suit for the manor of Newmarket brought by his kinsman Sir Edward Butler in 1394, which was easily defeated.

His illegitimate birth did not prevent Sir William Argentine from exercising his role in society. He represented Suffolk in parliament as a knight of the shire in 1393, 1395 and 1399. He had already been knighted, possibly for military service overseas, by the time of his first election in 1393. His standing in local society is further demonstrated by his appointment as sheriff of Norfolk and Suffolk at the end of that year. In 1399 he acted as cupbearer at Henry IV's coronation. This was in accordance with his tenure of Great Wymondley, a moiety of which was held by grand serjeanty for the service of rendering the king a silver-gilt cup at his coronation feast. William's father, Sir John, had performed this service at the coronation of Richard II. It is worth noting that Sir Ivo Fitzwaryn claimed the right to perform this role in the right of his wife, but Argentine prevailed, and in May 1400 strengthened his position by obtaining royal confirmation of a charter granted by King Stephen to one of his ancestors. Fitzwaryn's challenge may have represented one last attempt to secure the property, rather than a particular desire to perform this service, since the two were indivisibly linked. However, William was secure in possession by this stage, and the service later descended with the manor to the Allington family, remaining with the holders of the manor of Great Wymondley down to the coronation of William IV (1830–37).

When Sir William Argentine died, in possession of his estate, in 1419, his heir was his six-year-old grandson, John, but the boy died four years later, leaving his sisters, Elizabeth and Joan as coheirs to the estates, which were worth c £170 *per annum*. Sir William's widow subsequently sold the wardship of the girls to William Allington of Horseheath (Cambridgeshire). Allington evidently saw this as an opportunity to provide for his two sons. Elizabeth, the elder of the girls, was subsequently married to Allington's son and heir, William, and her sister Joan was married to his illegitimate half-brother. Robert, the illegitimate son, was perhaps unlucky as Joan died in May 1429, as most of her share of the Argentine estates then passed to William Allington junior, by right of his wife.

By the time that Sir John Argentine made provisions for his illegitimate son, the legal mechanisms for the post-mortem disposition of estates were well established. One of the earliest examples was the arrangement made by William, the last Vescy lord of Alnwick, almost ninety years earlier. William was the second son of William de Vescy (d. 1253) and had succeeded his childless brother, John, in 1289. After the death of William's son, also called John, the heir general appears to have been Gilbert de Aton, a distant cousin. However, William had an illegitimate son, known as William de Vescy of Kildare, son of a liaison with Debforgaill, daughter of the lord of Desmond. As a bastard, he could not inherit by common law, but he could benefit from the circumvention of the common law rules of inheritance.

The Vescys were a northern family whose rise to eminence had begun in the early-twelfth century with the marriage of Eustace FitzJohn, a minor baron and official of Henry I who held the manor of Saxlingham (Norfolk), to Beatrice, heiress of Yves de Vescy, the lord of Alnwick and Malton. During the ensuing two centuries the family successfully steered a tricky course between service to the English Crown and rebellion and by the end of the thirteenth century their range of landed interests had expanded to encompass Scotland, Wales and Ireland as well as their original powerbase in northern England. Through their mother, Agnes Ferrers, the Vescy brothers stood to gain a share of the Pembroke inheritance, though Agnes' longevity meant that they ultimately had little time to enjoy it. Her mother had been Sibyl, one of the daughters and coheirs of William Marshall, Earl of Pembroke. Agnes outlived her eldest son John and, when she died in 1290, it was William who inherited her estates in Kildare, an inheritance which seems to have affected the course of his life in more ways than the simply financial. A few months later he was appointed Justiciar of Ireland, a post which he held for four years, before being dismissed amid allegations of treason. Whilst the accusations of treason may have been unfair, Vescy was clearly engaged in local feuding which made his position untenable. Shortly after his dismissal, Vescy suffered another blow. His only son by his wife, Isabella de Periton, died at Conway (Wales), bringing the legitimate line to an end. By now, Vescy held the barony of Sprouston in Roxburghshire (Scotland); the liberty of Kildare (Ireland); Caerleon (Wales); Alnwick and Tughall (Northumberland); Malton, Langton, Brompton, Wintringham and Brind, Gribthorp, Thornton and Newsholme (Yorkshire); Caythorpe (Lincolnshire) and Eltham (Kent), as well as townhouses in Lincoln, Pontefract and London. The English lands alone had been estimated to be worth over £600 *per annum* in 1254, excluding the lands held in dower by Agnes de Vescy. He also had a tenuous claim on the Scottish throne through his grandmother Margaret, illegitimate daughter of William the Lion, King of Scots (1165–1214).

Simplified Vescy Family Tree

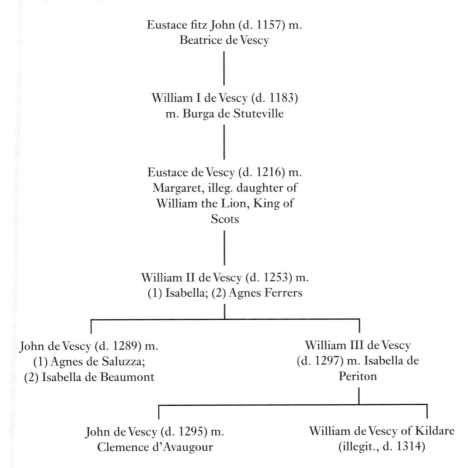

Eustace fitz John (d. 1157) m.
Beatrice de Vescy

William I de Vescy (d. 1183)
m. Burga de Stuteville

Eustace de Vescy (d. 1216) m.
Margaret, illeg. daughter of
William the Lion, King of
Scots

William II de Vescy (d. 1253) m.
(1) Isabella; (2) Agnes Ferrers

John de Vescy (d. 1289) m.
(1) Agnes de Saluzza;
(2) Isabella de Beaumont

William III de Vescy
(d. 1297) m. Isabella de
Periton

John de Vescy (d. 1295) m.
Clemence d'Avaugour

William de Vescy of Kildare
(illegit., d. 1314)

William de Vescy's plan was to convey the available parts of his Lincolnshire, Yorkshire and Northumberland estates, including the main family seat at Alnwick, to Anthony Bek, the powerful bishop of Durham. Bek then regranted the Lincolnshire and Yorkshire estates, though not Alnwick or Tughall in Northumberland, to William for life, with remainders to William de Vescy of Kildare and his heirs and then to William's right heirs. The manors in which William de Vescy of Kildare was to have reversions included Malton, Langton, Wintringham and Brompton in Yorkshire and Caythorpe in Lincolnshire. Newsolme was held in dower by Clemence, widow of William de Vescy's legitimate son John. Alnwick and Tughall were to remain to the bishop, in default of legitimate heirs of the body of William de Vescy senior. Eltham had previously also been granted to Bek.

As a legal device for the conveyance of estates to a bastard, the plan worked in the short term. William senior died on 19 July 1297. On 15 August of that year, an order was given to the escheator on this side of the Trent to release to William de Vescy of Kildare the manor of Caythorpe in Lincolnshire, and in accordance with settlement a similar order was given to the escheator North of the Trent regarding Malton, Langton, Wintringham and Brompton in Yorkshire. William de Vescy of Kildare did homage for Caythorpe on 6 May 1298, paying 100 shillings for his relief. He was presumably in possession of Malton by December 1298, when a writ was directed to his bailiffs concerning the delivery of a thief imprisoned there to the sheriff of Yorkshire. The barons of the Exchequer obviously regarded him as the legitimate successor to his father, for in 1299 and 1303 William de Vescy of Kildare obtained writs acquitting him of their demands for repayment of his father's and uncle's debts. Inquisitions post mortem show that he held the manors concerned at the time of his death and the juries were familiar with the terms of the enfeoffment. Their returns show that they knew that William de Vescy of Kildare was a bastard, but that he held the manors in fee tail and since he died without heir of his body, the next heir was the right heir of William de Vescy, whoever that might be. Their only problem was with the identification of the next heir. There seems to have been some doubt as to the identity of the right heir of William de Vescy senior and whilst Gilbert de Aton was eventually found to be the heir, he appears to have had some difficulty in obtaining livery of his inheritance. It is possible that his maternal ancestor Warin de Vescy, from whom his claim ultimately derived was also not legitimate, or so a pedigree printed in Dugdale's *Monasticon* would suggest. This may explain the absence of any protests at the time of the Vescy settlement. Whatever the reason, William de Vescy's enfeoffment worked. The bastard held the lands for his life and after his death without issue they were to return to the heir general, avoiding an escheat.

William de Vescy of Kildare thus received his estates, and received a personal summons to parliament in 1313 and 1314. Only his death at Bannockburn prevented him from saving the family line; in the event, with him, the male line of Vescys died out. The legal constraints surrounding William de Vescy of Kildare had therefore been at least partially circumvented. He had, however, only gained a portion of the Vescy inheritance and the question remains as to why William de Vescy senior transferred only the Yorkshire and Lincolnshire estates to his bastard son.

One theory is that he intended no such thing. There were later rumours that Bek had in effect swindled William de Vescy of Kildare out of this part of his inheritance. Some corroboration of the story may be provided by an undated petition in which William de Vescy of Kildare asked the king to enforce the covenants between his father and the bishop of Durham to invest him in the lands which his father gave to the bishop, of which he had no part yet, to his disinheritance. However, it is a little strange that such an important estate as Alnwick was not specifically identified, if it was the subject of this petition. The petition may possibly have related to the Yorkshire and Lincolnshire estates, or even Scottish ones, since it survived with records relating to Scotland. Yet this explanation also seems unsatisfactory as William de Vescy of Kildare seems to have received the Yorkshire and Lincolnshire lands fairly promptly, whilst no Scottish estates are mentioned in any of the surviving documents of the transactions between Vescy and Bek. In any case the main Scottish estate of Sprouston had been surrendered to the Crown. Even if Alnwick were the subject of the petition, however, it does not prove that William senior truly intended Alnwick to go to his bastard son, as the petition may reflect a bargaining position rather than a genuine grievance. Moreover, the extant records of the transactions seem to confirm that the reversion of Alnwick was never intended for William the younger. This great prize was perhaps the price of ensuring Bek's support.

Alexander Rose, in his history of the Percy family, noted that the surviving documents do not include an official record of the conveyance of Alnwick, merely a private copy, and suggests that the bishop may not have been above a little forgery. The Percy Chartulary contains a draft concord, dated at Stapleford on 29 October 1295 between William senior and Bek, in which it is clearly stated that in the event of Vescy's death without an heir of his body, the Yorkshire and Lincolnshire lands were to go to Willliam Vescy of Kildare, whilst Alnwick and Tughall were to remain to the bishop and his heirs. Rose argues that since no copy of this agreement exists in the Exchequer records, it may have been altered. A final concord relating to the Yorkshire and Lincolnshire manors was registered, and appears in the Feet of Fines, but the Alnwick conveyance exists only in a private copy in the Percy Chartulary. Whilst fraud is not impossible, there is little positive evidence to support it. The question arises of why Alnwick should have been dealt with in a separate fine if it was Vescy's intention to devise it in exactly the same way as the Yorkshire and Lincolnshire estates. On the other hand, there are official records acknowledging both Bek and William de Vescy of Kildare as successors to William senior's estates. On 2 March 1299, the sheriff of Northumberland was ordered not to pursue the bishop of Durham, tenant of certain of the lands held formerly by William de Vescy, deceased, for debts of William or his brother John, in accordance with letters patent issued by the king in consideration of William's surrender of Kildare and Sprouston to the crown. A similar order was issued to the sheriffs of York and Lincoln in respect of William de Vescy of Kildare. If Bek was involved in a swindle, it was a successful one. It is more likely, however, that the official record of the Alnwick conveyance merely went astray.

A more plausible explanation for Vescy's disposition of his estates is that he was limited by political constraints, both in the wider sense and in terms of national politics. He needed the assistance of a powerful friend in order to secure the transfer of his estates and there were few more powerful in the locality than the bishop of Durham. Bek may well have driven a hard bargain, Alnwick being the price of his support. Vescy was in a relatively weak position at the time, having been recently dismissed from his post of Justiciar of Ireland in 1294. It may be significant that Bek and Earl Warenne had been appointed as keepers of the northern counties on 5 October 1295. Alnwick was a strong fortress in a vulnerable area. Vescy had been replaced as Justiciar of Ireland following allegations of treason, and the family had a rather chequered history of rebellion interspersed with royal service. It may well be that sacrificing Alnwick was necessary in order to achieve royal support for his plans. Vescy appears to have been content to allow Kildare, another politically sensitive area, to revert to the Crown. In February 1297 he granted the liberty, castle and county of Kildare to the king, in return for which he was pardoned all his own debts to the Crown and those of his brother John, including debts from his period as justiciar of Ireland and Justice of the Forest beyond the Trent. He received a regrant of the estates for life only in June 1297. The Scottish estate of Sprouston was dealt with in the same way. The plan after 1295 appears to have been to turn his bastard son into a member of the English nobility who could carry on the family name even if the family seat was no more, rather than allow him to find a role in Scotland, where the Vescys had a weak claim to the throne, or among his Irish kin in Kildare, where he could potentially have been a thorn in the side of the Crown. Vescy had actually made a claim to the Scottish throne on the basis of his descent from William the Lion (via an illegitimate female line) following the death of Margaret, the Maid of Norway, in 1291, although he did not pursue it very energetically, and abandoned the attempt shortly before Edward pronounced his adjudication in November 1292. These events were nonetheless recent enough for Edward to have them in mind. However, the weakness of Vescy's position should not be exaggerated. He was reappointed as Justice of the Forest North of the Trent on 24 September 1295 and was sent to Gascony in the king's service in late 1295, receiving a grant that in the event of his death whilst in the king's service, the king would charge his heirs with the debts due from him at the Exchequer, and his executors should have free administration of his will. It should also be borne in mind that the Yorkshire estates were the most valuable, and that in the political situation of the time estates in Northumberland might have seemed more vulnerable. The estimated values in 1219 for the Yorkshire, Northumberland and Linconshire estates respectively had been £135 8s 4d, £101 13s 4d and £50. A final possibility is that William senior may simply have felt that it was not right or appropriate for a bastard to succeed to the whole estate.

Although he received livery of his estates almost immediately, it is likely that William Vescy of Kildare was still a minor when his father died. The later rumour against Bek was that he had been entrusted with the lands to keep them to the use of the young son until he came of age and that he broke this trust. Professor Paul Brand has kindly drawn my attention to litigation heard in 1298 in which William Vescy de Kildare was described as being of such a tender age that he had no discretion. If the child had been conceived whilst William senior was in Ireland as Justiciar (1290–94) he would indeed have been very young at the time of his father's death.

William de Vescy successfully managed to transmit a significant proportion of his estates to his illegitimate son, ensuring that the latter would be able to attain the same status in life. In this respect, William de Vescy of Kildare was a de facto heir of his father. However, there were limits to what could be achieved. In order to ensure success, he required the assistance of a powerful feoffee, Antony Bek, and the goodwill of the king. To obtain these, concessions needed to be made, which involved the sacrifice of the more politically sensitive parts of his estate, including the family seat of Alnwick itself. Although William de Vescy of Kildare acquired only a portion of his father's estate, there can be no doubt that he was intended as a substitute for a legitimate heir. The estates in Scotland, Ireland and Northumberland which did not fall to William de Vescy of Kildare did not pass to the right heir of William de Vescy senior, but were permanently alienated to the crown and to the bishop of Durham.

Other landowners at the turn of the fourteenth century also made use of legal devices to enable a bastard son to act as a substitute for a legitimate male heir. The Musard family was a gentry family with principal residences at Miserden (Gloucestershire) and Staveley (Derbyshire) The last of the legitimate male line, Nicholas Musard, as a clerk in orders could have no legitimate offspring, and when he died in 1300 his heirs were Sir Ralph de Frescheville, son of Nicolas's eldest sister Amice, Margaret, another sister and Joan, daughter of Nicholas' other sister Isabel. However, whilst his coheirs received shares in the manor of Staveley, which with a value of around £35 was the most valuable of the manors, Nicholas had previously made provision for his illegitimate children. His daughter Christiana was given lands in Staveley, whilst his son Malcolm received the larger part of the other two demesne manors of Miserden and Saintbury. Malcolm was a retainer of Hugh Despenser the elder, and already during his father's lifetime had granted Miserden to Despenser. Malcolm made his own base at Saintbury, obtaining a pardon in 1300 for having entered the manor without licence. There he led a lawless and violent gang, whose activities included an armed raid on the house of the rector of nearby Weston–sub–Edge. In 1305, a number of Worcestershire juries made presentments concerning his activities, but although he was fined for the Weston raids, and was for a time imprisoned in Worcester, he was indicted only for receiving his page, John Baldewyn, an outlaw who had been indicted for murder. Malcolm Musard was declared innocent, and went on to serve, though not as a reformed character, as chief forester of Feckenham. In May 1321 he was appointed constable of Hanley Castle, which had been surrendered into the king's hand by the younger Despenser. Musard had obtained the bulk of the family lands, though not the most lucrative manor. His tactics of alienating one of his manors to a more powerful protector and leading his own violent gang appears to have been successful in securing his future, despite his illegitimacy.

The family of Meinill had been established at Whorlton in Yorkshire since the end of the eleventh century. Nicholas Meinill, who inherited the estate in 1299, is not known ever to have married, but, as noted in the previous chapter, he fathered an illegitimate son, Nicholas, as a result of an adulterous liaison with Lucy, daughter of Robert de Thweng, who was then the wife of Sir William Latimer. In 1314 Nicholas Meinill settled a large part of his estate on this illegitimate son. The manors of Greenhow and Boynton were entailed on Nicholas Meinill the elder with remainder to Nicholas, son of Lucy Thweng and the heirs of his body, with reversion to the right heirs of Nicholas Meinill. The family seat of Whorlton, together with the manors of Seamer (Cleveland), Eston, Middleton, Carlton (Cleveland), Potto and Trenholme (Yorkshire) and the advowson of the church of Rudby, was similarly entailed, with remainder to Nicholas son of Lucy Thweng and the heirs male of his body. In addition, in 1315 he purchased the reversion of the moiety of the manors of Wooler, Hethpool, Heatherslaw, Lowick, and Belford, Northumberland, held by Mary Muschamp, one of the two coheirs of Robert Muschamp, to hold to him and the heirs of his body, with reversion to Nicholas, son of Lucy Thweng. He also obtained from Robert Huntercombe a moiety of the forest of Cheviot which was settled with reversion to Nicholas, son of Lucy. Nicholas' right heir was his brother John and he took steps to ensure that he was also provided for, with the reversion of the manor of Castle Leavington, following the death of their mother, Christine. Lucy Thweng and her new husband Robert Everingham also settled the reversion of the manor of Yarm (Yorkshire) on Nicholas, son of Lucy, in default of any heirs of Lucy's body by Robert.

Nicholas, son of Lucy, appears to have entered the estates without difficulty. On his father's death in April 1322 he succeeded, whilst not yet of age, to Whorlton and the other Meinill lands held of the archbishop of Canterbury. After the death of Mary Muschamp later the same year, he succeeded to the moiety of the Muschamp barony purchased by his father. There was an initial problem with the moiety of Cheviot, his father having apparently neglected to obtain a royal licence, but this was resolved in February 1327. His standing does not appear to have been unduly affected by the circumstances of his birth and he received a personal summons to parliament from January 1336. In this case then, the bastard entered into an estate which included the main family seat, and was in every sense *de facto* heir of his father. He died in 1341, leaving a 10-year-old daughter, Elizabeth as his heiress.

Another example of an illegitimate son succeeding to the main family seat can be found in the case of Thomas Foxley. The Foxleys were a family of knightly rank with estates in Berkshire, Hampshire and Kent. The founder of the family fortunes appears to have been Sir John de Foxley, a lawyer who profited from loyal service to the Crown during the reign of Edward II. He had also been bailiff to the abbot of Westminster. He acquired property in Bramshill (Hampshire) through his wife, Constance, and purchased land in the parish of Bray (Berkshire), which he obtained permission to impark in 1321, and in Rumboldswyke (Sussex). His son Thomas, who appears not to have taken knighthood, continued in the parental tradition of royal service, and was constable of Windsor Castle from 1328–61. It is his son, Sir John de Foxley (d. 1378) whose property dispositions and colourful marital history are of particular interest. John's first marriage, to Maud, daughter of his father's friend Sir John Brocas, Master of the King's Horse, was a runaway match, rather like Romeo and Juliet but with a somewhat happier ending. The couple, who may well have met at Windsor, ran away together in 1332, aged only about 14, and sought the help of the vicar of Bray, William de Handloo. The vicar duly married them. He was initially suspended for a year as punishment for having solemnised the marriage outside his own parish, but it seems the couple persuaded their now-resigned parents to intercede with the bishop. The couple had a son, William, and two daughters, Katherine, who married John Warbleton, and Margery, who married Robert Bullock. But John and Maud may not have lived entirely happily ever after. Following Maud's death John married his mistress, Joan Martin, with whom he already had three sons, Thomas, Richard and John. Despite his technical illegitimacy, Thomas succeeded to the manors of Bray and Bramshill, though his possession was challenged in 1412 by William Warbleton, grandson of Katherine. Thomas seems to have prevailed, and his position was later strengthened by quitclaims from Margery Hertington, the daughter of Margery Bullock. On Thomas' death in 1436 his estates passed to his daughter Elizabeth, wife of Sir Thomas Uvedale. Thomas' brother John was provided with the manor of Rumboldswyke (Sussex), valued at £20 *per annum* in 1411–12, sufficient enough for him to maintain a position among the minor gentry of Sussex. He died on 30 April 1419, leaving an infant daughter, Alice, as his heir.

There are numerous other examples of landowners without a legitimate son making arrangements to transfer some or all of their property to an illegitimate son. Sir Andrew Sackville, a successful soldier whose Sussex estates were augmented by the addition of four manors when his wife, Joan de la Beche, shared in the division of her father's estate, is a case in point. Sir Andrew had had two sons, Andrew and John, with Joan, but both appear to have predeceased him, as did Joan herself. His second marriage to Maud Lovat produced no children. However, by his mistress, Joan Burgess, he had a son, Thomas, and a daughter, Alice. In September 1365, as he was nearing sixty he determined to settle his estates on Thomas and Alice in default of surviving legitimate issue. There was no challenge to this disposition of his estates when Sir Andrew died in 1369 and Thomas gained possession of estates which have been estimated by Nigel Saul to be worth in the order of £200 *per annum*. It was not until the death of Sir Andrew's widow, Maud, in 1393 that a belated challenge was mounted by a distant cousin, Sir Andrew Sackville of Fawley, who claimed to be Sir Andrew's right heir. This challenge was unsuccessful, and although sporadic claims were made by the Fawley branch of the family over the next ninety years, the transfer to the illegitimate line remained secure. The illegitimate son married Margaret, a daughter of Sir Edward Dallingridge of Bodiam, one of the most powerful men in Sussex, and was a respected member of the Sussex gentry community who served as a knight of the shire on three occasions. His descendants were to include the Sackvilles of Knole, lords Buckhurst and earls, later dukes, of Dorset. It is worth noting, however, that when a challenge to the younger Thomas' possession of Joan de la Beche's share of the de la Beche inheritance was mounted during the reign of Henry IV by John FitzElys, a descendant of one of Joan's sisters and coheiresses, he massaged his pedigree to conceal his illegitimacy by making himself appear to be the son of his legitimate half-brother, Sir Andrew the younger.

Sir William Dronsfield was a member of a gentry family which had been established in Yorkshire by the mid-thirteenth century, and at the time of his death in 1406 he was sheriff of York and held the manors of West Bretton, Gunthwaite, Newhall, Burgh and Bulcliff with assorted holdings in the surrounding area. As a retainer of Henry Bolingbroke, Dronsfield took advantage of the royal favour after Bolingbroke seized the throne to make provision for his illegitimate son, Richard Kesseburgh, by means of a resettlement of his estates in August 1406. Failing any issue of Dronsfield and his wife, Grace, Kesseburgh was to have the reversion of the lands in Cumberworth, High Hoyland, Wickersley, Fryth, Carhouse, Sandal and Ingburchworth, with successive remainders to the heirs of his body and then to William Dronsfield's right heirs. The only significant exclusion was Dronsfield's principal seat, the manor of West Bretton, which was to remain to Dronsfield's right heirs. Kesseburgh was also to have land which William had purchased in Wollay and the remainder of purchased property in Bargh, in the event of the death of William Dronsfield's siblings Thomas, John and Joan without heirs. This was thus similar to the Vescy case of a century before in that the bastard succeeded to most of the land except the principal seat, although in this case the right heirs acquired the latter. In Dronsfield's will, made at the same time, he bequeathed to Richard Kesseburgh a tapestry bed with two pairs of sheets and two pairs of blankets.

Another supporter of Henry Bolingbroke, Sir John Pelham (d. 1429) also managed to transfer the bulk of his property to his illegitimate son, John, to the exclusion of his right heirs. In this case, there was not really an issue over the main family seat, for most of the property had been accumulated during Sir John's lifetime. Sir John's father and grandfather had served as county coroners and he had inherited only a smallholding at Warbleton (Sussex) and part of the manor of Gensing. He made his fortune in the service of the Lancastrian regime. After Bolingbroke successfully seized the crown in 1399 he was rewarded with offices and income, rising to become a leading figure in the government of Henry IV. Sir John was made a knight of the household and royal sword-bearer, keeper of the New Forest, and chief steward of the duchy of Lancaster estates south of the Trent. As constable of Pevensey castle he was entrusted with the custody of a number of high profile political prisoners, including Edward, Duke of York, Edmund and Roger Mortimer and James I of Scotland (1406–37). He was one of the executors of Henry IV's will. He seems to have been less fortunate in his marriages. In 1387 he allegedly mounted a night assault on the house of Sir John Shardelowe at Fulbourn, abducting Margaret, the widow of Shardelowe's son, and heiress of Sir Roger Grey. He then married Margaret, gaining control of her property. In 1399 or early 1400 he married another wealthy widow, Joan, widow of Sir Hugh Zouche. By the time of his death in 1429, Sir John's income from rents was in excess of £870 *per annum*, but his marriages produced no surviving legitimate children. The settlements he made during his lifetime in favour of his bastard son, John, to the exclusion of his right heirs, the children of his two sisters, were successful. Among the lands of which John Pelham the younger took possession were the manors of Crowhurst, Burwash and Bibleham and the rape of Hastings in Sussex, the reversions of which had been granted to his father by Henry IV, and which were collectively worth £51 10s 2¾d. Sir John junior also seems to have acquired at least part of the family land at Warbleton, which was not held in chief. Sir John senior also made his illegitimate son one of the executors of his will, along with his wife and two others, but John's illegitimacy is not explicitly stated in the will, where he is simply described as '*filium meum*'.

Some plans to enable a bastard son to inherit were only partially successful as another Lancastrian knight, Sir Henry Hoghton, was to discover. Sir Henry was the younger son of Sir Adam Hoghton of Hoghton, but was fortunate enough to be provided with an adequate estate from the family holdings, including lands at Mollington (Cheshire), the manor of Chipping (Lancashire) and lands in Alston, Hothersall and Dilworth. His prospects were further enhanced by his position within the retinue of John of Gaunt, Duke of Lancaster, and his association with the latter's son, later Henry IV. Hoghton's personal affairs were however rather tangled. In 1403 he obtained a dispensation to enable him to marry Joan Radcliffe, who was not only a former mistress, but was related to him in the second and third degrees. Furthermore, Sir Henry had previously had a relationship with a woman related to Joan in the third degree, who was perhaps the mother of his illegitimate son, Richard. Certainly, when his marriage to Joan proved childless, the couple attempted to settle property from Joan's inheritance upon the bastard. This property included the manors of Salesbury, Little Pendleton and Clayton-le-Dale as well as lands in Clitheroe, Oswaldtwistle, Preston, Ribchester and Dulton. This attempt met with considerable opposition from the Talbots, the rival claimants, and eventually after arbitration in 1449 Richard Hoghton was left with Little Pendleton and revenues of £20 *per annum* from Salebury.

Turning now to the end of the fifteenth century, Sir Richard Beauchamp, Lord St Amand, (d. 1508) had no legitimate heirs of his body and devised the bulk of his estates to his illegitimate son by Mary Wroughton, Anthony

St Amand. Anthony certainly managed to gain possession of some of these estates, including the manor of Ramerick (Hertfordshire) which he conveyed to St John's College Cambridge in 1520–21, and the manor of Grendon Underwood (Buckinghamshire) which he conveyed to the trustees of Thomas Pigott of Whaddon in 1520. He was still holding the manor of Ion in Lower Gravenhurst (Bedfordshire) in 1531. However, if he ever had possession of Basildon (Berkshire), he held it for only a very short time as it was sold by Sir John Hussey and his wife to Henry Bridges in 1509. He had to face a claim from Thomas Brook for the manor of Knotting (Bedfordshire), which was submitted to the archbishop of Canterbury for arbitration and decision was ultimately given in favour of Thomas. Anthony St Amand married Anne, daughter of Thomas West, Lord la Warre, with whom he had a daughter, Mary.

Henry Grey (d. 1496), last Lord Grey of Codnor, died without legitimate issue, though he had three illegitimate sons, Richard, Henry and Henry. His coheirs were his aunts, daughters of his grandfather Richard Grey, and their descendants. Lord Grey made some provision from his estate for his bastard sons. The manor of Ratcliffe-on-Trent (Nottinghamshire) was to go to Richard Grey and the heirs of his body, with reversion to the two younger illegitimate sons, both confusingly called Henry. The two Henries were to have the manors of Towton and Barton, Nottinghamshire. He also willed that the younger Henry, son of Katherine Finderne, was to marry Cicely Charlelton and that his cousin, Sir Thomas Barowe should pay £100 towards the marriages of Richard and the elder Henry. However, unlike Sir Richard Beauchamp, Lord St Amand, Grey chose not to settle the bulk of his estates on any of his illegitimate sons but instead sold the reversion of the family seat of Codnor, together with other manors in Derbyshire and Nottinghamshire to Sir John Zouche, the husband of one of his coheirs.

In some cases a father's attempts to settle the reversion of his estates on his illegitimate offspring ended in failure. John Chenduyt was a member of a family that had been established in Cornwall since the thirteenth century, and whose main seat in the county was the manor of Bodannon, which had been settled by his grandfather in fee tail. John was not entirely secure in his tenure; in 1407 an attempt had been made to deprive him of his estate on the grounds that it was forfeit to the Crown as the property of Sir Robert Tresilian, the former chief justice who had fallen foul of the Merciless Parliament. Although Chenduyt eventually proved that he held the property by inheritance from his father, he had to face further challenge from John Colshull I who had married Tresilian's widow. Chenduyt and his wife Joan, widow of Richard Glyvyan, had no legitimate offspring and in 1425 he settled the bulk of his estates by a fine levied at Westminster. According to this settlement, in default of heirs of John

Chenduyt's body the estates would descend to his illegitimate son Richard, with remainder to Joan, Chenduyt's illegitimate daughter, who was wife of John Pengelly, and in the event of their deaths without heirs of their bodies, successive remainders to William, Lord Botreaux, Sir Walter Hungerford and his wife Katherine, Sir William Talbot and his wife Alianora, John Tretherff, Ralph Trenewith and Ralph Botreaux. It is worth noting that the fine specifically referred to Richard and Joan as Chenduyt's bastard children, rather than identifying them by reference to their mother. Four years previously he had made direct provision for his illegitimate children by which Joan and her husband received lands in Penpethy and Bodwin, and Richard received the manors of Cant and Tremore. Chenduyt died on 13 December 1426. An inquisition post mortem held in Cornwall on 28 May 1427 found that Chenduyt had died seised of the manor of Bodannon in fee tail, and that his next heirs were his kinsmen Ralph Trenewith and Thomas Rescarrek, as descendants of the sisters of John Chenduyt's father, Thomas. A further inquisition held in October of the same year reported the 1425 settlement, a copy of which was shown to the jury. By this time, however, Richard Chenduyt was already dead. It was also found at the same time that John Chenduyt's lands in Penpethy and Bodwin had been granted in 1421 to Joan and John Pengelly and the heirs of Joan's body; with successive reversions to Richard Chenduyt, Sir Walter Hungerford and Katherine his wife and Sir William Talbot and Eleanor his wife etc. and that John and Joan were seised of this property. The manors of Cant and Tremore had likewise been settled in 1423 on Richard Chenduyt, with reversions to Joan Pengelly, William Lord Botreaux and the others named in the 1421 settlement. Copies of both these settlements were shown to the jury.

Chenduyt thus not only provided for his bastard offspring by settling certain lands on them during his own lifetime, but also attempted to settle the reversion of the bulk of his estate on them, in preference to his right heirs. Unfortunately for both him and them his plan failed. The death of Richard Chenduyt shortly after his father meant that he was unable to benefit, but under the terms of the 1425 settlement, Bodannon should have reverted to his sister Joan, wife of John Pengelly. However, in June 1428, an order was issued to the escheator to take the fealty of Thomas Rescarrek and to partition Bodannon into two equal portions, and deliver seisin to Thomas Rescarrek and John, son of Ralph Trenewith. Had Richard lived, he might have succeeded in retaining the estates. Whilst a live adult male bastard might have stood a good chance of keeping the estates passed on to him by his father, the husband of a bastard daughter found it much more difficult to secure possession.

However, disinherited heirs general did not always confine themselves to legal means of regaining estates from a bastard. Some turned to violence, particularly during the lawless times of the mid-fifteenth century. Sir John Basynges of Empingham, Rutland had an illegitimate son, John and daughter Alice. He had no legitimate offspring and his legal heir was his sister Alice, wife of Thomas Makworth. Sir John's plan for the post-mortem distribution of his estates was that his illegitimate children should receive the less important part of his estates and that the younger John should also have a life interest in his main seat of Empingham, to the disadvantage of his sister and heir, Alice, and her children. In May 1439, Sir John conveyed his Rutland and other midland estates to a group of local feoffees, including his cousin, William Lord Zouche of Harringworth. On 29 September, shortly after the death of his brother-in-law Thomas Makworth, Sir John instructed his feoffees to settle minor properties in the midlands, with a total value of around £5 *per annum*, including the manors of Egmonton (Nottinghamshire) and Roxham (Lincolnshire) on his son John and the heirs of his body, together with a life interest only in the family seat of Empingham, worth £20 *per annum*. His bastard daughter, Alice, was to have a life interest in land in North Luffenham, South Luffenham and Tixover, with reversion to John. In August 1445, Sir John made a further will, confirming the terms of the 1439 will, including John's life interest in Empingham, and further arrangements for his Kent estates, the issues of which were to be used for payment of his debts and a marriage portion for the bastard daughter, the property reverting to Sir John's right heirs after two years. Sir John died less than a month later, on 22 September 1445. Initially, all went smoothly and the juries in inquisitions post mortem held in Rutland, Nottinghamshire and Lincolnshire all referred to Sir John's settlement in favour of his bastard children.

From one point of view, it was only less important properties that were to be permanently alienated to the bastard, John. However, the Makworths were not prepared to wait. Despite, or possibly because of, the younger Basynges's swift re-enfeoffment of the property to more powerful feoffees, Sir John Talbot, Sir James Ormond, Ralph, Lord Cromwell and John Sutton, Lord Dudley, the Makworths took executive action. In January 1446, a servant of Cromwell was threatened by Alice's brother-in-law John Makworth, dean of Lincoln Cathedral, so that he dared not collect rents from the manor of Empingham. In the early morning of 23 September 1446, Alice's son, Henry Makworth and three accomplices broke into the manor house at Empingham and murdered John Basynges junior. Alice was able to use her late husband's connections with the Lancastrian regime to secure a pardon, and the Makworths were able to secure their possession of Empingham.

In June 1516 Thomas Stafford of Tattenhoe (Buckinghamshire) made a will which not only made significant provision of lands and tenements for his bastard son William, but attempted to pre-empt any trouble from his right heirs by threatening them that they would lose the reversions to which they were entitled under his settlement if they 'interrupt, vex or trouble the foresaid William Stafford ... of any part of my lands, tenements or hereditaments to him willed'. In the event of the bastard son William, son of Alice Denton, dying without heirs of his body, the reversion of the estates was to go successively to Thomas's nephew William, his second son, Thomas's nephew Humphrey, Humphrey's second son, John Constable, and the right heirs of Thomas Stafford. It appears that the other Staffords were not prepared to allow the estates to go to a bastard son without a fight, and litigation in Chancery followed.

In the inquisition post mortem on Thomas Stafford, his right heir was found to be his nephew Humphrey Stafford of Blatherwick (Northamptonshire), the son and heir of his eldest brother, Humphrey. The mother of William Stafford the bastard, Alice, who was widow of William Ingoldsby, accused Bentley and Humphrey Stafford of abducting him. A dispute arose later between William and Humphrey, and the latter sent the title deeds in a great coffer to Woburn Abbey (Bedfordshire) for safe custody. William Stafford, bastard, sued the abbot for their recovery, an action which the abbot considered to be malicious and vexatious. William also brought an action against Thomas Worley, the surviving feoffee. Eventually some form of compromise was reached and in 1525 there was an agreement by which William Stafford the bastard received grant of the manor of Tattenhoe to himself and his wife Eleanor for life for an annual payment of £10 to William Stafford of Bradfield. William the bastard evidently obtained Great Linford (Buckinghamshire), for he died seised of this manor in 1529. Thomas Stafford's attempts to provide for his bastard to take over his estates were thus only partially successful, despite the dire warnings in his will.

Some fathers of bastards made only limited provision for them. Thomas Montagu, 4th Earl of Salisbury (d. 1428) is a case in point. His legitimate daughter and heiress, Alice was preferred over his bastard son John, who received only 50 marks in Montagu's will, and his more distant male heir, his uncle Richard Montagu. Alice was married by February 1421 to Richard Neville (d. 1460), the younger son of Ralph Neville, Earl of Westmorland. The earldom and most of the late earl's estates went to his Alice and her husband, whose right to the title was confirmed by the Privy Council in May 1429, instead of to Richard Montagu, although Neville's right to the associated seat in parliament had apparently to be referred to the Lords, and was confirmed only until the king reached his majority. Richard Montagu received only a bequest of £100 and the lands which were held in tail male (including the manors of Amesbury and Winterbourne in Wiltshire and Canford in Dorset, though Thomas' widow held one-third of each of these in dower).

There are several points to be borne in mind when considering why Montagu did not attempt to do more for his bastard son. Firstly, his father had been executed and attainted for his part in the conspiracy of the earls of Kent and Huntingdon to murder Henry IV. Although Thomas Montagu had been granted seisin of the estates his father had held in fee tail on proving his age in 1409, it took longer for him to secure reversal of the attainder. A petition in 1414 was unsuccessful and it was not until 1421 that his petition to be fully restored as heir in blood was granted. Even then he recovered only entailed lands, not those held in fee simple. It would therefore have been difficult for him to attempt a resettlement in favour of a bastard. Secondly, by 1421 his daughter and apparent heiress had married, and the Nevilles would therefore have been interested parties. Furthermore, Salisbury may not have married his second wife until 1424, and the birth of a legitimate son was still a realistic possibility, since he was only aged about forty when he was fatally wounded at the siege of Orleans. Even so, the relative size of the cash bequests to his bastard son and to his heir male give an indication of Montagu's conception of the relative status of a bastard son and a legitimate uncle and heir.

At around the same time as Sir John Argentine was making arrangements to disinherit his legitimate daughters in favour of a bastard son, Otto Bodrugan was arranging the future succession to the Bodrugan estates. The Bodrugan family illustrates just how fragile the line of male succession could be. At the start of the fourteenth century they were a well-established and influential gentry family of Cornwall. By the time he died Sir Henry Bodrugan (*c*. 1263–1308) had an estate comprising eleven main manors and a number of lesser holdings. His son Sir Otto Bodrugan (d. 1331) had six sons who reached adulthood, Henry, William, Nicholas, Thomas, John and Otto. Yet by the end of the century there were no remaining legitimate heirs in the direct male line. Of Sir Otto's six sons Henry died just a few weeks after his father's death and before he obtained seisin of the estates. The only child of William's to reach maturity was a daughter, Elizabeth, the first wife of Sir Richard Cergeaux. After William's death in 1362 most of the Bodrugan lands passed into the hands of Elizabeth and her husband and they remained in Sir Richard's possession by courtesy after his first wife's death. ('Courtesy' was a right by which a husband could continue to occupy his deceased wife's estates for the term of his life, provided that a living child and heir had been born to the couple.) Little is known of Nicholas Bodgrugan, but no surviving offspring are recorded. Thomas and John both entered the church and were dead by 1362. It therefore rested with the youngest son, Otto, to preserve the family line. This he managed with only partial success as he had no legitimate son.

He did however have an illegitimate son, William, and a legitimate daughter, Joan, who married Ralph Trenewith, by whom she had two sons, Otto and William. In 1386 Otto senior chose to settle the reversion of the Bodrugan estates (most of which were still in the possession of Sir Richard Cergaux) on his legitimate grandsons rather than his illegitimate son. Although Otto junior died young, William survived, changed his name to Bodrugan and thus continued the Bodrugan line. A separate settlement made by his father in 1382 had given the illegitimate William a reversion in one messuage, one carucate of land and 100s of rent at Markwell and Carburrow after the death of Cergeaux. This was not the first time that Markwell had been the portion of an illegitimate Bodrugan child, for William Bodrugan (d. 1307), Archdeacon of Cornwall (an uncle of the earlier Sir Henry who died in 1308), had granted it to the husband of his illegitimate daughter, Elizabeth, Adam de Markwell. Under the settlement of 1386 William also had a reversionary interest in the manor of Tregrehan, but only in the event of the deaths of his legitimate nephews and nieces without heirs of their bodies. In favouring a legitimate grandson through the female line rather than an illegitimate son, Otto Bodrugan thus took a different approach from that of Sir William Argentine. One key difference in this case is that much of the family estate was not in Otto's hands. Reassembling the patrimony after the death of Sir Richard Cergaux was to prove a difficult enough task without the additional factor of illegitimacy to complicate matters.

Although William Bodrugan the bastard did not fare particularly well in terms of landed settlement, he was at least able to maintain the status of a gentleman. He represented Helston in the parliament of April 1384 and Launceston in the parliament of February 1388. It has been suggested that these elections owed more to his father's standing in the locality than his own abilities. If so, this would indicate closer family ties and more willingness on the part of his father to provide for his illegitimate son than the landed settlement might suggest. His integration into the wider Bodrugan family can be demonstrated by his support of his legitimate nephew and heir to the Bodrugan estate, William Bodrugan (alias Trenewith), in a dispute with the Trevarthian family, and his witnessing of charters both of his nephew and his father's wife. He was also involved with his nephew, William, in trying to regain control of the manors of Tremodret and Trevelyn from Richard Cergeaux's widow and daughters by fairly unscrupulous means. In 1402 it was found that Bodrugan's case rested on a forged document. Forgery may have been a family speciality: Sir Henry Bodrugan (see Chapter One), the grandson of William's legitimate nephew, was accused of illegally altering wills and testaments to his own advantage in the 1470s.

Simplified Bodrugan Family Tree

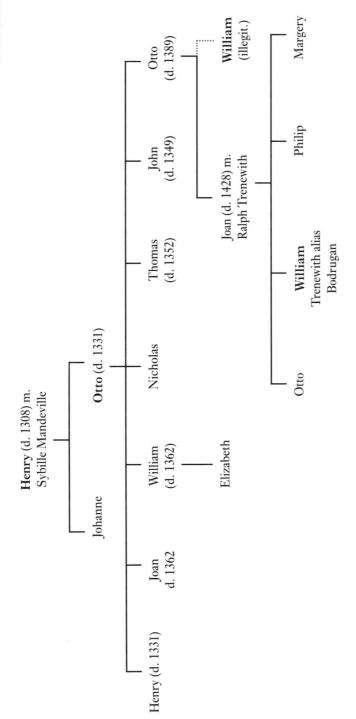

Sir Roger Bertram (d. *c.* 1272) of Mitford, Northumberland, whose only legitimate heir of his body was a daughter, Agnes, gave the manor of Throphill to his bastard son, Thomas. Agnes inherited Mitford and Felton, but Sir Roger alienated most of his extensive possessions. Bertram's actions may simply have been due to financial problems, rather than concern over illegitimate status, for he was said to have been 'indebted to divers Jews' and in the *Quo Warranto* proceedings it was noted that the fences of one of the properties he sold had fallen into decay when in his possession, owing to his poverty.

John Wilcotes (d. 1422) of Great Tew, Oxfordshire, a younger son who acquired a landed estate in Oxfordshire through an advantageous marriage, was another landowner who did not favour his illegitimate son over the legitimate female line. He left instructions that his widow was to have possession of all of his estates for the duration of her life, and after her death Great Tew was to pass to their elder daughter Elizabeth and Dean and Chalford to the younger daughter Margaret. His illegitimate son Thomas was to have only a reversionary interest in these estates in the event of his half-sisters' failure to have issue, but he was provided with other lands and tenements in Gloucestershire and Worcestershire. In the event, Thomas did acquire at least part of the estate, but it took time, during most of which he was serving in France. There was a long dispute over the performance of John Wilcotes' last will and it was over twenty years before his widow obtained possession of Dean and Chalford. Eventually, Thomas Wilcotes gained possession of Dean and Chalford, which he ultimately gave to Oriel College Oxford.

In an unusual case from the fifteenth century a mother was able to secure the transmission of at least part of her husband's estate to a bastard line. Sir Peter Bessels (d. 1425) of Bessels Leigh, Oxfordshire had no legitimate children. In his will, he left a life interest only in land at Longworth to Thomas, described as the son of Margery Haines, Bessels' second wife, with further provision for Thomas' education. The reversion of this property, together with the rest of Bessels' estates, save Bessels Leigh and Kingston, which were given to Margery for her life, and King's Brompton which was given to Barlinch Priory, were to be sold and the proceeds were to go towards the payment of Bessels' debts and charitable purposes. Thomas was subsequently known as Thomas Bessels, and may have been a pre-nuptial bastard of Peter Bessels and Margery, though it is possible that he was Margery's son only. Margery was certainly ultimately more generous, though she went against the provisions of her late husband's will. Having outlived Bessels by some 50 years, she was able to settle his manors of Radcot and Grafton on William, the son of Thomas, and his heirs, with remainders to Thomas' other sons and their heirs. On William's death the manors passed to his daughter Elizabeth, widow of Richard Fettiplace.

The intentions of Sir William Sturmy (d. 1427), a diplomat and speaker of the House of Commons, are unclear. Sturmy was another landowner who had no legitimate son, though he had a bastard son called John. His heirs were his daughter Agnes and John Seymour, son of his elder daughter Maud. The circumstances were similar to those in which Sir John Argentine had arranged to transfer his property to his illegitimate son William some twenty-five years earlier. Sir William may or may not have belatedly attempted to follow Argentine's example. After his death, there were allegations of fraud involving John Sturmy and a cousin, Robert Erle, concerning a supposed deathbed enfeoffment of the manors of Wolf Hall, Stichcombe, Standen, Stapleford and Burbage and lands in Pickedwood and Crofton (Wiltshire). According to depositions in the case, Sir William had died at Elvetham on a Friday evening, having earlier that day sealed letters of attorney to William Tournay, to deliver seisin of the manors concerned to John Benger and other feoffees. It was claimed that John Sturmy and Robert Erle swore the servants to keep Sir William's death secret until the following Sunday, one of Robert Erle's men being instructed to admit no one. Meanwhile, on the Saturday, William Tournay met John Benger in Marlborough and they rode together to Pickedwood, Stichcombe, Durley (part of Burbage) and Wolf Hall, where he duly delivered seisin. Whether Sir William really elected to make a deathbed enfeoffment with a view to providing for his illegitimate son, or whether it was a deliberate fraud on the latter's part is uncertain. John Sturmy was certainly an executor of Sturmy's will, which had been made in London a couple of days earlier. Either way John Sturmy did not derive much benefit from the supposed enfeoffment. The case dragged on into the 1450s, but the manor of Crofton and main family seat of Wolf Hall passed into the Seymour family. Sir William had taken some responsibility for his illegitimate son's future, ensuring his position in local society. In 1422, he secured John Sturmy's election to the Commons for Ludgershall, along with his grandson and heir, John Seymour. Robert Erle represented Great Bedwyn in the same parliament.

Sir Thomas Cobham of Sterborough (Surrey) had a legitimate daughter, Ann, from his marriage to Ann, the daughter of Humphrey Stafford and widow of Aubrey de Vere, who was his heiress. Aged four at her father's death, she was married first to Edward Blount, Lord Mountjoy, who died whilst still a minor, and then to Edward Burgh. However Sir Thomas left his manor of Pentlow (Essex) with the advowson of the church and also land and the advowson of the church in Cavendish (Suffolk) and some lands in Kent to his illegitimate son Reginald. He also bequeathed a number of items of plate to Reginald, who would appear to have been a minor, since he was only to receive them on reaching the age of twenty or on his marriage. In the event of Reginald's death before coming into his inheritance, these items were to be sold and the funds distributed for the good of the souls of Sir Thomas and of Reginald. Reginald's mother was apparently a sister of Sir Gervase Clifton, who is described as Reginald's uncle in the will, in which he is named as one of Reginald's trustees.

John Berney of Reedham (d. 1460), uncle of Margaret Paston, never married. In his will he left his illegitimate son, Osbert Berney, a messuage in Reedham and a life interest only in the Norfolk manors of Shipdam and Turtevilles in Little Witchingham, along with all his movable property. The reversion of the manors went to John Berney, the representative of the main line of the family. John was also to have the manor of Caston straight away, but was required for the first three years to contribute £20 towards Osbert's maintenance, Osbert being still under age. Osbert subsequently found employment in the service of his Paston cousins.

Sir Edward Poynings (1459–1521), Deputy Lieutenant of Ireland and the son of Robert Poynings (d. 1461) and his wife, Elizabeth Paston, had no legitimate son to succeed him. His son John had predeceased him, but he had three illegitimate sons and four daughters. He made provision for these illegitimate children in his will of 27 July 1521, leaving his manor of Westenhanger in Kent, to the eldest, Thomas, but most of his estates, with a value of £427 4s ¾d, passed to Henry Percy, Earl of Northumberland. This was in accordance with the terms of an earlier agreement with Percy concerning the reversion of the estates which Poynings held of the inheritances of Robert, Lord Poynings and Sir Guy Brian. It seems that his illegitimate sons were born relatively late in Poynings' life and after the agreement of 1504. Sir Edward's will of 1521 provided that his servant Edward Thwaytes should have the revenues of Westenhanger for twelve years until Thomas, the eldest, came of age, and another son, Adrian, was attending Gray's Inn in 1533. Thomas and Adrian both enjoyed successful careers as soldiers and courtiers. Thomas was present at the coronation of Anne Boleyn in 1533, and was made a knight of the Bath during the celebrations. In 1545 he was created Baron Poynings and appointed lieutenant of Boulogne. Adrian served in his brother Thomas' retinue and continued to serve in Boulogne and Calais after his brother's death. He was knighted by Queen Elizabeth on her accession. Poynings' daughters may have been a little older than his sons. Joan married Thomas, Lord Clinton (d. 1517) in around 1510 and was the mother of Thomas Clinton, Earl of Lincoln. Although Sir Edward was constrained in his ability to provide for his illegitimate children from his estates, they were able to follow in their father's footsteps in terms of a diplomatic and military career.

Sir Richard Nanfan of Trethewel (Cornwall) and Birtsmorton (Worcestershire) died in 1507, leaving no male heir of his body, though he had at least two legitimate daughters and two bastard sons, John and William. Sir Richard left lands in Birtsmorton, which had been purchased by his grandfather in 1424/5, to his bastard son John in his will. The Nanfans were an old Cornish family and Sir Richard's Cornish lands passed to James Erisey, his heir general and one of the executors of his will. John eventually gained possession of Birtsmorton, although only after a suit against Richard Nanfan's widow, Margaret. In his will, Nanfan also bequeathed his 'great red horse that came from Calais' to his bastard son John, who was also the residuary legatee. William, who was born by 1485, received little in the way of direct provision from his father, but benefitted through patronage by means of connections with Cardinal Wolsey. He represented Dorchester in the parliament of 1529.

By the end of the fifteenth century the degree of freedom which landowners enjoyed to settle their estates as they wished was reducing. The example of Sir William Gresley of Drakelow (d. 1521), related by Susan Wright in her study of the Derbyshire gentry in the fifteenth century, is one such case where a landowner's attempt to provide for his illegitimate offspring was hampered by an existing entail. The Gresley estates had been entailed, mainly in tail male, by William Gresley's father, Sir John, in 1475. William apparently tried to break the entail by means of a legal procedure known as common recovery to enable him to use all of the patrimony, including Drakelow, for the performance of his last will. According to this will part of the estate was go to Alice Tawke, the mother of his four bastard sons, for her life, with successive remainders to her issue and William's brothers, and the other part would go to Alice and William's eldest son, Anthony, and his issue, with remainders to his brothers. After William's death the case went to Chancery, where it was held that as William had held only the use of the property his attempt to break the entail was invalid and his brother George was the rightful heir. He had, however, also made some provision from newly-purchased land. In February 1511 he settled lands in Snarestone (Leicestershire), which he had recently purchased from John Corbett, on Alice with successive remainders to her sons Anthony, Thomas, Humphrey and Edward and the right heirs of William. Simon Payling has pointed out how the popularity of general entails in the fourteenth and fifteenth centuries meant that families lacking a direct male heir frequently found that so much of the estate was already tied up that it was not possible to disinherit female heirs in favour of male collaterals with any certainty of success. The same problem would obviously have applied to any attempt to favour an illegitimate son.

The examples above all involve cases where there was no surviving legitimate son to inherit and carry on the family name. What happened to bastards where there was a son and heir? In many cases the bastard was treated in much the same way as a legitimate younger son, with some form of landed settlement and/or an advantageous marriage. John Lovel of Minster Lovell (d. 1287) made provision for his elder, illegitimate son, John, by conveying to him the manor of Snorscombe (Northamptonshire). His position thus seems similar to that of a younger legitimate son, in that he was provided with a small portion of the family estate, but also made his own way through military service.

In his will of December 1442, Edward Tyrell of Downham (Essex) left his bastard son John property in Rettendon and South Hanningfield together with the reversion of a property called Barons in Downham. Tyrell was from a well-established Essex family, the younger son of Walter Tyrell of Avon (Hampshire) and brother of John Tyrell (d. 1437) of Heron in East Horndon (Essex). Although he was a younger son, Edward had played an important role in county affairs. He had at various times served as escheator of Essex and Hertfordshire, sheriff of Essex and Hertfordshire and had been a knight of the shire for Essex in 1427, 1432, and 1435. His own income was assessed at £135 *per annum* in 1436. He held property in Cambridgeshire, Essex and Middlesex, though his manor of Downham was leased from his brother. His Cambridgeshire estates, which he had inherited from his mother, the daughter and heiress of Edmund Flambard, went to his legitimate son, Edward.

William Lord Bonville of Chewton (1392–1461) had a legitimate son and three daughters from his first marriage to Margaret, the daughter of Reynold, Lord Grey of Ruthin. He also had an illegitimate son, John, from a relationship with Isabel Kirkby. Both his grandfather and father had acquired substantial property through marriage, and Bonville was one of the most powerful and wealthy landowners in the south west, with estates concentrated in Devon, where his principal seat was Shute, and around Chewton Mendip in Somerset. He received a personal summons to parliament as Lord Bonville of Chewton in 1449. His income was valued in 1435 at around £900 *per annum*, placing him in a good position to be able to provide for his illegitimate son. He settled the manors of Little Modbury and Meavy, together with land in Ivybridge (Devon), on John and Alice, his wife. Alice was the daughter and heiress of William Dennis of Combe Ralegh and, through her, John obtained the manors of Combe Ralegh (Devon) and Alleston (Somerset) and founded a cadet branch of the family.

The Montforts had settled at the manor of Beaudesert near Henley-in-Arden, Warwickshire soon after the Conquest, and their landholdings in Rutland and Berkshire can be traced back at least to the early twelfth century. Peter was the legitimate younger son of John de Montfort (d. *c.* 1296) and as such was originally intended for the Church. He had been instituted to the rectory of Ilmington (Warwickshire), one of the de Montfort manors, in 1312 as a clerk in minor orders when he was presumably in his late teens. Following the death of his elder brother John at Bannockburn in 1314 his plans changed. In 1316 he was summoned for military service against the Scots and the following year he obtained a dispensation from the Bishop of Worcester for non-residence and for not taking further orders for three years. He eventually resigned the rectory of Ilmington on 5 May 1320 and, as Peter de Montfort, knight, he presented his successor in October of the same year.

Peter de Montfort had three illegitimate children as a result of a liaison with one Lora Astley of Ullenhall ((close to Henley-in-Arden), two sons, John and Richard, and a daughter, Alice. It would appear that the elder son John, at least, must have been born whilst Peter was still expecting to follow a Church career as a younger son, for Peter settled an annuity of £50 from the issues of his manor of Remenham (Berkshire) on him as early as 1313. After succeeding to the family estate he made settlements of his property in which these illegitimate children were included. In 1324 he settled the manors of Remenham (Berkshire) and Ilmington on himself and the heirs of his body with successive remainders to John, son of Lora of Ullenhall, and his issue and Alice, sister of John. It should be noted in this context that Remenham and Ilmington were not recent acquisitions but had been held by the de Montforts of the Earls of Warwick for a century and a half by this date. In 1326 he settled Whitchurch and an estate in Little Brailes (Warwickshire) on himself with remainder to John, and also Ullenhall. At this stage it appears that he was unmarried. This had changed by 1338–39, when he settled the manor of Gunthorpe (Nottinghamshire) on himself and his wife Margaret (daughter of Lord Furnivall), and their heirs, with successive remainder to John, son of Lora de Ullenhall and the heirs of his body, Richard, brother of John and the heirs of his body and Alice, wife of Fulk de Penebridge, who was presumably the illegitimate daughter.

By 1349, however, Peter had a legitimate son and heir, Guy, and resettled his estates, apparently on the occasion of Guy's marriage to Margaret, daughter of Thomas Beauchamp, Earl of Warwick. The reversion of Whitchurch was now granted to Guy de Montfort and Margaret his wife, with reversion to Thomas, Earl of Warwick. His eldest illegitimate son, John, received a life interest in Hinton (then in Wiltshire). Guy predeceased his father and on the latter's death the bulk of his estates, including Beaudesert, passed to the Earl of Warwick in accordance with the settlement of 1349. The precise details of the descent of the property are not entirely clear, but John de Montfort appears to have retained Remenham, Monkspath, Ilmington and Ullenhall, as these were still in the family in the time of John's grandson, William de Montfort. John was able to add to his estate through his marriage to Joan de Clinton, heiress to the Warwickshire manor of Coleshill. He represented Warwickshire in parliament as a knight of the shire in 1361–62. John had a son, Baldwin de Montfort, with

Joan and thereby founded the family of Montfort (later known as Mountford) of Coleshill. Baldwin's son William was to consolidate the family fortunes through his marriage to Margaret, the heiress of Sir John Peche, by which means he acquired a further ten Warwickshire manors. In this case a bastard son who received a landed endowment succeeded in establishing himself in county society and founding a cadet branch of the family.

Peter de Montfort also provided his second illegitimate son, Richard, with a small landed estate. In 1363 he settled the manor of Odes on himself for life, with remainder to Richard and his wife, Rose. Richard acquired half the manor of Lapworth through his marriage to Rose, daughter of Sir Hugh de Brandeston (d. 1362), and received a bequest of plate in his father's will, of which he was an executor. Like his brother, he served as a knight of the shire, in the parliament of October 1363, though he was less successful in founding a family line, the eventual heirs being his granddaughters, one of whom married John Catesby. Peter de Montfort had ensured that his illegitimate sons received an adequate livelihood from the family estates. De Montfort's relationship with the mother of his illegitimate sons was a long term one and she was mentioned in his will.

Sir John Arundell of Lanherne had extensive estates in the south-west and at the time of his death in 1435 held twenty-four manors in Cornwall and nine more in Devon, together with other land, providing him with a total income from land in the order of £300 *per annum*. In 1418 Sir John made a settlement of part of his estate in favour of what appear to have been five bastard children. His eldest legitimate son, John (b *c.* 1392), had married Margaret, a daughter and coheir of Sir John Burghersh, the previous year. Under the 1418 settlement, the manors of Tolverne, Respery, Treveneague and Penberthy with various other land, messuages and rents, including a ferry across the river Tolverne, were to remain after his death to Emmeline Wode, to hold during the life of her daughter Agnes, who appears to have been the mother of Arundell's bastard children. After Agnes' death, the manors of Tolverne and Respery were to remain to Edward Arundell, son of Agnes and the heirs of his body with successive remainders to his brothers Richard and Thomas and sisters Anne and Margaret and the heirs of their bodies, whilst Treveneague was to remain to Richard and Penberthy to Thomas and the heirs of their bodies, with successive remainders to their siblings and a final reversion to Sir John's right heirs. However, this settlement was superseded by various arrangements made in the 1420s following the death of Sir John's eldest son and heir, John, in favour of his two surviving legitimate sons, Thomas and Renfrew. In 1428 Tolverne and Respery, two of the manors mentioned in the 1418 settlement, were granted along with three other Cornish manors to feoffees to the use of Thomas, on condition that after Sir John's death they would maintain a chantry of five chaplains and a clerk to pray for the soul of Sir John and his kin. Treveneague and Penberthy were jointly settled on Thomas and his wife Elizabeth. None of the illegitimate children were mentioned in Arundell's will of 1433, so it is possible that, like his eldest son, they predeceased him. The rather curious nature of the 1418 settlement suggests that the children of Agnes may perhaps have been quite young at the time it was made.

The Cheshire knight, Sir John Arderne, had two illegitimate sons, Thomas and Walkeline, who were pre-nuptial bastards born before Sir John's marriage in 1346 to his third wife and former mistress, Ellen Wasteneys. His heir male was Peter de Arderne, his second and surviving son by his first wife Alice Venables. Peter inherited the manor of Alvanley and acquired part of the manor of Bredbury, subsequently known as Harden Hall, through his wife Cicely, the heiress of Adam de Bredbury, to whom he was espoused in 1331, at the age of four. In 1347, with the licence of the Prince of Wales, as Earl of Chester, Sir John had settled his manors of Aldford, Alderley and Etchells and the advowsons of the churches of Aldford and Alderley on himself and his wife Ellen, with successive remainders to Thomas, son of Ellen and the heirs male of his body, Walkeline, brother of Thomas and the heirs male of his body and the heirs of the bodies of John and Ellen. In this case the provision for the bastards took place after the marriage of Sir John to their mother. Although they could not be formally legitimated by this marriage, they were nevertheless products of a regular relationship, and in his provision, Sir John seems to have preferred the offspring of this relationship to those of his first marriage, despite their technical illegitimacy. Thomas followed a military career, serving with the Black Prince in Spain and at Poitiers. He died in 1391 and is commemorated in an elaborate tomb in the church at Elford, Staffordshire. The manors passed to his son John, but the latter had no male heir of his body and his daughter and heiress, Matilda married Thomas de Stanley.

Sir Theobald Trussell (d. 1368) of Flore, Northamptonshire, had a son and daughter with his mistress Katherine before later marrying her and having a legitimate son, John. After his death, most of the property passed to John, but Sir Theobald had transferred the manor of Nuthurst (Warkwickshire) to his elder and illegitimate son, Alfred. In contrast, Sir Richard de la Ryvere was an elder illegitimate son who was apparently privileged over legitimate younger sons. Richard was the son of Sir William de la Ryvere (d. 1301) of Beedon (Berkshire) and a woman called Sara Middleton. Sir William also had three legitimate sons: John, Robert and Walter, all of whom were still minors when their father died. Sir William acquired a holding of land in Denchworth which was settled on Richard, with remainders to his legitimate half-brothers in

March 1301. This much is not so remarkable, but in May 1301, perhaps whilst on his deathbed, Sir William granted the principal family manor of Beedon to John and to Richard and the heirs of John, and made another grant the same day to Richard for life, with remainder to John and his heirs. The bastard son thus acquired the principal family manor for life. Unfortunately we do not know the name of Sir William's wife. It is possible that he married Sara de Middleton, with John, Robert and Walter being born after the marriage, but there seems to have been an age gap between Richard and his younger siblings which might suggest a different mother.

Sir William de la Ryvere's arrangement for an illegitimate son to have a life interest in the main family manor in preference to legitimate sons was extreme, but there are other cases where bastards held property during the minority of the legitimate son and heir. One example is the arrangement made in the late-fifteenth century by Sir John Pilkington (d. b. 1478), a member of a cadet branch of a Lancashire knightly family, whose main residence was in the West Riding of Yorkshire. He also held lands in Lancashire, Lincolnshire, Derbyshire and the City of London. The total value of his estate was in excess of £200 *per annum*. When he made his will in June 1478, his legitimate son, Edward, was still under age. He accordingly made arrangements for the custody of his lands during his minority. His brother Charles was to have custody of Bradley, whilst his illegitimate son, Robert, described as his bastard son in the will, was to have custody of Elphaborough and other lands in Sowerbyshire and Aringden Park. Once Edward reached the age of twenty-four, Robert was to have lands in Wistow; he was also to have Greenhirst. Sir John also settled on Robert the reversion of lands granted to Edward in tail male. Sir John died on 29 December 1478. We do not know how this settlement would have worked out when Edward came of age, for he died in 1486, aged about seventeen and Robert thus became ultimate heir, succeeding to the majority of Pilkington's property, except for lands granted to Pilkington by Edward IV which were to go to his lawful male heirs. He married firstly, Alice, daughter and heiress of James Burrell; and secondly, Alice, daughter of William Bernard of Knaresborough, by whom he had a son, Arthur, who was his heir and from whom the Yorkshire branch of the Pilkington family descended. Robert Pilkington must have been born before Sir John's marriage in 1464, since he would appear to have been of age in 1478. It is said that his mother was Elizabeth Lever of Darcy Lever. In 1485 John Barnard esquire made a will with a rather similar arrangement in which his son Thomas was to enjoy the profits and issues of his demesne in Brington (Northamptonshire) during the minority of John Barnard, the son and heir.

These examples show that given the right circumstances, the implications of illegitimacy for inheritance could be overcome by the development of legal

Above left: Medieval childbirth. (Tarker/Bridgeman Images)

Above right: Monumental brass to John Foxley (d. 1378) and his two wives in St Michael's Church, Bray, Berkshire, England. (Oosoom at English Wikipedia)

Conisbrough Castle, South Yorkshire. Birthplace of Prior William de Warenne. Reconstruction drawing by Alan Sorrell showing the castle as it may have looked in the 13th century. (©English Heritage)

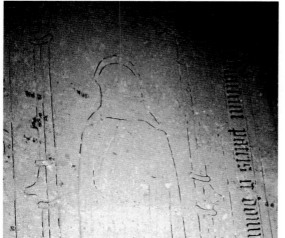

Above: Castle Acre Priory, Norfolk. Prior's House viewed from south west. (©English Heritage)

Left: Tomb of Emma of North Bradley. (Image courtesy of jmc4 at Flickr)

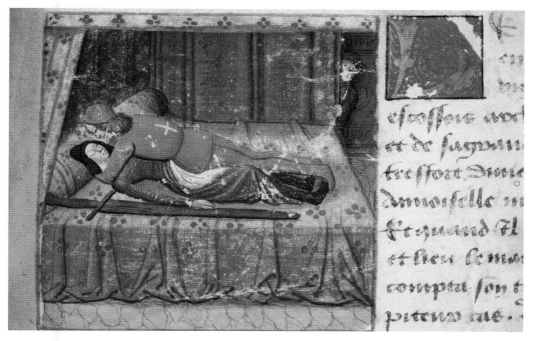

Above: A bed scene, from 'Les Cent Nouvelles Nouvelles', 1462. (Ms Hunter 252 fol.12r, Glasgow University Library, Scotland/Bridgeman Images)

Below: A marriage illustration from the commentaries of Johannes Andreae on Papal Decretals. French School, 14th-century. (Ms 364 fol.166, Bibliothèque Municipale, Laon, France/Bridgeman Images)

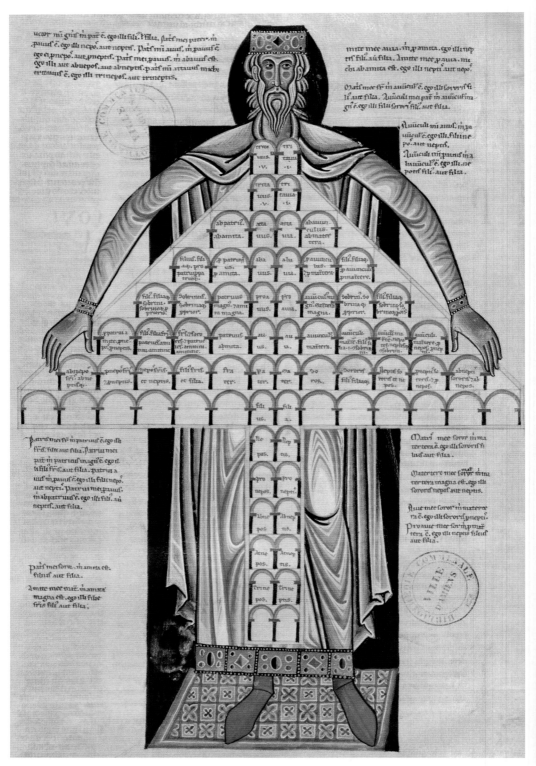

Ms 360 f.264v. Tree of Consanguinity. French School, 14th-century. (Bibliothèque
Municipale, Amiens, France/Bridgeman Images)

Above left: Richard Fitzalan, 3rd (10th) Earl of Arundel (*c.* 1307–1376) and Eleanor, Countess of Arundel. Engraving, 1785. (Private Collection/Bridgeman Images)

Above right: Earl Warenne justifying his title to his estates. Illustration for *The Pictorial History of England* (W & R Chambers, 1858). (Private Collection ©Look and Learn/ Bridgeman Images)

Sir James Dandele [de Audley] of the Order of the Garter, wearing a blue Garter mantle over plate armour and surcoat displaying his arms. (British Library, London, UK ©British Library Board. All Rights Reserved/Bridgeman Images)

Above left: Faked Wellesbourne Tomb, Hughenden Parish Church, UK.

Above right: Court of King's Bench, Westminster. English School, 15th-century. (Inner Temple, London UK/Bridgeman Images)

Below left: 'The Bastard Dunois': Jean d'Orleans (1409–1468). Count of Dunois, w/c on paper. (Thierry Bellange (1594–1638) / Maison Jeanne d'Arc, Orleans, France / Bridgeman Images)

Below middle: William Longespée, 1st Earl of Salisbury (d. 1226), after a mid-13th-century manuscript in Cambridge University Library. Litho. (Henry Shaw (1800–1873 / Private Collection / The Stapleton Collection / Bridgeman Images)

Below right: The Eagle and Child Crest of Sir Thomas Stanley, Lord Stanley, Earl of Derby, 1483–1504. Chromolitho. (William St John Hope (1854–1919) / Private Collection / © Look and Learn / Bridgeman Images)

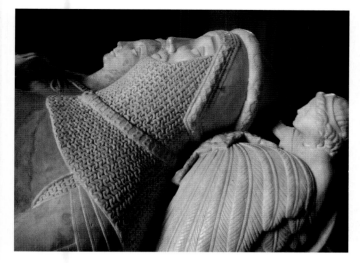

Above left: Tomb of Sir Thomas Arderne (d. 1391) in St Peter's Church, Elford, Staffordshire. (Photo by kind permission of Aidan McRae Thomson)

Above right: Edmund, from Shakespeare's 'King Lear'. Illustration from *Trachtenbilder für die Bühne (Costumes for the Stage)* by Bruno Kohler (Max Pasch, Berlin, 1890). German School, 19th-century, colour litho. (Private Collection / © Look and Learn / Bridgeman Images)

Below: Tomb of Sir Thomas Arderne (d. 1391). The Arderne Tomb, St. Peter's Church, Elford, Staffordshire, England, 1848–1849. Hand-coloured engraving. (Edward M. Richardson (1812–1869) / Private Collection / Bridgeman Images)

THE ARDERNE TOMB (SOUTH VIEW) ELFORD CHURCH, STAFFORDSHIRE.

Wills also provide examples of bastards being accepted as part of the family by members of the same generation. Sir Robert Swillington (d. 1391), having prospered through service to Edward III and John of Gaunt had an annual landed income in the order of 2,000 marks when he died. In his will he left only a small legacy of £20 to his bastard son Thomas Hopton, but Thomas was apparently treated as part of the family. Sir Robert's son and heir, Sir Roger (d. 1417), granted his illegitimate half-brother a life interest in a small property in Ufton (Derbyshire) and, in making a careful settlement of his estates, included a reversionary interest to Thomas Hopton and his sons, after his own two legitimate sons John and Robert, their sons, their daughters and his own daughter Margaret. Whilst it would have seemed most unlikely at the time that the reversions would fall in to the benefit of Thomas's son John, the inclusion of Thomas in the settlement shows that he was accepted as part of the family, and given preference over more remote legitimate relations. Sir Roger also bequeathed ten marks to Thomas in his will, in which Thomas was named as an executor. As it happens, by 1430, everyone else included in Sir Roger's settlement had died and John Hopton, the son of a bastard, became the ultimate heir to the family fortune.

Inclusion of an illegitimate sibling in the will of a legitimate half-brother was not particularly unusual, though the generosity of provision varied. This contrasted with the situation in Florence, where Thomas Kuehn was unable to find any examples of brothers and sisters leaving property to illegitimate siblings. John Leventhorpe (d. 1435) of Hertfordshire, the loyal servant of the House of Lancaster, left a relatively small sum to his illegitimate brother, William. William was to receive only 6s 3d in comparison with twenty shillings for various members of Leventhorpe's legitimate kin. Thomas Bataill (d. c. 1396) of Otes and Matching in Essex, who represented Essex in the parliaments of 1390 and 1394, had a bastard son and daughter as well as legitimate offspring. The will of his legitimate son and heir, John, dated 21 February 1397/8 included bequests of ten marks to Thomas, his father's bastard son, and forty shillings to Maud, Thomas' sister. To place these sums in context, John Crabbe, a servant, was to receive forty shillings, as was the vicar of Matching. John's sister, and eventual coheir, Margaret, was to receive £20 on her marriage.

Cecilia, widow of Sir Thomas Kyriell (d. 1461) made a will in April 1472 in which she bequeathed her jewels, lands in in Sandwich (Kent), vestments and the utensils in her manor of Westhanger to John Kyriell, but in the event that he should die beyond the seas, another John Kyriell, a bastard, was to have the utensils. Cecilia was daughter and coheir of John Stourton of Preston Plucknett, Somerset (d. 1438) and the widow of John Hill of Spaxton, Somerset (d. 1434). Sir Thomas Kyriell, her second husband, was a seasoned military campaigner who fought in France in the 1430s, and been active in local government in Kent. He had joined the Yorkist cause in 1460, and was executed after the second battle of St Albans.

Integration of bastards into the family worked both ways. William de Vescy of Kildare, the illegitimate son who inherited William de Vescy's Yorkshire and Lincolnshire property, appears to have been on good terms with his father's widow, Isabella de Periton, and to have felt some responsibility for her welfare. Before he set out on campaign in 1314, he obtained a grant on behalf of Isabella that nothing should be taken for the king's use from her manor of Tughall against the wishes of Isabella, William or their bailiffs. John Lovel of Snorscombe was closely associated with his legitimate half-brother. In 1287 he accompanied the younger Sir John Lovel into Wales in the king's service and both had letters of protection on going abroad in July 1287 and June 1288. As noted above, William, the illegitimate son of Otto Bodrugan, assisted his legitimate nephew in his attempts to reclaim the family lands.

Contrasts with Elsewhere

In Wales, concubinage and the recognition of illegitimate children were customary practices. This was slowly eroded over the course of the thirteenth century, but before this, a number of Welsh princes under native rule were bastards. The custom was also prevalent in Denmark and other Nordic areas. In parts of continental Europe where the *ius commune* prevailed, most notably the Iberian Peninsula and Italy, legitimation of bastards was possible. This provided a realistic option for parents who wanted a bastard to inherit in the absence of a legitimate heir of the body, though much depended on the circumstances and type of illegitimacy. The relative ease with which legitimation could be achieved meant that it was possible for a bastard to become the heir in the absence of legitimate sons, and it was also useful to have illegitimate sons in reserve. Manfredo Repeta of Vincenza had four legitimate sons, and three illegitimate, born after his wife ceased to bear children. Two of his legitimate sons and the two eldest bastards died in infancy. The youngest bastard, Riccardo, was born in the family home and integrated into the lineage through the names he was given. The most extreme example of bastard succession in Italy is probably the House of Este of Ferrara, which was led by princes of illegitimate birth for a period of almost 150 years until 1471, because of a preference for legitimated bastards over legitimate daughters. In France, illegitimate children could theoretically acquire noble status from their father, but this did not confer rights of inheritance unless they were legitimated. The situation was complicated by customary laws which differed according to region. In the Holy Roman Empire, illegitimate offspring of nobles could not acquire noble status without legitimation; and although possible, legitimations were rare as only legitimation by subsequent marriage provided inheritance rights; legitimation by rescript did not. Illegitimate sons of German nobles tended instead to be destined for the Church, whereas it seems illegitimate daughters were more likely to be married off than sent to a nunnery, though this cannot be certain as records of female illegitimate children are scarce.

In some parts of continental Europe there are records which allow a more systematic analysis of provision for bastards. As noted in the introduction, under the Florentine *castato* tax, introduced in 1427, bastards were tax-deductible as a personal expense. Thomas Kuehn's study of bastardy in Renaissance Florence based on these records suggests that the traditional notion of a 'golden age' of bastards is difficult to sustain. He stresses the 'deep indelible stain of dishonour' borne by bastards, and the generally limited nature of testamentary provision for them. However, he did note that they were in some cases used as a form of insurance policy for the continuation of the family line in the absence of a legitimate male heir, as legitimation was possible. In the meantime, they were less expensive to provide for than legitimate offspring. Florentines were generally concerned to provide bastards with a sufficient living, or in the case of bastard daughters, a modest dowry. The Florentine records also provide a source which allows specific provision for illegitimate daughters, which are normally more difficult to trace, to be identified. Fathers were able to invest in a civic fund, the *Monte delle doti*, in order to provide a future dowry for their daughters. Julius Kirshner and Anthony Molho have shown that this fund was used to provide for bastard daughters as well as for legitimate ones, though the dowries they could expect were on average much smaller. Whereas the overall average dowry for all daughters, legitimate or otherwise, was 405 florins, for illegitimate daughters the average was only 232 florins. In cases where individuals made investments for both legitimate and illegitimate daughters the bastard daughters were generally provided with a dowry between a quarter and a third of that of their legitimate siblings.

James Grub, in a study of Renaissance families in the Veneto, also stressed the value of illegitimate sons as potential substitute heirs, and further suggests that procreation of bastards tended to occur mainly when men did not have wives capable of conceiving, that is before and after marriage and when their wives had passed childbearing age. He also found that illegitimate daughters were less well-favoured, being five times more likely than their legitimate siblings to be sent to a convent and, when married, receiving significantly lower dowries and being married down the social scale.

The concept of nobility as an inherited status was much weaker in England than the rest of Europe. Status was for the most part defined by wealth and lifestyle rather than blood. The examples in this chapter have shown how many fathers were able to make provision for the livelihood of their illegitimate children. In some cases, where there were no legitimate sons, bastards were able to inherit most, if not all, of the family estate and continue the family line. In other cases they were endowed with sufficient estates to start a cadet branch of the family. Others were less fortunate. Bastard daughters were provided with the means to secure a marriage, though generally the provision was less generous than that of their legitimate sisters. Bequests and even landed endowments from other family members testify to the fact that illegitimate children were often regarded as part of the family, despite the legal fiction of *fillius nullius*. The next chapter will look at other opportunities for bastards and the role that they could play in wider society.

Chapter 5

Social Status, Career and Opportunities for Bastards

In the south ambulatory of Westminster Abbey, close to the tomb of King Richard II, is a marble slab. It was once inlaid in brass with the figure of a knight, surmounted by a canopy and surrounded by a marginal inscription. What little remains of the brass has now been removed for safe-keeping, but in the eighteenth century enough was visible for John Dart to print an English translation in his history of the abbey: 'Under this is buried Sir John Golofre, called Lord of Langley, natural son of Sir John Golofre knight by Johannet Pulham'. Who was this Sir John and why did he merit a tomb in Westminster Abbey?

Sir John was the illegitimate son of a Midland knight, another Sir John Golafre (d. 1379), who owned manors in Buckinghamshire, Oxfordshire, Berkshire and Wiltshire. The elder Sir John had no legitimate children. It is not entirely clear from surviving records whether Sir John senior made any landed provision for his illegitimate son, but whilst it appears that his nephew and right heir, John Golafre (d. 1442), the son of his younger brother Thomas Golafre, did not acquire all the family estates until after the death of the illegitimate Sir John, the latter's main source of income seems to have been from service to the Crown. The elder Sir John used his connections to secure his illegitimate son a place in the household of Richard II. His second wife, Isabella, was the daughter of Sir John Brocas, a household knight of Edward III and well-connected at court, and widow of Thomas Missenden, an esquire of Edward III. By 1384 the younger John was an esquire of the king's chamber in receipt of a fee of £20 *per annum*. He was knighted in 1385, and his fee increased to 100 marks, payable from the manor of Wallingford. Two years later he was appointed Keeper of the King's Jewels and Plate. He was by this time one of the most highly regarded of Richard's chamber staff. His work also involved him in a range of diplomatic missions. In 1387 he was tasked with visiting France to arrange a peace conference with Charles VI. Some years later, he was sent to Poland to enlist support for a crusade against the Turks, though he was not really a diplomat so much as a fighting man. He served with the king in Scotland in 1385, and on the first of Richard's Irish expeditions, and was also well known on the tournament circuit. He was entrusted with developing the military capacity of the royal household: ensuring that all the yeomen of the household carried bows and had regular archery practice—the intention being to provide Richard with a personal bodyguard. Golafre was also granted the custody and maintenance of royal castles such as Wallingford and Nottingham. His role at court enabled him to benefit from royal patronage though custody of forfeited estates. Nigel Saul has estimated his income from these sources to have been in the region of £300–£400, which was a perfectly respectable income for one of knightly status, though far from excessive given that his position at court would have involved significant expenses. Although he married a co-heiress, Philippa, daughter of Sir John de Mohun and widow of Lord FitzWalter (d. 1386), her mother sold the greater part of the reversion of her estates, disinheriting her daughters. Golafre therefore seems to have been largely dependent for his income on the fees he received from the Crown. He died at Wallingford in 1396. In his will, as well as bequests to his family, he left his best horse, a badge of the white hart, a stone with a sapphire set in it, a cup and a golden chain to the king. He desired his body to be buried in the Grey Friars' church at Oxford, but as he lay dying he received a request from the king to allow his body to go to Westminster Abbey. This was not the first time that Richard had interfered in the interment of one of his servants. A year earlier, he had similarly requested that the body of John Waltham, Bishop of Salisbury and his former treasurer, be buried in the abbey, despite Waltham's request to be buried in Salisbury cathedral. Nigel Saul has noted that, at the time, Richard was using Westminster Abbey as a mausoleum for royal servants rather as the French kings were using St Denis in Paris, and that he seems to have relished the opportunity for displaying his power over his subjects by controlling their destinies even after death. It nevertheless says something about the status of bastards in medieval England that the illegitimate son of a middling knight could be honoured in this way, and without any concealment of the nature of his birth.

Public Office

In some of the Italian city states, there were attempts to control the participation of bastards in public life, though not always with great success. Stanley Chojnacki found that attempts by members of the Venetian aristocracy to insinuate their illegitimate children into the patriciate were sufficiently widespread enough to be a concern for the city government, which attempted to control this through legislation. In 1376 the Great Council narrowly passed a measure to prevent the illegitimate sons of nobles from inheriting their fathers' status. It was not universally popular, passing only on the third reading, and even then, with just fifty-one per cent of the vote. As with many prohibitive measures, the fact that such a rule was needed suggests that bastard sons had previously acquired noble status. The legislation was apparently unsuccessful. However, the Council's concern appears to have been less to do with illegitimacy as such than with the need to control admission of individuals of dubious status to the elite. The likelihood of a bastard having a mother of low birth was as at least as much of an issue as the illegitimate birth itself. Forty-six years later, this was made more explicit when a further measure was passed, with rather more enthusiasm, which aimed to deny noble status to any sons of noble fathers and mothers of servile status, even if they were legitimate. In 1526, the Council of Ten introduced a requirement for the registration of all noble marriages to address a situation in which many bastard sons had achieved noble status. A Florentine law of 1404 prevented anyone of illegitimate birth from sitting on the major executive and legislative councils of the city and from various other posts, although with limited success, since a further measure was enacted in 1428 setting a fine of 500 florins for bastards who filled such an office despite their origins.

Given the lack of concern with bloodline as a determinant of nobility in England, such concern as was expressed about illicit sexual activity tended to be aimed more at the licentious behaviour of the parents than the possible products of their adulterous liaisons. In contrast with the situation in Venice and Florence, where bastards themselves could be excluded from membership of the civic elite, at least in theory, political and administrative activity by bastards does not appear to have been an issue in England. Illegitimate sons could and did fill local administrative posts and a number of them secured election to parliament. As noted in Chapter Four, illegitimate birth did not prevent Sir William Argentine from exercising his role in society. He represented Suffolk as a knight of the shire in 1393, 1395 and 1399. He had already been knighted, possibly for military service overseas, by the time of his first election in 1393. His standing in local society is further demonstrated by his appointment as sheriff of Norfolk and Suffolk at the end of that year. William's illegitimacy was apparently no bar to his service as cup-bearer to Henry IV. On the other hand, it has been suggested that William's lavish expenditure on building a tower for the parish church of his main residence of Halesworth may have been prompted by a desire to make his mark upon the community and counteract any remaining stigma associated with the circumstances of his birth.

Sir Nicholas Stafford (1331–1394) was, as we have already seen, an illegitimate son of Richard, Lord Stafford of Clifton (d. 1380) who was originally destined for the church. Instead, he married Elizabeth, heiress of Thomas Meverel and thus became a substantial landowner with estates in Staffordshire, Derbyshire and Herefordshire. His early years were spent on military service in France, but from 1372 onwards, he increasingly devoted himself to administration of the estates of the earl of Stafford, and to local government. He served as sheriff of Staffordshire in 1372–77 and 1375–76, and served as a justice of the peace for seventeen years. He was elected to parliament as a knight of the shire for Staffordshire on nine occasions between January 1377 and November 1390. He was chief steward of the estate of the earls of Stafford, responsible for the administration of estates worth around £3,000 year between 1383 and 1391. He was also highly regarded by the merchant community: he and his wife were admitted to the Holy Trinity guild at Coventry.

James Nash (d. 1400) of Hereford followed his father, Richard Nash, into the legal profession, and, again like his father, was elected to parliament on several occasions, representing Hereford in 1390, 1397 and 1399. Both James and Richard appear to have been in the service of the Earl of March. Shortly after the deposition of Richard II, James was appointed Crown Attorney in the court of the King's Bench. His illegitimacy appears not to have been in doubt; on 9 June 1400, following his death, a commission was set up to enquire what lands he held in the city and county of Hereford, in which he was described as a bastard who had died without heir. His standing in the community is perhaps indicated by the willingness of the mayor and commonalty of Hereford to comply with the post-mortem wish of his father for the foundation of a chantry in Hereford cathedral to offer masses daily for the souls of himself and his son.

William Thickness (d. c. 1403) was, according to a deposition made in September 1378, the child of a 'secret marriage' some 50 years previously between William Thickness (d. c. 1385) of Newcastle-under-Lyme (Staffordshire) and Katherine Swynnerton. Since William the elder's first wife was still alive at the time, this 'marriage' cannot have been valid and William the younger was clearly illegitimate. He certainly had no share in his father's estates, which were settled on Thomas, the son of a later marriage to Margery Audley. His financial independence was secured by an advantageous marriage to Alice, the widow of Hugh Hough of Shavington, but he was nevertheless able to benefit from his father's influence within the borough. He was first became bailiff in 1370, and was thereafter very active in local government. He served a total of nine times as mayor, and by 1389 was one of the senior members of the Newcastle merchant guild. He represented Newcastle in parliament on six occasions between 1378 and 1388.

Sir Alfred Trussell (c. 1349–1419) was a pre-nuptial bastard, born before the marriage of his father Sir Theobald Trussell to his mistress Katherine. Most of his father's estates in Leicestershire and Northamptonshire went to his younger, legitimate brother, John, but as noted in Chapter Four, Alfred did receive the manor of Nuthurst from his father, and he gained a further nine manors belonging to another branch of the Trussell family through marriage to Katherine, daughter of Sir William Trussell of Kibblestone. Like his younger brother, he was a retainer of Thomas, Earl of Warwick, one of the Lords Appellant. Perhaps because of this association he became more involved in public office following the deposition of Richard II. He sat as a knight of the shire for Warwickshire on four occasions from 1399 to 1407 and was sheriff of Warwickshire and Leicestershire 1402–23, and escheator 1407–08.

Sir Thomas Sackville (d. 1432), as seen in the previous chapter, succeeded to his father's estates despite his illegitimate birth and married the daughter of a prominent local knight, Sir Edward Dallingridge (the builder of Bodiam Castle). He assisted his father-in-law in resisting the officials of John of Gaunt, Duke of Lancaster, poaching in the latter's parks and preventing Gaunt's steward from holding courts. When one of the duke's under-foresters was killed in 1384, Sackville was suspected of abetting the culprits. Elected as a knight of the shire for Sussex in 1394, 1395 and 1397, he came under suspicion after Henry IV seized the throne. Although he was appointed to a commission of array by the new regime in December 1399, he was arrested a month later on suspicion of involvement in the Epiphany plot to restore Richard II to the throne, and only released when his brother-in-law Sir John Dallingridge, who had been a retainer of Henry's, provided surety. He was sheriff of Surrey and Sussex in 1406–07, but may have been heavy-handed: the tenants of the royal manor of Witley in Surrey complained to the King's Council about his behaviour. Despite this, he continued to serve on royal commissions from time to time and appears to have been well-regarded by members of the local gentry community, among whom he was much in demand as a trustee. Whatever his faults, his illegitimate birth does not appear to have been a stumbling block to his career.

Robert Holme (d. 1433) appears to have been illegitimate, since his father's will, drawn up in 1396 refers to his two wives (both deceased) and to Beatrice Forden, the mother of his only son. His father Robert and uncle Thomas (d. 1406) were among the most influential men in York in the late- fourteenth century, and wealth and family connections ensured that the younger Robert was able to occupy a similar place in society to his father. He was a principal beneficiary in his father's will, receiving his house in Goodramgate along with the rest of his extensive property in the city, large quantities of silver plate and the sum of 1,000 marks. He was sheriff of York in 1388–89, mayor 1413–14, MP in 1414, a member of the council of twenty-four by c. 1420 and member of the council of twelve from c. 1416 to 1424.

Edmund Ford (d. 1440), who represented Bath in the parliament of February 1388, was a member of a prominent Bath family who had invested their wealth in property outside the city. Edmund did not acquire the bulk of his father's property until after the death of his younger brother, Thomas, and it therefore seems likely that he was, like Alfred Trussell, a prenuptial bastard. Although he served only once as an MP for Bath, he appears to have become a respected member of the community in Somerset, Gloucestershire and Wiltshire. He was in demand as a trustee and was twice entrusted with the keeping of the property of a mentally deficient heir.

William Fulbourn (d. *c.* 1441), who represented Cambridgeshire in the parliament of December 1421, was probably an illegitimate son of William Fulbourn (d. 1391), rector of St Vigor's church, or of a close relative of his since he was named as heir to the latter's property, and was described as 'William Fulburne the younger, son of Alice Whytyng of Fulburne' in documents in which he was associated with the elder William. A lawyer by profession, he was employed by the bishop of Ely, and acted for a number of the East Anglian gentry. He was a justice of the peace for a period of 20 years.

John Selman (d. after 1442) was probably an illegitimate son of the John Selman (d. 1426) who sat as MP for Plympton Erle on five occasions. The younger John followed his father into the legal profession, and like him, spent part of his career in the service of the earls of Devon. He was engaged in a legal dispute over his father's estate, when one of the feoffees refused to hand over part of the property on the grounds that John Selman the elder had no legitimate issue and that he himself was entitled to the property. However, despite this, he managed to maintain a certain position in society, and was to represent the borough of Plympton Erle in parliament on ten occasions.

Edward Bertram, the illegitimate son of John Bertram, alias Ogle of Bothal, served as sheriff of Newcastle and represented the city in parliament in 1435. Henry Tuddenham, the illegitimate son of Thomas Tuddenham was admitted to the freedom of Ipswich in 1450, and served as MP for Truro in 1455–56 and Farnham in 1460–61. John Wood, who sat as an MP for both the city and county of Worcestershire and had a successful career as a lawyer and administrator, was possibly the illegitimate son of Sir John atte Wood (d. 1391) of Wolverley. He certainly eventually came into possession of Sir John's Worcestershire properties. It is clear that illegitimacy was no bar to public office.

Royal Service

Hugh of Cressingham was the illegitimate son of William of Cressingham (Norfolk) and a woman called Emma. He was at least in minor orders, but was initially employed as a clerk in the courts at Westminister. From 1282 to 1286 he was steward of the bishop of Ely. He then entered royal service as steward of Queen Eleanor. After her death in 1290, he continued in service to King Edward I. Initially, he prospered. In 1292 he was one of the commissioners to audit the debts owed to Henry III, and shortly afterwards he was employed as a senior justice on the northern circuit. After the Yorkshire eyre was prorogued in 1294 he became involved in military operations, raising troops to suppress a Welsh revolt. On 1 August 1295 he was one of the justices and councilors summoned to parliament and in August 1296 he was appointed as treasurer in the administration set up to administer Scotland following the deposition of King John. He set up an English–style exchequer at Berwick, where he did not endear himself to the Scots, partly because of his heavy-handed approach to Scottish debtors, but also simply because he was effectively the head of the English occupying government. Ultimately he was unable to control the rebellion led by William Wallace, and was killed at the battle of Stirling Bridge in 1297. He was so hated by Scots that they flayed his body and divided his skin into strips. Wallace is said to have made a sword-belt from one of the pieces. Cressingham left an illegitimate daughter, Alice, and possibly a son, Hugh.

The career of John Golafre described above demonstrates the possibilities for an illegitimate son to prosper through service to the Crown. His contemporary, William Lisle, also relied on service to the Crown for the greater part of his livelihood. William Lisle was the illegitimate son of Robert, 3rd Lord Lisle of Rougemont (d. 1399). His father had no legitimate issue, and disposed of the bulk of his estates during his lifetime. In November 1368 he had surrendered 86 knight's fees to the Crown and in return had been granted an exemption for life from attending parliament or performing any form of service to the Crown or payment of tenths or fifteenths against his will. William seems to have made his own fortune largely through military service to the Crown in Ireland and France and to a lesser extent through marriage.

On 23 November 1392 he was retained for life by Richard II, for which he was granted forty marks per year, and on 13 March 1394 this annuity was increased to £40. On 11 February 1397, he and his wife Amy FitzElys were granted a further annuity of £30. His marriage to Amy, who was the widow of John FitzElys of Waterperry (Oxfordshire), brought him a life interest in the manor of Waterperry. He later acquired the manor of Great Wilbraham (Cambridgeshire) from his uncle. Lisle's career in royal service was not unduly inconvenienced by the change of dynasty in 1399. His annuities were confirmed on 5 October 1399 and in August 1401 he received a further grant for life of two tuns of wine a year, and he served Henry IV as both a soldier and diplomat. He fulfilled a range of duties, including as an envoy to treat with the Burgundians in 1404, as lieutenant to the earl of Warwick as captain of Calais, and as sheriff and escheator of Oxfordshire and Berkshire. He was elected as a knight of the shire for Oxfordshire in April 1414, 1417 and 1426. The question that remains is why Lord Lisle, who had no legitimate heir of his body, disposed of the bulk of his estates and chose not to make greater provision for his illegitimate son. The proceedings before the king's council in the case brought by John Windsor suggest a possible explanation. Lord Lisle explained in a letter that he was unable to attend in person as he could not travel because of 'the very great infirmity and malady from which I suffer and have long suffered' and had therefore appointed attorneys, among them his brother and his illegitimate son, to represent him. This letter was written in 1390, but it is at least possible that Lord Lisle may have already started to suffer from some illness or infirmity as much as twenty-two years earlier, which would explain why he had surrendered the 86 knight's fees in return for exemption from attending parliament or performing service.

William Herbert (d. 1469), 1st Earl of Pembroke (the first full-blooded Welshman to enter the English peerage), had two illegitimate sons, Richard and George, from a relationship with Maud, daughter of Adam ap Howell Gwyn. The elder, Richard (d. 1510), known as Richard Herbert of Ewyas, prospered in the service of Henry Tudor as a gentleman usher and later as constable of Abergavenny castle. The legitimate line of the Herberts ended when Richard's half-brother, William died in 1490, but Richard's second son, William, was later created Earl of Pembroke in his own right. Richard has an impressive tomb in the Priory church of St Mary, Abergavenny.

Sir John Pelham (d. 1429) sent his illegitimate son John to represent him on Henry V's Agincourt campaign, where he was knighted. The younger John later became a chamberlain of the household of Queen Katherine of Valois, and married one of her ladies-in-waiting.

Military Service

Many bastard sons of the nobility and gentry made their fortunes as soldiers, though not necessarily in the same way as John Pelham did. During the fourteenth century, illegitimate sons were to be found in the retinue of several earls. As noted earlier, both Aymer de Valence, Earl of Pembroke and John de Warenne, Earl of Surrey, had illegitimate sons who were knighted and served in their fathers' retinues, whilst Sir Thomas de Lancaster, an illegitimate son of Thomas, Earl of Lancaster served with Edward III in France. Sir Thomas Mortimer served in the retinue of his legitimate brother Edmund Mortimer, 3rd Earl of March (d. 1381). When the earl was appointed as Lord Lieutenant in Ireland, in 1379, Thomas acted as his deputy. He subsequently headed the Mortimer council during the minority of his nephew, Roger Mortimer, 4th Earl of March (1374–1398), a position to which he was appointed by the group of magnates, comprising the earls of Warwick, Arundel and Northumberland, and Lord Neville, who held the wardship of the young earl. Mortimer had been a close companion of his legitimate half-brother, Edmund (d. 1381), the third earl, and seems in his exercise of family responsibilities to have behaved remarkably unlike the villainous bastard of literature. Thomas was associated with the Lords Appellant, which later led to Roger risking royal displeasure when instead of obeying a commission to arrest his uncle, he allowed him time to flee the country.

Military service in France seems to have served as a useful outlet for the illegitimate sons of the higher nobility, both English and continental during the late 1420s and 1430s: bastard sons of Thomas Montagu, Earl of Salisbury, Richard Beauchamp, Earl of Warwick, Thomas Duke of Clarence and John, Duke of Bedford were all actively engaged there, where they encountered Jean Dunois, the Bastard of Orléans, the Bastard of St Pol and the Bastard de Sauveuses, to name just a few. John, the illegitimate son of Thomas Montagu, 4th Earl of Salisbury (d. 1428) and generally referred to as the Bastard of Salisbury, was captain of Gournay and Gerberoy (1430–31), captain of Argentan (1431– 34) and captain of Fresnay (1446–48). In 1431 he fought at the siege of Louviers under Lords Willoughby and Beaumont, leading a mobile detachment of ten men at arms and thirty-three archers from the garrison of Argentan. He served again under Lord Willoughby the following year, and in 1434 he served under the earl of Arundel, acting as his lieutenant at St Lô. He was described in the early 1440s as Lord of Montgomery, but probably derived little in the way of income from this estate. John, Bastard of Clarence, served in France, retrieving the corpse of his father, Thomas, Duke of Clarence, who had been killed at the battle of Baugé in 1421, for which service he received a grant of an annuity of £100 *per annum* from the Irish manors of Newcastle-Lyons, Esker, Tassagard and Crumlin. However, he was not well provided for. At one stage, he petitioned the Commons to ask his uncle, King Henry V, on account of his poverty, to be sent to France or elsewhere to serve the king, or to make other provision for his sustenance. In July 1431 he was granted the office of constable of the castle of Dyvelyn in Ireland. His cousin Arthur, the illegitimate son of Humphrey, Duke of Gloucester, was, along with other members of his father's retinue, arrested and convicted of treasonable conspiracy after Gloucester's death.

Sir Hugh Johnnys (*c.* 1410–1485), an illegitimate member of the Vaughans of Bredwardine (Herefordshire) earned a name for himself in the service of John VIII, Emperor of Constantinople, having been knighted at the Holy Sepulchre in Jerusalem. He was later Knight Marshal of France under the Duke of Somerset. In 1468 Edward IV appointed him one of the Poor Knights of Windsor.

The political upheaval of the Wars of the Roses provided military opportunities for Thomas Neville, the illegitimate son of William Neville, Lord

Fauconberg and Earl of Kent (d. 1463), though the details of his life, other than his appearance in chronicles as 'Bastard Fauconberg' are largely undocumented. He certainly performed military service at sea against the Hanse, for which he was paid £50 in March 1470, but he joined his cousin Richard Neville, Earl of Warwick in his invasion of England the following October, deputizing for him as admiral, but he failed to prevent Edward IV's invasion from Burgundy. In April 1471, Bastard Fauconberg landed in Kent and raised an army.

Sir James Audley (d. 1369), one of two illegitimate sons of Sir James Audley of Stratton Audley (d. 1334), was a founder member of the Order of the Garter. His illegitimate birth was clearly not an insuperable barrier to membership of an order which required martial renown, gentle birth and an unblemished reputation. Feats of military prowess were sufficient to make up for any deficiencies of birth. Another bastard member of the order was Charles Somerset ('Bastard Somerset') the illegitimate son of Henry Beaufort, 2nd Duke of Somerset, who was elected to the Order of the Garter by June 1498.

A number of bastard-begetters were also among the companions of the Garter, among them Sir Walter Mauny (elected 1359); Edmund Holand, Earl of Kent (elected 1403); William, Lord Roos of Helmsley (elected 1403); John Cornwall, Lord Fanhope (elected 1409); Sir John Dabrichecourt (elected 1413); Thomas Montagu, Earl of Salisbury (elected 1414); William de la Pole, Earl, and later Duke of Suffolk (elected 1421); William, Lord Bonville (elected 1460). Begetting illegitimate children was clearly not seen as a barrier to membership.

The Church

It was the increasing concern of the Church from the eleventh century onwards to regulate marriage that had made illegitimacy an issue, but in practice the attitude of the Church towards those of illegitimate birth was less clear cut than it might seem. A career in the Church, often involving churches over which the family had rights of advowson, was another way of ensuring the livelihood of family members. In the 1270s, one Richard de Vescy, an illegitimate kinsman of the Vescy family of Alnwick, was provided for by means of a Church career, although subsequent events suggest that perhaps a military role might have been more to his liking. He was presented to the Church of North Ferriby by Lady Agnes de Vescy in 1272, having previously been presented to a moiety of the church of St Mary, Castlegate, York, by the prior and convent of Kirkham. A Richard de Vescy, clerk, possibly the same individual, also received a lease of the manor of Gripthorp (Yorkshire) from John de Vescy in 1271. Although he had received assistance from the Vescy family thus far, in 1280 there seems to have been some sort of disagreement. Richard de Vescy was presented to the church of Escrick by Roger Lascelles, knight, and received a dispensation for illegitimacy and confirmation of orders on 3 April. Meanwhile, William de Cliff was presented to North Ferriby by Agnes de Vescy. Vescy was reluctant to relinquish it, and he forcibly resisted Cliff's entry, assisted by his son Reginald. Either North Ferriby was a more desirable benefice, or Vescy had hoped to hold both. It is probably significant that in 1279, Walter Giffard had been succeeded as Archbishop of York by William Wickwane, who took a much harder line against pluralists. North Ferriby may in fact have slightly more lucrative; in 1291 it was worth £33 6s 8d, whereas Escrick was worth £30. Vescy and his accomplices were subsequently excommunicated and the fruits of Escrick were sequestrated. In December 1280, a Richard de Vescy (perhaps the same one) made arrangements to go overseas. The following January, William de Monceus was presented to North Ferriby by Lady Agnes, and the church of Escrick was declared vacant. Vescy was readmitted on the presentation of Roger Lascelles only in July 1282.

It might be thought that the Church was less of an option for illegitimate sons, since bastards were in theory barred from careers in the church, but in practice illegitimate birth was not an insurmountable obstacle. Provided the necessary dispensations were obtained, the Church provided an outlet in which noble bastards could pursue a similar career to a legitimate younger son, often taking advantage of family connections, as a number of Warenne bastards did. John, Lord Grey of Codnor (d. 1392) petitioned the pope for a prebend at Lincoln or Southwell on behalf of his illegitimate son Nicholas in 1355. The illegitimate son of the Sussex Knight Sir William de Etchingham (d. 1326) became a monk at Robertsbridge, a Cistercian abbey of which Sir William was a patron. In 1391 John Curteys' will left a life interest in certain lands to William Curteys on condition that he became a priest as soon as possible '*post legitimation suam*', presumably referring not to legitimation as such but to a dispensation.

However, as the canon law distinguished between different categories of illegitimacy, making a distinction between simple bastards who were sons of an unmarried man and an unmarried woman, those who had been born in adultery and those who were children of clergy, the circumstances of the illegitimate birth were significant. Dispensations therefore usually provided some detail as to the nature of the birth defect, and sometimes also on the rank or identity of the parents, and this needed to be accurate. John de Saunford, a canon of St Paul's, London, received dispensations on account of illegitimacy in 1364 and 1367 and subsequent provisions of benefices and canonries of Wells and St John's, Beverley, but when it subsequently came to light that he was an adulterine bastard, his mother having been married to someone other than his father at the time of his birth, some doubt was cast on the validity of the dispensation and the provision of benefices. Robert Dalton, a priest of York, initially concealed, when he sought a dispensation as the son of an unmarried man and married woman, the fact that his parents were related and had been living together in concubinage and further confirmation of his dispensations was therefore required when this came to light in 1401.

The effects of the plague were probably at least partly responsible for a relaxation in attitudes towards illegitimacy in the mid-fourteenth century. The need to ensure that there were enough ordained priests to administer the sacraments during the plague years certainly led the Church to show more flexibility in its attitude towards those of illegitimate birth. In 1349 there was a marked increase in the number of licences obtained by English bishops to enable them to dispense a fixed number of clerks of illegitimate birth to be ordained priests, although in some cases the distinction between different types of illegitimacy was retained, limiting the numbers of clerical or adulterous parentage who might be included.

In addition to dispensations for different types of bastardy there were also different levels of dispensation. The basic dispensation enabled the applicant to take orders and hold or exchange a benefice, but would not allow them to accept a preferment or dignity without further dispensation. In some cases, however, a dispensation might expressly include a dignity or office, or even state that the applicant need not mention the defect in future. For example, in 1393, when John Howbert, the rector of Garthorp, who is described as being of knightly (*militari*) race, and who originally received a dispensation allowing him to be ordained and hold a benefice with cure, received an extension permitting him to hold and exchange two other compatible benefices, it was stated that he need not mention his illegitimacy in future.

John Leversegge, a merchant and leading citizen of Kingston-upon-Hull, had been employed as receiver of the lordship of Beverley and two other manors for Thomas Arundel when he was Archbishop of York, which may have helped him in 1401 to secure the necessary papal dispensations for his illegitimate son, Richard, to take holy orders. Richard was granted the most generous form of dispensation, which permitted him to be promoted to all, even holy orders; to hold any mutually compatible benefices with and without cure, including canonries and prebends and elective dignities, major or principal respectively, offices in metropolitan, cathedral or collegiate churches; to resign them simply or for exchange as often as he pleased; and not to need to mention his illegitimacy and dispensation in future graces. He was described in the dispensation as the son of an unmarried man and unmarried woman, and so was presumably born before Leversegge's marriage.

The infamous military commander and mercenary Sir John Hawkwood had an illegitimate son, John, who was intended for a church career. In 1373 the bishop of London was mandated to ensure that he was a more fit and proper person than his father, before granting a dispensation which would enable him to hold any number and kind of benefices, including elective dignities. Sir John later married Donnina, an illegitimate daughter of Bernabò Visconti. Sir John Thornbury, another English mercenary, also obtained papal dispensations in 1373 for his illegitimate sons to enter the Church. In 1374 the bishop of Bologna was issued with a mandate to grant a dispensation to Thornbury's sons Philip and Justan to be ordained and hold up to three benefices. Philip was at the time a student at Bologna. The following year this was extended to allow Philip to hold a major elective dignity. Philip was subsequently appointed by Pope Gregory XI (1371–78) to the Lincoln prebend of Caistor, though it later transpired that the bshop of Bologna had not acted on the mandate to grant a dispensation and Thornbury was required to resign it. His appointment led to the disappointment of John Wyclif, who had expected to be appointed and had apparently already paid £13 6s 8d as the first payment of annates. Thornbury senior was a leader of mercenaries in the papal service, which presumably had helped to smooth the way for the original dispensations and appointment. Thornbury had a legitimate son, also called Philip, who inherited his estates in Hertfordshire.

John Lound, rector of Dacre (Cumberland), was a bachelor of canon and civil law and had received a dispensation to be promoted to holy orders and hold a benefice by 1428, when he received a further dispensation to hold an additional incompatible benefice. He eventually became chancellor to the bishop of Durham. His father was probably the Yorkshire MP, Sir Alexander Lound, whose legitimate son and heir, Alexander, received a papal indult to use a portable altar together with John Lound in November 1428. The fifteenth-century career of John Wensley, the son of another MP, Sir Thomas Wensley, followed a similar path. He too studied canon law, and eventually became vicar-general to the bishop of Coventry and Lichfield, and archdeacon of Stafford.

With the right dispensations, education and patrons, there was no reason why an illegitimate son should not rise to a high rank within the Church. During the fifteenth century both York and Canterbury had an archbishop of illegitimate birth: John Stafford, Archbishop of Canterbury, 1443–52 and Laurence Booth, Archbishop of York 1476–80. Stafford's was probably the most successful Church career by an illegitimate son of a noble or gentle family during the late-medieval period. The bastard son of Sir Humphrey Stafford of Southwick Court (Wiltshire) and Hooke in Dorset, he rose to the heights of Archbishop of Canterbury and Chancellor of England. Stafford's mother was a local woman called Emma, of North Bradley, and his father was a member of a cadet branch of the Stafford family, who had acquired his manor of Southwick through his marriage to the heiress Alice de Greville. Humphrey Stafford had a legitimate son, Sir Humphrey (d. 1442), with whom John was closely associated. In his will the younger Sir Humphrey left his illegitimate half-brother a pair of silver-gilt flagons, a silver gilt figure of John the Baptist and an Arras tapestry, and also appointed him as executor. The Staffords built a fine mortuary chapel at the church of St Joseph in North Bradley to house the tomb of the archbishop's mother, Emma. Stafford's career began with papal dispensations for illegitimacy, a lengthy period of study at Oxford and the acquisition of a string of benefices. In the 1420s the focus of his career shifted from church administration to royal administration. He served as Keeper of the Privy Seal from February 1421 until December 1422, when he was appointed as Treasurer. In February 1432 he was appointed as Chancellor, an office he was to fill for an unbroken period of over seventeen years. Although he undoubtedly had support from his wider family during the early stages of his career, much was also due to his own evident administrative ability. During his period of royal service he obtained further promotion within the Church. He was elected Bishop of Bath and Wells in 1424 and was Archbishop Chichele's own choice of successor at Canterbury. His administrative and political skill is demonstrated by the fact that he managed to retain the office of chancellor for so long during the turbulent times of Henry VI's minority and, despite a close association with Suffolk's party which led to his resignation in 1450 at the time of Suffolk's impeachment, he never faced any allegations of wrongdoing. The worst charges that can be laid against him are that his performance as archbishop, whilst administratively competent, was lacklustre. It was also alleged by his contemporary, the Oxford theologian and opponent of clerical abuses, Dr Thomas Gascoigne, that he had sons and daughters by a nun while he was bishop of Bath and Wells.

Laurence Booth (c. 1420–1480) was an illegitimate son of John Booth of Barton in Eccles (Lancashire) an MP. He studied civil and canon law at Cambridge, taking his degrees in 1448. By that time he had already received a papal dispensation for promotion to holy orders as the son of unmarried parents and had been ordained priest in 1446. His early career benefitted from the support of his elder, and legitimate, half-brother, William Booth (d. 1464) who was Bishop of Coventry and Lichfield from 1447 and Archbishop of York from 1452. He succeeded his brother as Chancellor to Queen Margaret in 1451 and this paved the way for political advancement as Keeper of the Privy Seal on 24 September 1456. In August 1457 he was appointed Bishop of Durham. His close association with the queen and the Lancastrian court led to something of a change of fortunes following the Yorkist victory, but although he had to resign the privy seal, he submitted to Edward IV after the battle of Towton in 1461, and became his confessor. He was not entirely trusted, however, and in face of combined Scottish and Lancastrian incursions in the north in 1462, Booth was stripped of his episcopal estates and forced to reside in Cambridge (where he had been Master of Pembroke College since 1450). His estates were restored in 1464, but he was kept under close oversight for the next few years. He survived the readeption of Henry VI and restoration of Edward IV, serving as Chancellor of the realm from 27 July 1473 to 27 May 1474. He was appointed Archbishop of York on 31 July 1476. During the final four years of his life, as archbishop, he was mindful of his family relationships, with various nephews and great-nephews securing lucrative appointments.

The appointment of archbishops of illegitimate birth was not confined to the fifteenth century. Although neither province appears to have had an illegitimate archbishop during the fourteenth century, three of the archbishops of York who held office during the thirteenth century were of illegitimate birth: Geoffrey, illegitimate son of Henry II, Archbishop of York, 1191–1212; Sewall de Bovill, Archbishop of York, 1256–57; John le Romeyn, Archbishop of York, 1286–96. There was also an election of an illegitimate candidate to Canterbury: Ralph Nevill in 1231.

Perhaps the most notorious case of provision for a bastard through the Church was that made by Cardinal Thomas Wolsey for his son, Thomas Winter, born c. 1510, whom he publicly acknowledged as his 'nephew'. Winter was sent to the university at Louvain at the tender age of nine, and also studied in Paris, though he does not appear to have excelled at academic work, and in the meantime his father ensured that he was provided with numerous preferments. Whilst still under age, Winter held three archdeaconries (York, Richmond and Suffolk), and was chancellor of Salisbury, and Dean of Wells, as well as various prebends and rectories, with a total value in the order of £2,700, although it appears that Winter received only a relatively small proportion of the revenues, the majority being retained by Wolsey. However, this was lavish provision by any standards, and rather too lavish for some. The extent of the provision made for Winter formed the basis of charges laid against Wolsey in 1529. Winter was one of two illegitimate children fathered by Wolsey with his concubine, 'Mistress Lark'. The other, a daughter called Dorothy, was also destined for the Church, being sent to Shaftesbury Abbey (Dorset). Although the provision made for Winter was generous, if not, as A. F. Pollard viewed it, scandalous, Wolsey's nepotism was not unique, as Peter Gwyn has pointed out, and among the various nephews and kinsmen who benefitted from the largesse of Wolsey's colleagues were certainly other illegitimate sons. William Warham, the so-called nephew of Archbishop Warham, may, like Winter, have been an illegitimate son, but there is no definite evidence on this point. When Wolsey eventually married his mistress off, he allegedly provided her with a dowry at the expense of Sir John Stanley, who was himself the bastard son of James Stanley, Bishop of Ely (d. 1515), imprisoning him for a year in the Fleet prison until he relinquished a farm which he held of the Abbot of Chester. Sir John was said to have been so upset by his treatment that he became a monk at Westminster, though this story, which formed article thirty-eight of the charges against Wolsey, has not been substantiated.

Another of Wolsey's contemporaries was an illegitimate son of the Stanley family. Edward Stanley (d. 1523), 1st Baron Monteagle and brother of James Stanley, the bishop of Ely mentioned above, had three illegitimate children; two sons, Edward and Thomas, and a daughter, Mary, in addition to his legitimate son and daughter. Thomas was provided for by a Church career. After attending Oxford, he was consecrated as Bishop of Man in 1510, an appointment that was made possible through his family's position since 1405 as lords of Man, which gave them control of the Manx church. He was also rector of several northern parishes.

The Church could of course provide a livelihood for illegitimate daughters as well as sons. Sir John Golafre's illegitimate daughter Alice (the sister of Richard II's loyal servant) was abbess at the Augustinian abbey of Burnham (Buckinghamshire). In 1403 she had received a dispensation, as daughter of an unmarried man and an unmarried woman to hold any dignities, even abbatial or principal, of her order. Sir Walter Mauny's two illegitimate daughters, Mailosel and Maplesant, were both nuns. In his will, Sir Walter left them 200 marks and 100 marks respectively.

Studies of bastardy in continental Europe have been facilitated by the opening of the papal penitentiary archives, containing details of dispensations to enable those of illegitimate birth to become clergy. Ludwig Schmugge used this material to compile a database of 37,916 dispensations that were registered in the papal penitentiary between 1449 and 1533. His analysis suggests that there were fewer opportunities for bastard sons of the nobility in the German Empire. He found that canonries and bishoprics were almost unobtainable for bastards from German noble houses, whereas those from Spain fared much better. This was perhaps partly because of the stricter way in which noble status was defined in the German Empire.

Guilds

Illegitimacy could prove a problem for townsmen seeking membership of English guilds or admission to municipal freedom. This was not because bastards were regarded as inferior in themselves, as seems to have been the case with some continental guilds, but because the principal means of gaining admission was by inheritance as the son or daughter of a member, or in some cases by marriage to the daughter of a member. In 1408 the Borough Court of Nottingham ruled that a bastard was not entitled to sue as a burgess. Interestingly, it was the plaintiff in the case, a prenuptial bastard, who raised this issue, when the defendant objected that he was not bound to answer as he was suing as a non-burgess. The plaintiff won his case. The status of the bastard daughter of Walter Dyer, a cloth trader and freeman of Wells (Somerset), presented a particular difficulty for the authorities. One of the five ways of obtaining freedom of Wells was by marriage with the daughter of a burgess. It seems that the rule was not clear as to whether the daughter had to be legitimate. In 1425, Peter Boghyar, alias Tankard, the husband of Dyer's bastard daughter, was admitted as a freeman following the usual admission process for a 'stranger', which included a fine of ten shillings, but it was recorded that in the event that the muniments proved that the bastard daughter had freedom of the borough, the fine would be refunded. Boghyar was later given an opportunity to prove his case that he was entitled to freedom of the borough through his marriage, but it seems that the matter was not easily resolved, as he was again ordered to appear before the convocation in 1437 to prove he had freedom of the borough because he married the bastard daughter of Walter Dyer. In this instance, marriage to a bastard was not viewed as an impediment to guild membership, but as a potential aid to membership.

Richard, the illegitimate son of John, Duke of Bedford (d. 1435), third son of Henry IV, may have received relatively little provision from his father, save a life interest in the castle, lands and lordship of 'Harapute' (Haye-du-Puits, Normandy), but in 1436, as 'Richard Bedford, Bastard of Bedford' he was made an honorary member of the Guild of Merchant Taylors of the Fraternity of St John the Baptist in the City of London. He seems to have acquired an interest in London property through marriage to Isabel, widow of Nicholas Rickhill of Essex.

The situation in continental Europe was a little different, though practice varied from state to state. Membership of most Florentine guilds was not initially affected by illegitimacy, although bastards were excluded from the guild of notaries. This did not necessarily mean that defects of birth did not matter at all; in some cases bastards were not allowed to hold offices within the guild. Allowing them guild membership was a pragmatic matter, which enabled them to earn an honest living. This approach contrasts with that in Ghent and some German towns, in which bastards were strictly prohibited from most guild membership, and members who begat or married bastards might have their membership revoked. (The Ghent Tanner's guild, which did not discriminate, was an exception.) In Frankfurt at the turn of the fourteenth century, attitudes to illegitimacy were more generally liberal, and bastards had access to similar opportunities as those of legitimate birth; only children of priests were regarded in a negative light. By the end of the Middle Ages, however, the city's guilds had become less accommodating towards those of illegitimate birth. In 1455, the weavers' guild tried to expel a member because he had married a woman who was a pre-nuptial bastard. On this occasion the city council intervened on the side of the weaver, who was permitted to remain within the guild. During the sixteenth century, a number of Frankfurt guilds, including bakers, tailors, shoemakers, bookbinders, barbers and brewers amended their statutes to exclude those of illegitimate birth. By the end of the century, most of the guilds required both membership applicants and their spouses to be of legitimate birth, and such requirements were supported by the city council. Strict standards of proof of legitimacy were required.

Marriage

Marriage was the principal way of providing for daughters, legitimate or otherwise. But bastard daughters were more difficult to place on the marriage market. In around 1275, Nicholas Meinill thought that his ward Robert le Gower would be an ideal husband for an illegitimate daughter of his relative John de Stuteville. Robert felt differently and fled. His reluctance might not have been entirely due to his prospective bride's illegitimacy though; the York Assize records reveal that when Meinill subsequently sold the marriage to one of his knights, William de Roseles, Gower also refused to marry the latter's daughter and was fined the sum of eighty marks, twice the value of the marriage.

Joan, the wife of Thomas Stonor II (d. 1474), is generally believed to have been an illegitimate daughter of William de la Pole, Duke of Suffolk, born in Normandy. The close local association of the two families lends some plausibility to this theory. It is also true that Joan was born overseas, as she received letters of denization in 1453.

An illegitimate son would not be the ideal choice of husband for an heiress, but some illegitimate sons were provided for in this manner. Philip Marmion (d. 1291) of Tamworth had a total of four legitimate daughters from his two marriages. He was able to provide for his bastard son Robert through his acquisition of the wardship of Isabel, the daughter and heiress of Giles FitzRalph. As a result of his marriage to Isabel, Robert acquired the manors of Nether Whitacre, Perry Croft and Glascote (Warwickshire). John Rous of Imber (Wiltshire) had two legitimate sons: William and John, by his wife Isolde, the eldest daughter and coheiress of Sir Philip Fitzwaryn of Great Chalfield

(Wiltshire). He also had several bastard children. By Alice Phillips, daughter of John Phillips of Imber, he had an illegitimate son, Richard, who married Alice Percy, daughter and heiress of John Percy of West (or Little) Chalfield. Another bastard son, Thomas, farmed East Chalfield manor from his legitimate half-brother William Rous. Two illegitimate daughters married into local families. Margaret married William Pylehous of Holt, and Alice married John Wolley of Bradford.

Randle Mainwaring of Over-Peover (Cheshire) had a large family of legitimate children: John, William, Randle, Elizabeth, Cicely, Joan, Agnes and Margaret, as well as illegitimate sons and three illegitimate daughters. Hugh, his bastard son by Emma Farrington married Margaret, sister and eventual heir of Ralph Croxton, of Croxton.

Sir Nicholas Stafford (1331–1394), the bastard son of Richard, Lord Stafford (d. 1380) was, like Peter de Montfort, intended originally for the Church, but this plan was superseded by marriage to Elizabeth, daughter and heiress of Thomas Meverel, who brought him extensive estates in Staffordshire and Derbyshire. Together with the influential family connections that had probably contributed to the advantageous marriage, this meant that he was able to become a notable landowner who served as knight of the shire for Staffordshire on nine occasions.

A variation on marriage to an heiress was marriage to a wealthy widow. William Thickness (d. *c.* 1403) of Newcastle-under-Lyme was, according to a deposition made in 1378, the child of a 'secret marriage' contracted by his father, William Thickness (d. 1385) with Katherine Swynnerton during the lifetime of his first wife, with whom he had no issue. William senior remarried after the death of his first wife, and it was the son of this later marriage on whom he settled his estates. William junior was however able to achieve financial independence through his marriage to Alice, the widow of Hugh Hough of Shavington.

The Beauforts

No discussion of the status of bastards in late-medieval England is complete without reference to the most famous of them all: the Beauforts. I have left them until the end as John of Gaunt's illegitimate children by his mistress Katherine Swynford, John, Henry, Thomas and Joan Beaufort were exceptional even among the bastards of the late-medieval English nobility. As children of John of Gaunt, they were not merely the offspring of the most powerful magnate of the time, but also benefited from their close connections with the Crown as cousins of Richard II and half-siblings of Henry IV. As previously noted, following Gaunt's later marriage to Katherine in 1396, Richard formally legitimated them in parliament. They were accorded a place in the duke's household alongside their legitimate siblings. John and Thomas were present when their half-brother Henry Bolingbroke, the future Henry IV, was admitted to the fraternity of Lincoln Cathedral in February 1386.

John, the eldest of the Beauforts, was created earl of Somerset a few days after his formal legitimation in February 1397. In September of that year he was made Marquess of Dorset and Somerset as a reward for supporting Richard in his action against the duke of Gloucester and the earls of Arundel and Warwick. At around the same time he married Margaret Holland, daughter of Thomas Holland, 5th Earl of Kent. Born around 1371, John had already gained a reputation for military prowess. In 1390 he jousted at St Ingelvert and joined the duke of Bourbon's crusade to Mahdiyya, in north Africa. He was knighted by December 1391. In 1394 he was crusading in Lithuania. He had been elected to the Order of the Garter in September 1396, at the same time as the marriage of his parents was ratified and the couple's children declared legitimate by papal authority, but the year before the formal recognition of his legitimacy in parliament. He was appointed constable of the royal castle of Wallingford in November 1397 and constable of Dover Castle and warden of the Cinque Ports in February of the following year. In May 1398 he was appointed admiral of the north and west and later as king's lieutenant in Aquitaine in August 1398. When his half-brother Henry Bolingbroke seized the crown in 1399, he initially raised troops to support Richard, but surrendered to Henry without a fight, and after Richard's deposition became a loyal and trusted supporter of the regime, notably as chamberlain of England from November 1399 and a key figure at court. He was Constable of Calais from 1401 until his death in 1410.

The second son, Henry, was marked out for a clerical career. His subsequent acquisition of both political power and wealth (he became known as 'the Rich Cardinal') invite comparisons with Wolsey. The irregularity of his birth did not prevent him from becoming one of the wealthiest individuals in the kingdom, or from eventually achieving the dignity of cardinal. If his path to the latter office was not entirely straightforward, it was for political reasons rather than concerns about his earlier illegitimate status. Born c. 1375, he studied at Peterhouse, Cambridge, in 1388–89 and then at Queen's College, Oxford between 1390 and 1393. In 1396 he was provided by papal bull to the deanery of Wells, and became chancellor of the University of Oxford in April 1397, having also been ordained deacon at around the same time. In February 1398 Pope Boniface IX (1389–1404) was persuaded to remove the serving bishop of Lincoln and provide Henry Beaufort in his place. During the early years of Henry IV's reign, Henry Beaufort was seldom at court. During this period he had an affair with Alice Fitzalan, which resulted in the birth of an illegitimate daughter, Jane or Joan. However, from the autumn of 1402, when he was appointed to the king's council, he became more involved in politics. In February 1403, he was appointed Chancellor of England, and continued to hold this position until March 1405, by which time he had been appointed to the see of Winchester, as successor to William Wykeham. On the accession on Henry V, Henry Beaufort again became chancellor. He resigned the role in 1417 to go on pilgrimage—a journey that conveniently took him by way of the Council of Constance, where he supported the election of Odo Colonna as the next pope. So far, so good, but then came a political misjudgment. Shortly after Colonna had duly been elected as Martin V (1417–31) he rewarded Beaufort for his support by naming him a cardinal and appointing him legate *a latere*, while allowing him to retain his see of Winchester *in commendam* and exempting him from the jurisdiction of Canterbury. Not surprisingly, this alarmed Henry Chichele, the archbishop of Canterbury, who protested to the king in no uncertain terms. King Henry was also very concerned about the grant of legatine powers, having no wish to see a permanent papal representative at the English court, even one who was also his half-uncle. He forbade Beaufort to accept these dignities, on pain of losing his bishopric and his wealth. Beaufort by this time had continued with his pilgrimage to the Holy Land, setting sail from Venice on 10 April 1418. It was almost a year later, in March 1419 that Beaufort met Henry V at Rouen, on his way back to England. He failed to convince the king of his good intentions, and returned to England, where his activities were kept under scrutiny by his cousin Thomas Chaucer, a trusted royal servant. It was only in 1421, when the king was desperately in need of funds for a new expedition, that Beaufort received some measure of reinstatement, in return for a loan of £17,666, secured on the customs of Southampton. This was not the first time that Beaufort had loaned money to the crown, which was now significantly in his debt.

Henry V died in 1422, and his two brothers, John, Duke of Bedford and Humphrey, Duke of Gloucester assumed the regency in France and England respectively, or in Gloucester's case, attempted to do so. But the council, possibly orchestrated by Beaufort, declined to allow Gloucester the title or powers of regent, allowing him only the title of protector. The rivalry between Beaufort and Gloucester was to be a defining feature of the minority of Henry VI, along with the consequences of the government's continued indebtedness to Beaufort, as the needs for further financing of the war effort in France led to further loans. By October 1425 the tension had escalated to such an extent that the armed retinues of Gloucester and Beaufort were confronting each other on London Bridge. Bedford returned to England in order to defuse the situation, and a settlement was reached in parliament the following February. Beaufort was forced to resign from the chancellorship and withdraw from membership of the council, but in return, Bedford procured from Martin V the cardinalate that Beaufort had been unable to accept in 1419. Cardinal Beaufort's illegitimate daughter Joan married Sir Edward Stradling of St Donat's, Glamorgan and Halsway, Somerset, sometime around 1423. In his will, the cardinal left her two dozen dishes, four chargers, twelve salt-cellars and a 100 pounds in gold. He also bequeathed £400 to 'John, Bastard of Somerset', probably an illegitimate son of his elder brother.

The youngest of the male Beauforts, Thomas, born *c*. 1377, joined the retinue of Richard II in July 1397. In 1399 he transferred his allegiance to his half-brother Henry IV, becoming a loyal supporter of the Lancastrian regime. He was elected to the Order of the Garter in 1400. In 1416 Thomas was created Duke of Exeter. He became one of Henry V's most trusted commanders, and was named in a codicil to the king's will as governor to the infant Henry VI.

Joan was the youngest of the Beauforts, having been born *c*. 1379. She was betrothed in 1386 to one of Gaunt's retainers, Sir Robert Ferrers of Oversley, Warwickshire. The couple married in 1392, and Joan bore two daughters in quick succession. By November 1396 Ferrers had died, and Joan, who had now been declared legitimate by papal bull, married Ralph Neville, 6th Baron Neville of Raby and later 1st Earl of Westmorland, with whom she had nine sons and five daughters, including William Neville, Earl of Kent, Edward Neville, 1st Baron Bergavenny, Katherine Neville, Duchess of Norfolk and Cicely Neville, who married Richard, Duke of York.

As the illegitimate offspring of the most powerful magnate of their day and grandchildren of Edward III, the Beauforts were of course far from typical. All the same, their remarkable success demonstrates the gap that could exist between legal theory and actual practice. Whilst none of the other bastards in this chapter were formally legitimated in parliament, their illegitimacy seems at most to have been a financial difficulty rather than a problem for their social standing.

Chapter 6

The End of an Era?

T he fifteenth century may perhaps have been the golden age of noble bastards as Jacob Burckhardt believed, but in England there was no corresponding age of opportunity for bastards at the highest levels of landed society, the illegitimate offspring of earls, marquises and dukes. For those slightly lower down the social ladder, if there ever was such a golden age, it was, if anything, slightly earlier. The most striking examples of landed provision for bastards, and in particular of bastards becoming *de facto* heirs in the absence of legitimate offspring, those of Vescy, Meinill, Sackville, Kerdiston and Argentine, occurred in the fourteenth century and the turn of the fifteenth century. As the fifteenth century progressed, it seems to have become more difficult to make significant provision for a bastard. In part this was a consequence of the very legal devices that had enabled provision for bastards in the first place. As estates became increasingly tied up in complex settlements and entails, the freedom of landowners, such as Sir John Basynges and William Gresley, to make provision was restricted.

The fourteenth century also provided other opportunities for illegitimate offspring. The effects of the Black Death in the middle of the century led to an increase in the number of dispensations granted to clerics of illegitimate birth, in order to fill vacancies. The ability of landowners to settle estates according to their own inclinations rather than strict rules of primogeniture was of equal benefit to legitimate younger sons and illegitimate sons, as was the opportunity to acquire a livelihood from military endeavour. The wars in France provided a potentially lucrative outlet.

A gradual shift in attitudes towards bastards appears to have begun during the fifteenth century as the landed classes became more concerned with pedigree and coats of arms as a symbol of status. By the sixteenth century, attitudes towards bastard children in general were much harsher, partly as a result of the Elizabethan Poor Law. Whilst there was little danger of illegitimate children from the landed classes becoming a charge on the parish, what Richard Helmholz has described as the 'contemporary mania about bastard children' may have encouraged such families to edit their pedigrees to remove any suggestion of illegitimate ancestry. What we know of illegitimate children often comes from chance survivals.

Whilst it is just possible to identify three separate members of the Paston family who fathered bastards, despite the huge quantity of surviving documents relating to this particular family and all the scholarship that has been carried out upon them, there remain scant traces of illegitimate children. Sir John Paston's illegitimate daughter Constance is mentioned only in Margaret Paston's will, and not in any of the letters at all. The illegitimate children of John Paston III and Edmund are referred to only obliquely. The details of the Rous family of Imber and Great Chalfield survive mainly through the chance survival of a cartulary compiled with great care by their kinsman Thomas Tropenell in the second half of the fifteenth century to prove his own property rights. Since Tropenell's purpose was to defend his own claim, it was in his interests to ensure that illegitimate children were clearly identified as such. He therefore made it clear that John Rous, senior, had many bastards but only two legitimate children, William, from whom Tropenell later acquired the manor of Great Chalfield, and John. William, like his father, had many bastard children, but had no surviving legitimate offspring, and John the younger had only a bastard son. Families that survived into the sixteenth century, when attitudes were changing, as the Pastons did, may well have concealed or destroyed such evidence of illegitimacy in the pedigree.

The landowning classes of Tudor England took a great interest in heraldry and genealogy. Well-established families used genealogy to demonstrate that they were superior to upwardly mobile social climbers, whilst families of more recent gentility used it to disguise their comparatively lowly origins. A living could be made by fake heralds, such as the glazier William Daykins, who posed as Norroy King of Arms, swindling ninety hopeful gentlemen in the process. Whilst not everyone went to the lengths of the Wellesbournes of Hughenden (Buckinghamshire), who not only tinkered with their pedigree, but forged monuments in their parish church to support it, it is clear that pedigrees were edited by later generations. Some of this falsification of the records may well have concealed illegitimacy. For example, in the late eighteenth century, the Reverend John Watson, attempting to support the claim of the Warren family of Poynton to the earldom of Surrey, made the case that Sir Edward Warren, the founder of the family, was legitimately descended from the second earl, rather than being a bastard of the last earl. Watson's theory relies on the less than credible assumption of a coincidence of there being two different ladies named Maud Nerford alive at the same time, one of whom was the mistress of the last earl, and one of whom was the wife of a 'Sir Edward Warren' who was legitimately descended from the second earl. In making this case he appears to have relied on the evidence of a pedigree which purported to have been prepared by the sixteenth century heralds and early genealogists Sir Robert Glover and his father-in-law William Flower, but which was of as doubtful provenance as the Warren family themselves. In this particular case, the absence of any contemporary evidence for Sir John Warren, father of Sir Edward Warren, and his father Sir John Warren is compounded by the mention of a son called Edward, clearly illegitimate, in the will of the last earl, which was contained in a register of Archbishop Zouch that was 'unfortunately lost' when Watson was compiling his work, although it subsequently made a reappearance. In the sixteenth century the Hopton family manufactured a pedigree and tampered with the quarterings of their arms to disguise their origins and how they came to acquire the Swillington estates. As noted above, Sir John Pelham's will did not mention his son's illegitimacy, but a deed by which Sir John Pelham conveyed property to his illegitimate son appears to have been subject to later amendment to substitute '*unico*' for '*bastardo*' after the words '*filio meo*'. Other pedigree redactions may be more difficult to identify.

The story of the medieval English bastard, then, is one which begins in the early thirteenth century, by which time the definitions of marriage and legitimacy had become sufficiently clear for illegitimacy to be a meaningful term, and a bar to inheritance. Opportunities for bastards opened up as the landed classes found ways to distribute their property as they wished, aided by the burgeoning legal profession, and the Hundred Years War provided opportunities for impoverished younger and illegitimate sons to make their fortunes. Towards the end of the fifteenth century, the freedom to dispose of landed property reduced once more as estates became encumbered by entails, and whilst it was still possible to make a fortune by training as a lawyer, the opportunities for advancement through military endeavour had dried up. In the sixteenth century, changing religious attitudes and the rise of Puritanism, combined with an increased concern about illegitimacy in the wake of the Poor Law, changed attitudes towards illegitimate children at a time when the nobility and gentry were becoming more conscious of their pedigree. The age of the medieval English bastard was over.

Glossary

Affinity	An impediment to marriage, similar to **consanguinity** but brought about by sexual intercourse with a person related in the prohibited degrees.
Annates	A tax paid on appointment by the recipient of an ecclesiastical benefice.
Consanguinity	An impediment to marriage being related in the prohibited number of degrees to the intended spouse.
Enfeoffment to use	A legal agreement in which land was granted to a person or group of persons on the understanding that they would do as the original owner instructed, which was used as a mechanisim for controlling descent of property.
Entail	A means of settling property so as to control or limit the way in which it can be inherited by generations.
Escheat	Reversion of property to the Crown or feudal lord on the death of a tenant with no heir.
Ex soluto et soluta	A form of illegitimacy where both parents were single and would bave been able to marry without impediment.
Godsib	A particular form of **affinity** caused by the spiritual relationship of godparent and godchild.
Hidalgo	A member of the lower nobility or gentry in Spain.
Inquisition Post Mortem	A royal inquiry following the death of a tenant-in-chief to determine what property they held and whether the heir was of age in order to assess the rights and dues to the Crown.
Mulier	A legitimate child.
Naturales	Illegitimate children born to a couple who were free to marry without impediment.
Oyer and terminer	A commission issued to judges authorizing them to hear criminal cases.
Prebend	A stipend assigned to a canon or member of the chapter of a cathedral or collegiate church.
Pre-contract	An impediment to marriage arising from a previous contract of marriage.
Seisin	Possession of land.
Spurii	Illegitimate children born to a couple who could not have married lawfully.

Annex

Dramatis Personae

The following is intended to aid readers in keeping track of individuals, particularly where they appear in different contexts in different chapters, or where there are multiple individuals with similar names.

It is not intended as a comprehensive list of all family members in each generation.

Cross references to individuals with their own entry in the list are highlighted in **bold text**.

Name	Chapters	Dates	Parents	Siblings	Spouse	Children
Allington, Robert (illeg.)	4		**William Allington (d. 1446) and ?**	**William Allington (d. 1459)**	**1.Joan Argentine** 2.Mary Brews	Jane Allington, Ann Allington
Allington, William	4	d. 1446	William Allington and Denise Malet		Joan Burgh	**William Allington, Robert Allington (illeg.)**
Allington, William	4	d. 1459	**William Allington (d. 1446) and Joan Burgh**	Robert Allington (illeg.)	Elizabeth Argentine	
Arderne, John	4	d. 1349	John Arderne and Margaret	Peter Arderne, Margery Arderne, Matilda Arderne, Agnes Arderne	1. Alice Venables, 2. Joan Stokeport 3. Ellen Wasteneys	**Peter Arderne, Thomas Arderne (illeg.), Walkeline Arderne (illeg.),** Matilda (m. Thomas Stanley)
Arderne, John	4	1369–1408	**Thomas Arderne (d. 1391)**			
Arderne, Peter	4		John Arderne and Alice Venables	**Thomas Arderne (illeg.), Walkeline Arderne (illeg.)**	Cicely Bredbury	**John Arderne (d. 1408)**
Arderne, Thomas (illeg.)	4	d. 1391	John Arderne (d. 1349) and Ellen Wasteneys	**Peter de Arderne (half-brother), Walkeline Arderne (illeg.)**		
Arderne, Walkeline	4		John Arderne (d. 1349) and Ellen Wasteneys	**Peter de Arderne (half-brother), Thomas Arderne (illeg.)**		
Argentine, Elizabeth	4		John Argentine (d. 1382) and Margaret Darcy	Joan Argentine, Maud Argentine, William Argentine (illeg.)	Baldwin St George	Baldwin St George

Name	Chapters	Dates	Parents	Siblings	Spouse	Children
Argentine, Elizabeth	4		John Argentine and Margery Calthorpe	Joan Argentine	William Allington (d. 1459)	Margaret Naunton
Argentine, Joan	4		John Argentine (d. 1382) and Margaret Darcy	Maud Argentine, Elizabeth Argentine, William Argentine (illeg.)	Bartholemew Naunton	
Argentine, Joan	4	d. 1429	John Argentine and Margery Calthorpe	John Argentine (d. 1423) Elizabeth Argentine	Robert Allington (illeg.)	
Argentine, John	4	d. by 1318			1. Joan Brian 2. Agnes Bereford	John Argentine (d. 1382)
Argentine, John	4, 6	d. 1382	John Argentine (d. 1318) and Agnes Bereford		Margaret Darcy	Joan Argentine, Maud Argentine, Elizabeth Argentine, William Argentine (illeg.)
Argentine, John	4		William Argentine (illeg.) and Isabel Kerdiston	William Argentine, Giles Argentine	Margery Calthorpe	John Argentine (d. 1423), Joan Argentine (d. 1429), Elizabeth Argentine
Argentine, John	4	d. 1423	John Argentine and Margery Calthorpe	Joan Argentine (d. 1429), Elizabeth Argentine		

Name	Chapters	Dates	Parents	Siblings	Spouse	Children
Argentine, Maud	4		John Argentine (d. 1318) and Agnes Bereford	Joan Argentine, Elizabeth Argentine, William Argentine (illeg.)	Ivo FitzWaryn	
Argentine, William (illeg.)	4, 5	d. 1419	John Argentine (d. 1382)	Joan Argentine, Maud Argentine and Elizabeth Argentine	1.Isabel Kerdiston 2.Joan Hadley 3.Margery Parles	John Argentine, William Argentine, Giles Argentine
Arundel, Edmund	Intro		Richard FitzAlan, Earl of Arundel (d. 1376) and Isabella Despenser		Sibyl, daughter of William Montagu, Earl of Salisbury	Elizabeth Arundel (married Sir John Meryett), Philippa Arundel (married 1. Richard Cergaux, 2. John Cornwall), Katherine
Arundel, Philippa	2	d. 1399		Edmund Arundel	1. Sir Richard Cergaux; 2. John Cornwall, Lord Fanhope	
Arundell, Edward (illeg.)	Intro		Sir John Arundell of Lanherne, Agnes Wode	John Arundell, Thomas Arundell, Renfrew Arundell, Richard Arundell (illeg.), Thomas Arundell (illeg.), Anne Arundell (illeg.), Margaret Arundell (illeg.)		

Name	Chapters	Dates	Parents	Siblings	Spouse	Children
Arundell, John	4		**Sir John Arundell of Lanherne**	Thomas Arundell, Renfrew Arundell, **Edward Arundell (illeg.)**, Richard Arundell (illeg.), Thomas Arundell (illeg.), Anne Arundell (illeg.), Margaret Arundell (illeg.)	Margaret Burghersh	
Arundell, John (of Lanherne)	Intro, 4	d. 1435				**John Arundell,** Thomas Arundell, Renfrew Arundell, Philippa Arundell, Joan Arundell **Edward Arundell (illeg.),** Richard Arundell (illeg.), Thomas Arundell (illeg.), Anne Arundell (illeg.), Margaret Arundell (illeg.)
Audley, James	5	d. 1334				**James Audley (illeg.),** Peter Audley (illeg.)
Audley, James (illeg.)	5	d. 1369	**James Audley (d. 1334) and Eve Clavering**	Peter Audley (illeg.)		
Barnard, John	4	d. 1485				John Barnard, Thomas Barnard (illeg.)

Name	Chapters	Dates	Parents	Siblings	Spouse	Children
Basynges, Alice	4			John Basynges (d. 1445)	Thomas Makworth (d. 1439)	Henry Makworth
Basynges, Alice (illeg.)	4		John Basynges (d. 1445)	John Basynges (illeg.)		
Basynges, John	4, 6	d. 1445		Alice Basynges		John (illeg.), Alice (illeg.)
Basynges, John (illeg.)	4	d. 1446	John Basynges (d. 1445)	Alice Basynges (illeg.)		
Bataill, Thomas	4	d.c. 1396				John Bataill, Thomas Bataill (illeg.), Maud Bataill
Beauchamp, Richard, Lord St Amand	4	d. 1508				Anthony St Amand (illeg.)
Beaufort, Charles ("Bastard Somerset")	5		Henry Beaufort, 2nd Duke of Somerset (1436–1464)			
Beaufort, Edmund, 1st Duke of Somerset	3	1406–1455	John Beaufort (d. 1410) and Margaret Holland	John Beaufort (d. 1444)		
Beaufort, Henry, Cardinal	1, 5	1375?–1447	John of Gaunt (1340–1399) and Katherine Swynford	Henry IV (half-brother); John Beaufort, Thomas Beaufort, Joan Beaufort		Jane Beaufort

Name	Chapters	Dates	Parents	Siblings	Spouse	Children
Beaufort, Henry, 2nd Duke of Somerset	5	1436–1464	**Edmund Beaufort** (d. 1455) and Eleanor Beauchamp			**Charles Beaufort** (illeg.)
Beaufort, Jane	5		**Cardinal Henry Beaufort** and Alice FitzAlan (widow of John Charlton of Powys)		Sir Edward Stradlyng	
Beaufort, Joan	1, 5	1379–1440	**John of Gaunt** (1340–1399) and Katherine Swynford	Henry IV (half-brother), **John Beaufort, Henry Beaufort, Thomas Beaufort**	1. Robert Ferrers, 2. **Ralph Neville, Earl of Westmorland**	Elizabeth Ferrers, Mary Ferrers, Richard Neville, Earl of Salisbury (d. 1460), William Neville, George Neville, Robert Neville, Edward Neville, Henry Neville, Thomas Neville, John Neville, Cuthbert Neville, Katherine Neville, Eleanor Neville, Cecily Neville, Joan Neville

Name	Chapters	Dates	Parents	Siblings	Spouse	Children
Beaufort, John, Duke of Somerset		1404–1444	John Beaufort (d. 1410) and Margaret Holland	Edmund Beaufort	Margaret Holland	John Beaufort, Edmund Beaufort, John 'Bastard of Somerset' (illeg.)?
Beaufort, John, Marquess of Dorset	1, 5	c. 1371–1410	John of Gaunt (1340–1399) and Katherine Swynford	Henry IV (half-brother), Henry Beaufort, Thomas Beaufort, Joan Beaufort		
Beaufort, Thomas, Duke of Exeter	1, 5	1377–1426	John of Gaunt (1340–1399) and Katherine Swynford	Henry IV (half-brother), John Beaufort, Henry Beaufort, Joan Beaufort	Margaret Neville	
Beaumont, Eleanor	1				Richard FitzAlan (d. 1376)	
Beaumont, William	1	d. 1453		Philip Beaumont	Joanna Courtenay	
Beaumont, John	3		Henry Bodrugan (d.c. 1503) and Joanna Courtenay			
Beck, Nicholas	2			Elizabeth Beck		Elizabeth Beck, Margaret Beck
Bedford, John, Duke of	4	1389–1435	Henry IV and Eleanor Bohun	Henry V, Thomas, Duke of Clarence, Humphrey Duke of Gloucester	1. Anne of Burgundy 2. Jacquetta of Luxembourg	Richard (illeg.), Mary (illeg.)
Bedford, Richard	4		John, Duke of Bedford (d. 1435)	Mary (illeg.)	Isabel, widow of Nicholas Rickhill.	

Name	Chapters	Dates	Parents	Siblings	Spouse	Children
Bereford, Agnes	4	d. 1375	William Bereford (d. 1326) and Margaret Plessy	Edmund Bereford (d. 1354), Joan Bereford, Margaret Bereford	1. John Argentine (d. 1318), 2. John Nerford, 3. John Maltravers	John Argentine (d. 1382)
Bereford, Baldwin (illeg.)	Intro	d. 1405	Edmund Bereford (d. 1354)	John Bereford (illeg.)		
Bereford, Edmund	Intro, 4	d. 1354	William Bereford and Margaret Plessy	Agnes Bereford		John Bereford (illeg.) Baldwin Bereford (illeg.)
Bereford, John (illeg.)	Intro	d. 1356	Edmund Bereford (d. 1354)	Baldwin Bereford (illeg.)		
Bereford, Osbert	4			William Bereford (d. 1326)		Simon Bereford
Bereford, Simon	4		Osbert Bereford			
Bereford, William	4	d. 1326		Osbert Bereford	Margaret Plessy	Edmund Bereford (d. 1354), Agnes Bereford (d. 1375), Joan Bereford, Margaret Bereford
Berney, John	4	d. 1460				Osbert Berney (illeg.)
Berney, Osbert (illeg.)	4		John Berney (d. 1460)			

Name	Chapters	Dates	Parents	Siblings	Spouse	Children
Bertram, John (of Bothal)	5	c. 1382–1450	Sir Robert Ogle (d. 1409) and Joan Heton	Sir Robert Ogle	1. Isabel Heron, 2. Joan Ludham	William Bertram, Edward Bertram (illeg.)
Bertram, Roger (of Mitford)	4	d.c. 1272	Roger Bertram and Agnes	Agnes, Isabel, Christina and Ada	Ida	Agnes, Thomas (illeg.)
Bessels, Peter	4	1363–1425	Sir Thomas Bessels (d. 1378) and Katherine Leigh		1. Joan Cateway, 2. Margery Haines	Thomas Bessels (illeg.)?
Bessels, Thomas (illeg.)	4	d. 1458	**Margery Haines and? Peter Bessels**			William Bessels
Bodrugan (alias Trenewith), William	4		**Joan Bodrugan** and Ralph Trenewith	Otto Trenewith		
Bodrugan, Henry	4	c. 1263–1308			Sybille Mandeville	**Otto Bodrugan** (d. 1331), Johanne
Bodrugan, Henry	1	c. 1426–c. 1503	William Bodrugan (d. 1441) and Philippa Arundell of Lanherne		**Joanna Courtenay**	John 'Beaumont'?
Bodrugan, Joan	4	d. 1428	Otto Bodrugan (d. 1389)	**William Bodrugan** (illeg.)	Ralph Trenewith	Otto Trenewith, **William Bodrugan** (alias Trenewith)

Name	Chapters	Dates	Parents	Siblings	Spouse	Children
Bodrugan, Otto	4	d. 1331	**Henry Bodrugan** (d. 1308) and Sybille Mandeville	Johanne		Henry Bodrugan, **William Bodrugan,** (d. 1362), Nicholas Bodrugan, Thomas Bodrugan, John Bodrugan, **Otto Bodrugan** (d. 1389), Joan Bodrugan
Bodrugan, Otto	4	d. 1389	**Otto Bodrugan** (d. 1331)	Henry Bodrugan, **William Bodrugan** (d. 1362), Nicholas Bodrugan, Thomas Bodrugan, John Bodrugan, Joan Bodrugan		**Joan (m. Ralph Trenewith),** William (illeg.)
Bodrugan, William	4	d. 1362	**Otto Bodrugan** (d. 1331)	Henry Bodrugan, Nicholas Bodrugan, Thomas Bodrugan, John Bodrugan, **Otto Bodrugan** (d. 1389)		Elizabeth Bodrugan (m. **Richard Cergaux**)
Bodrugan, William (illeg.)	4, 5		Otto Bodrugan (d. 1389)	**Joan Bodrugan (half-sister)**		
Bonville, John (illeg.)	4		**William Bonville** (d. 1461) and Isabel Kirkby		Alice Dennis	Elizabeth, Florence and Anne
Bonville, William	4, 5	1392–1461			Margaret Grey	William Bonville (d. 1460) and 3 daughters, **John Bonville (illeg.)**

Name	Chapters	Dates	Parents	Siblings	Spouse	Children
Booth, Laurence, Archbishop of York (illeg.)	5	1420–1480	William Booth (d. 1422)	William Booth d. 1464 (half-brother)		
Booth, William, Archbishop of York (d. 1464)	5		William Booth (d. 1422)	Laurence Booth d. 1480 (illeg. half-brother)		
Bourchier, Anne	3		Henry Bourchier, Earl of Essex (d. 1540)		William Parr	1 son (illeg.)
Brackenbury, Robert	3	d. 1485	Ralph Brackenbury		Agnes	Anne, Elizabeth, 1 son (illeg.)
Bradgate, John (illeg.)	4		John Bradgate		Katherine	Thomas, Ann
Brice, William	3					
Brocas, Maud	4		Sir John Brocas		John de Foxley	William de Foxley, Katherine de Foxley, Margaret de Foxley
Brokholes, Geoffrey	3			Margery Brokholes	Ellen Roos (d. 1419)	Joan Brokholes, Margery Brokholes
Brokholes, Joan	3		Geoffrey Brokholes and Ellen Roos	Margery Brokholes	Robert Armburgh	
Brokholes, Margery	3		Geoffrey Brokholes and Ellen Roos	Joan Brokholes	John Sumpter	John Sumpter (d. 1420), Christine, Ellen

Name	Chapters	Dates	Parents	Siblings	Spouse	Children
Brunston, John (illeg.)	4		**Thomas Brunston**	Thomas Brunston, William Brunston, John Brunston junior, Robert Brunston, Richard Brunston, Katherine Bruston, Isabel Brunston (half-siblings)		
Brunston, Thomas	4	d. 1424			Joanna	Thomas Brunston, William Brunston, John Brunston junior, Robert Brunston, Richard Brunston, Katherine Bruston, Isabel Brunston, **John Brunston (illeg.)**
Burgess, Joan	4					**Thomas Sackville (illeg.), Alice Sackville (illeg.)**
Burgh, Thomas, Lord Burgh	3	d. 1550	Edward Burgh and Anne Cobham		1. Agnes Tyrwhitt, 2. Alice London	Edward Burgh, **Thomas Burgh,** William Burgh
Burgh, Thomas			**Thomas, Lord Burgh** (d. 1550) and Agnes Tyrwhitt	Edward Burgh, William Burgh	Elizabeth	
Burton, Alice (illeg.)	Intro	*fl.* 1432				

Name	Chapters	Dates	Parents	Siblings	Spouse	Children
Burton, Robert	4	d. 1360	Matilda de Burton	Thomas Burton, John Burton and William Burton, Alice, Cecilia		Alice **Burton** (illeg.)
Burton, William	4		Matilda de Burton	Robert de Burton, Thomas de Burton and John de Burton, Alice, Cecilia		
Cantilupe, Nicholas	1	d. 1371			Katherine Paynell	
Case, William	4	d. 1494				2 sons (illeg.)
Cely, George	3	1458–1489	Richard Cely (d. 1482) and Agnes Andrew	Robert Cely (d. 1485), **Richard Cely (d. 1493)**	Margery Punt	Richard, Avery, George, John, Edmund; 1 illeg. child
Cely, Richard	3	d. 1493	Richard Cely (d. 1482) and Agnes Andrew	Robert Cely (d. 1485), **George Cely (d. 1489)**	Anne Rawson	Margaret, Isabel and Barbara
Cergeaux, Richard	4	d. 1393	Richard Cergeaux and Margaret Seneschal	Michael Cergeaux	1.**Elizabeth Bodrugan**, 2. **Philippa Arundel**	Richard, Alice and Elizabeth
Chaworth, Thomas	4	d. 1347				Thomas Chaworth, John (illeg.), Alice (illeg.), Ellen (illeg.)
Cheddar, Richard	4	d. 1437		Thomas Cheddar	Elizabeth Cantelo	Jane Cheddar, John Cheddar (illeg.)

Name	Chapters	Dates	Parents	Siblings	Spouse	Children
Chenduyt, Joan	4		John Chenduyt (d. 1426)	Richard Chenduyt (illeg.)	John Pengelly	
Chenduyt, John	Intro, 4	d. 1426		Thomas Chenduyt	Joan (widow of Richard Glyvyan)	Richard Chenduyt (illeg.), Joan Chenduyt (illeg.)
Chenduyt, Richard (illeg.)	4	d. 1427	John Chenduyt (d. 1426)	Joan Chenduyt (illeg.)		
Clarence, Thomas Duke of	5	d. 1421	Henry IV and Margaret Bohun	Henry V, John Duke of Bedford, Humphrey Duke of Gloucester, Blanche, and Philippa	Margaret Holland	
Clarendon, Roger	Intro		Edward, the Black Prince			
Clavering, Eve	3	d. 1369	John FitzRobert, Lord Clavering (d. 1332) and Hawise Tibetot		1. Thomas Audley (d. 1308), 2. Thomas Ufford (d. 1314), 3. Thomas de Benhale	John Ufford, Robert Ufford, Edmund Ufford, [with James Audley d. 1334, cousin of first husband], James Audley, Peter Audley (d. 1359)
Cobham, Reginald (illeg.)	4		Thomas Cobham (d. 1471)			
Cobham, Thomas	4	d. 1471	Reginald Cobham		Ann Stafford	Ann Cobham, Reginald Cobham (illeg.)

Name	Chapters	Dates	Parents	Siblings	Spouse	Children
Cokayn, John	4	d. 1504				Thomas, Jane (illeg.)
Cokeryngton, William (illeg.)	Intro		John Cokeryngton			
Colas, Henry	1	d. 1413	Henry Colas senior			Walter Colas (illeg.)
Colas, Walter	1	d. 1413	Henry Colas (d. 1413)			
Conyers, John (of Ormsby)	Intro		John Conyers			Thomas (illeg.)
Corbet, Thomas	1		John Corbet		Amice	John L'Estrange (illeg.)?
Cornwall, John, Lord Fanhope	Intro, 4, 5	d. 1443	Sir John Cornwall (d. 1392?)		1. Philippa (d. 1399), widow of Sir Richard Cergaux and daughter of Edmund Arundel, 2. Elizabeth, Lancaster	John (illeg.), Thomas (illegit.)
Courtenay, Joanna	1		Sir William Courtenay		1. William Beaumont, 2. Henry Bodrugan (d. 1503)	John 'Beaumont'
Curteys, William (illeg)	5		John Curteys?			

Name	Chapters	Dates	Parents	Siblings	Spouse	Children
Dabrichecourt, John	4, 5	d. 1415				Richard, 5 daughters, 2 sons (illeg.)
Dalton, Robert (illeg.)	Intro, 5		John Dalton			
Darcy, Margaret	4	d. 1383	John Darcy		John Argentine (d. 1382)	**Joan Argentine, Maud Argentine, Elizabeth Argentine**
de la Beche, Joan	4		John de la Beche		**Andrew Sackville, d. 1369**	Andrew Sackville, John Sackville
de la Pole, William, Duke of Suffolk	5	1396–1450	Michael de la Pole 1ˢᵗ Earl of Suffolk and Katherine Stafford	Michael de la Pole, 2ⁿᵈ Earl of Suffolk	Alice Chaucer	John de la Pole, 2ⁿᵈ Duke of Suffolk, Joan (illeg.?)
Despenser, Constance	3	1375–1416	Edmund of Langley, Duke of York and Constance (illeg.), daughter of Pedro the Cruel of Castile		Thomas Despenser, Earl of Gloucester (d. 1400)	Richard (d. 1414), Elizabeth and Isabella (m. 1. Richard Beauchamp, Earl of Worcester, 2. Richard Beauchamp, Earl of Warwick), **Eleanor** (illeg.—with **Edmund Holland, Earl of Kent**)

Name	Chapters	Dates	Parents	Siblings	Spouse	Children
Despenser, Isabella	1		Hugh Despenser the Younger (d. 1326)		**Richard FitzAlan (d. 1376)** (annulled)	**Edmund Arundel** (bastardised)
Dronsfield, William	4	d. 1406	John Dronsfield		Grace	Richard Kesseburgh
Egerton, Ralph	4	d. 1528				Richard Egerton, Ralph Egerton (illeg.), Mary Egerton (illeg.) other illeg. daughters.
Etchingham, William	5	d. 1326	William Etchingham (d. 1294) and Katherine	Robert Etchingham (d. 1327), Simon Etchingham, Richard Etchingham	Eve Stopham	Joan (d. by 1325), **William (illeg.)**
Etchingham, William (illeg.)	5		**William Etchingham (d. 1326)**	Joan (half-sister)		
Fauconberg, Anastasia	3		**Ralph Neville of Raby** and Euphemia Clavering		Walter Fauconberg d. 1314	
Ferrers, Agnes	4	d. 1290	William de Ferrers, Earl of Derby and Sibyl (daughter and co-heiress of William Marshal, Earl of Pembroke)		William de Vescy (d. 1253)	**John de Vescy, William de Vescy** (d. 1297)

Name	Chapters	Dates	Parents	Siblings	Spouse	Children
Ferriby, John	4	1470			Margaret, widow of Thomas Roos	2 sons, Margaret, 1 son (illeg.)
FitzAlan, Alice			**Richard FitzAlan, Earl of Arundel (d. 1376) and Eleanor Beaumont**	**Edmund Arundel** (bastardised half-brother), Richard FitzAlan (d. 1397), John Arundel, Thomas Arundel, Joan, Mary, Eleanor	**Thomas Holland, Earl of Kent (d. 1397)**	**Thomas Holland,** later **Earl of Kent and Duke of Surrey** (d. **1400**), Richard (d.*c.* 1396), **Edmund Holland, Earl of Kent**, Eleanor (d. 1405) Joan (d. 1434), Margaret Holland, m.1 **John Beaufort, Earl of Somerset, 2. Thomas, Duke of Clarence**; Eleanor (d.*c.* 1420), who married Thomas Montagu, Earl of Salisbury, Elizabeth (d. 1423), Bridget
FitzAlan, Edmund, Earl of Arudel	2	1285–1326			Alice de Warenne	**Richard FitzAlan** (d. 1376), Edmund, Michael, Alice FitzAlan, Aleyne, Jane

Name	Chapters	Dates	Parents	Siblings	Spouse	Children
FitzAlan, Richard, Earl of Arundel	1, 2	1313–1376	Edmund FitzAlan and Alice de Warenne		1. Isabella Despenser (annulled), 2. Eleanor Beaumont	Edmund Arundel (bastardised), Richard FitzAlan (d. 1397), John Arundel, Thomas Arundel, Joan, Alice, Mary, Eleanor
FitzPayne, Ela	3				1. John le Mareschal, 2. Robert FitzPayne	
FitzWalter, Walter, Lord FitzWalter	4	1400–1431	Walter FitzWalter (d. 1406) and Jane Devereux		Elizabeth Chydyok	Elizabeth, Maria (illeg.), Gabrielle (illeg.)
Fitzwilliam, Thomas (illeg.)	Intro		John Fitzwilliam			
Flemming, Robert (illeg.)	3	1416–1483	Robert Flemming			
Ford, Edmund	5	d. 1440	Henry Ford and Maud	Thomas Ford (half-brother)	Joan	
Foxley, John	4	d. 1378	Thomas Foxley and Katherine Ifield		1. Maud Brocas, 2. Joan Martin	William Foxley (d. 1376), Katherine Foxley, Margery Foxley, Thomas Foxley (illeg.), Richard Foxley (illeg.), John Foxley (illeg.)

Name	Chapters	Dates	Parents	Siblings	Spouse	Children
Foxley, John	4	d. 1419	John de Foxley (d. 1378) and Joan Martin	William de Foxley, Katherine Foxley, Margery Foxley, Thomas Foxley (illeg.), Richard Foxley (illeg.)	Isabel Fowler	Alice Foxley (d. 1421)
Foxley, Katherine	4		John Foxley (d. 1378) and Maud Brocas	William Foxley, Margery Foxley, Thomas Foxley (illeg.), Richard Foxley (illeg.), John Foxley (illeg.)	John Warbleton	Thomas Warbleton, Margaret Warbleton, Elizabeth Warbleton
Foxley, Margaret	4		John Foxley (d. 1378) and Maud Brocas	William Foxley, Katherine Foxley, Thomas Foxley (illeg.), Richard Foxley (illeg.), John Foxley (illeg.)	Robert Bullock	Margery Bullock (m. John Hertington)
Foxley, Richard	4	d. 1408	John Foxley (d. 1378) and Joan Martin	William Foxley (d. 1376), Katherine Foxley, Margery Foxley, Thomas Foxley (illeg.), John Foxley (illeg.)		
Foxley, Thomas	4	d. 1360	John Foxley and Constance		Katherine, daughter and co-heiress of Sir John Ifield	John Foxley (d. 1378)
Foxley, Thomas	4	d. 1436	John Foxley (d. 1378) and Joan Martin	William Foxley, Katherine Foxley, Margaret Foxley, Richard Foxley (illeg.), John de Foxley	1. Margaret Lytton, 2. Theobalda de Marys	Elizabeth (married Thomas Uvedale)

Name	Chapters	Dates	Parents	Siblings	Spouse	Children
Foxley, William	4	d. 1376	**John Foxley (d. 1378) and Maud Brocas**	**Katherine Foxley, Margery Foxley, Thomas Foxley (illeg.), Richard Foxley (illeg.), John Foxley (illeg.)**		
Fulbourn, William	5	d.*c.* 1441	Alice Whityng			
Gaunt, John of Duke of Lancaster	1,5		Edward III		1. Blanche of Lancaster, 2. Constanza of Castile, 3. Katherine Swynford	**Henry IV, Elizabeth of Lancaster, John Beaufort, Henry Beaufort, Thomas Beaufort, Joan Beaufort**
Gaveston, Piers, Earl of Cornwall	2		John Gaveston		Margaret de Clare	Joan, Amie (poss illeg.)
Gippyng, alias Lincoln, Thomas	Intro				Joanna	Beatrice (illeg.,) Juliana (illeg.)
Girlington, John	4					Robert Girlington (illeg.), William Girlington (illeg.)
Gloucester, Antigone (illeg.)	4		**Humphrey, Duke of Gloucester**	Arthur (illeg.)	Henry Grey, Count of Tankerville	Henry Grey, Lord Grey of Powis

Name	Chapters	Dates	Parents	Siblings	Spouse	Children
Gloucester, Arthur	5		**Humphrey, Duke of Gloucester**	Antigone (illeg.)		
Gloucester, Humphrey Duke of	4	d. 1447	Henry IV and Eleanor Bohun	**Henry V, John, Duke of Bedford, Thomas, Duke of Clarence**	1. Jacqueline of Hainalt, 2. Eleanor Cobham	**Arthur (illeg.), Antigone (illeg.)**
Godyn, John	Intro	d. 1469	John Godyn			Thomas (illeg.)
Golafre, Alice (illeg.)	5		**John Golafre (d. 1379)** and Johannet Pulham	**John Golafre (illeg.)**	Phillipa de Mohun	
Golafre, John	5	d. 1379		Thomas Golafre	2. Isabella Brocas (widow of Thomas Missenden)	**John Golafre (illeg.), Alice Golafre (illeg.)**
Golafre, John (illeg.)	5		**John Golafre (d. 1379)** and Johannet Pulham	**Alice Golafre (illeg.)**		
Grandison, Otto	4	d. 1359	William de Grandison and Sibyl Tregoz	Peter de Grandison	Beatrice Malemayns	Thomas, Elizabeth, William (illeg.)
Gresley, William	4, 6	d. 1521	John Gresley	George Gresley		[with Alice Tawke] Anthony (illeg.), Thomas (illeg.), Humphrey (illeg.), Edward (illeg.),

Name	Chapters	Dates	Parents	Siblings	Spouse	Children
Grey, Henry (of Codnor)	4	d. 1496	Henry Grey of Codnor (d. 1464) and Margaret Percy			Richard Grey (illeg.), Henry Grey snr (illeg.), Henry Grey jnr (illeg.)
Grey, John	5	d. 1392	Richard Grey of Codnor and Joan Fitzpayn		1. Eleanor, 2. Alice de Lisle	Henry, Nicholas (illeg.)
Haines, Margery	4	d. 1484			1. **Sir Peter Bessels** (d. 1425), 2. William Warbleton	**Thomas Bessels** (illeg.)
Hale, Richard (illeg.)	Intro		John Hale			
Hankford, John (illeg.)			**Richard Hankford** and Elizabeth Were William Hankford			
Hankford, Richard			**Richard Hankford** and Elizabeth Were			**John Hankford** (illeg.) **Richard Hankford** (illeg)
Hankford, Richard (illeg.)			**Richard Hankford** and Elizabeth Were			
Hastings, Laurence, Earl of Pembroke	Intro	d. 1348	John Hastings (d. 1325) and Juliana Leybourne (d. 1367).		Agnes (d. 1368), third daughter of Roger (V) Mortimer, first Earl of March	John Hastings, **William Hastings** (illeg.)

Name	Chapters	Dates	Parents	Siblings	Spouse	Children
Hastings, William (illeg.)	Intro	d. 1349	Laurence Hastings, Earl of Pembroke	John Hastings		
Hawkwood, John	5	d. 1394	Gilbert Hawkwood (d. 1340)	John Hawkwood	Donnina Visconti (illeg.), daughter of Bernabo Visconti	Gianetta, Caterina, Anna, John, John (illeg.) other sons and daughters
Herbert, Richard (of Ewyas)	5	d. 1510	William Herbert (d. 1469)	William Herbert, George Herbert (illeg)	Margaret Cradock	William Herbert, Earl of Pembroke (d. 1570)
Herbert, William, Earl of Pembroke	5	d. 1469	Sir William ap Thomas (d. 1445) and Gwladus, d. of Dafydd Gam			William Herbert, Richard Herbert (illeg.), George Herbert (illeg.) Thomas (illeg.)
Herle, John	Intro		John Herle			
Herle, Thomas (illeg.)	Intro		Sir John Herle		Joan	
Heydon, John	3		John Heydon		Eleanor Winter	
Hoghton, Henry	4		Sir Adam Hoghton		Joan Radcliffe	Richard (illeg.)

Name	Chapters	Dates	Parents	Siblings	Spouse	Children
Holland, Edmund, Earl of Kent	5	c. 1383–1408	**Thomas Holland, Earl of Kent** (1350–1397), and Alice FitzAlan	Thomas Holland, Earl of Kent (d. 1400), Richard, Eleanor (d. 1405), Joan (d. 1434); Margaret Holland (d. 1439), wife of John Beaufort, Earl of Somerset, and **Thomas, Duke of Clarence**, Eleanor (d. c.1420), Elizabeth (d. 1423), and Bridget	Lucia Visconti (1380–1424)	Illeg. daughter, Eleanor, with **Constance Despenser** (c. 1375–1416)
Holland, Henry, Duke of Exeter	4	1430–1475	**John Holland, Earl of Huntingon and Duke of Exeter** (d. 1447) and Anne Stafford (d. 1432)	William (illeg.), Thomas (illeg.)	Anne of York (daughter of Richard, Duke of York)	Anne (m. Thomas Grey)
Holland, Isabella	2,3		Robert Holland, Lord Holland (d. 1328) of Upholland, Lancashire, and Maud Zouche (d. 1349)	**Thomas Holland, Earl of Kent** (c. 1315–1360), Robert (d. 1373), Alan (d. 1359), Margaret (d. 1349), and Matilda		

Name	Chapters	Dates	Parents	Siblings	Spouse	Children
Holland, John, Earl of Huntingdon		c. 1352–1400	Thomas Holland, Earl of Kent (c. 1315–1360) and Joan (1328–1385), d. of Edmund of Woodstock, Earl of Kent	Thomas Holland, Earl of Kent (d. 1397), Maud (d. 1392), Joan (d. 1384)	Elizabeth Lancaster	Richard (d. 1400), John Holland, Earl of Huntingdon and Duke of Exeter (1395–1447), Edward, Count of Mortain (d. 1418), Constance (d. 1437), 1 further sister
Holland, John, Earl of Huntingdon, Duke of Exeter	4	1395–1447	John Holland, Earl of Huntingdon (d. 1400) and Elizabeth Lancaster	Richard (d. 1400), Edward, Count of Mortain (d. 1418), Constance (d. 1437), 1 further sister	1. Anne Stafford (d. 1432), 2. Beatrice, illeg. daughter of João I, king of Portugal and widow of Thomas Fitzalan, Earl of Arundel (d. 1415) 3. Anne Montagu	Henry Holland, Duke of Exeter (d. 1475), William (illeg.), Thomas (illeg.)
Holland, Thomas, Earl of Kent		c.1315–1360	Robert Holland, Lord Holland (d. 1328) of Upholland, Lancashire, and Maud Zouche (d. 1349), daughter and coheir of Alan.	Robert (d. 1373), Alan (d. 1359), Isabella, mistress of John de Warenne, Earl of Surrey (d. 1347), Margaret (d. 1349), Matilda	Joan (c. 1328–1385), d. of Edmund of Woodstock, known as the Fair Maid of Kent.	Thomas Holland (d. 1397), John Holland (d. 1400), Maud (d. 1392), Joan (d. 1384)

Name	Chapters	Dates	Parents	Siblings	Spouse	Children
Holland, Thomas		1350–1397	Thomas Holland, Earl of Kent (c. 1315–60) and Joan (1328–1385), d. of Edmund of Woodstock, Earl of Kent	John Holland, Earl of Huntingdon and Duke of Exeter; Maud (d. 1392), Joan (d. 1384)	Alice (c. 1350–1416), daughter of Richard (II) Fitzalan, Earl of Arundel	Thomas Holland, later Earl of Kent and Duke of Surrey (d. 1400), Richard (d. c.1396), Edmund Holland, Earl of Kent, Eleanor (d. 1405) Joan (d. 1434), Margaret Holland, who married John Beaufort, Earl of Somerset, and then Thomas, Duke of Clarence; Eleanor (d.c. 1420), wife of Thomas Montagu, Earl of Salisbury, Elizabeth (d. 1423), Bridget

Name	Chapters	Dates	Parents	Siblings	Spouse	Children
Holland, Thomas, Earl of Kent and Duke of Surrey		c. 1374–1400	**Thomas Holland, Earl of Kent** (1350–1397), and Alice FitzAlan (d. 1416)	**Edmund Holland**, Richard, Eleanor (d. 1405), Margaret (d. 1434), Joan (d. 1439), wife of **John Beaufort, Earl of Somerset, and Thomas, Duke of Clarence**, Eleanor (d.c. 1420), wife of Thomas Montagu, Earl of Salisbury, Elizabeth (d. 1423), Bridget, a nun	Joan, daughter of Hugh Stafford, Earl of Stafford (d. 1386)	
Holme, Robert	5		Beatrice Forden			
Hopton, Thomas	4		Robert Swillington and Joan Hopton			John Hopton
Howard, Edward	4	1476/7–1513	Thomas Howard, 2nd Duke of Norfolk (d. 1524) and Elizabeth Tilney (d. 1497)	Thomas Howard, 3rd Duke of Norfolk	Alice Morley	2 sons (illeg.)
Howbert, John	5					
Ipstones, John	2	d. 1394	John Ipstones (d.b. 1364) and Elizabeth, sister of Nicholas Beck		Elizabeth Corbet	William Ipstones

Name	Chapters	Dates	Parents	Siblings	Spouse	Children
Ipstones, William	2		John Ipstones (d. 1394) and Elizabeth Corbet		Maud Swynnerton	
Johnnys, Hugh	5	1410–1485				
Kerdiston, Isabel	4		William de Kerdiston (illeg.)		William Argentine (illeg.)	
Kerdiston, Maud	4		John Kerdiston	Roger Kerdiston (illeg.), William Kerdiston (illeg.)	John de Burghersh	John de Burghersh
Kerdiston, William	4, 6		John Kerdiston		1. ?, 2. Alice de Norwich, 3. Margery Cobbold	Maud Kerdiston, Roger Kerdiston (illeg.), William Kerdiston (illeg.), Isabel Kerdiston
Kerdiston, William (illeg.)	4	d. 1361	William Kerdiston and Alice Norwich	Maud Kerdiston (half-sister), Roger Kerdiston (illeg.)		
Kesseburgh, Richard	4		William Dronsfield (d. 1406)			
Kirkebrunne, William (illeg.)			John Kirkebrunne			
Lacy, Alice de	2		Henry de Lacy, Earl of Lincoln		Thomas, Earl of Lancaster (d. 1322)	

Name	Chapters	Dates	Parents	Siblings	Spouse	Children
Lancaster, Elizabeth	3	1364?–1425	John of Gaunt (1340–1399) and Blanche of Lancaster (1346?–1368)	Henry IV, Phillipa, Henry Beaufort (half-brother), John Beaufort (half-brother), Thomas Beaufort, (half-brother) Joan Beaufort (half-sister)	John Holland, Earl of Huntingdon (1352–1400), John Cornwall, Lord Fanhope	
Lancaster, Thomas	5		Thomas, Earl of Lancaster (d. 1322)	John Lancaster (illeg.)		
Lancaster, Thomas, Earl of	2	c. 1278–1322	Edmund, Earl of Lancaster and Leicester (1245–1296) and Blanche of Artois	Henry	Alice de Lacy	Thomas (illeg.),John (illeg.)
Le Brun, Ada	1		John Le Brun		Hubert de Multon (annulled)	William Lebrun
Le Brun, William	1		Hubert de Multon and Ada Le Brun			

Name	Chapters	Dates	Parents	Siblings	Spouse	Children
Leek, John	Intro, 4		John Leek		Jane Foljambe	John, Anne, Susan (illeg.), Elizabeth (illeg.), Dorothy (illeg.), with mistress Anne Mainwaring
Leventhorpe, William (illeg.)	4			John Leventhorpe (d. 1435)		
Leversegge, Richard	5		John Leversegge			
Lisle, William (illeg.)	5		Robert, Lord Lisle of Rougemont (d. 1399)			
Lound, John (illeg.)	5		Alexander Lound	Alexander Lound		
Lovel, John (of Minster Lovell)	Intro, 4	d. 1314	John Lovel	John Lovel of Snorscomb (illeg.)		
Lovel, John (of Snorscomb) (illeg.)	Intro, 4		John Lovel	John Lovel of Minster Lovel (d. 1314)		
Ludlow, Thomas (illeg.)	Intro		John Ludlow			

Name	Chapters	Dates	Parents	Siblings	Spouse	Children
Mainwaring, Hugh (illeg.)			Randle Mainwaring (d. 1456)	John Mainwaring, William Mainwaring, Randle Mainwaring, Elizabeth Mainwaring, Cicely Mainwaring, Joan Mainwaring, Ellen Mainwaring, Agnes Mainwaring, Margaret Mainwaring, Thomas Mainwaring (illeg.), Randle Mainwaring (illeg.), 3 more daughters (illeg.)	Margaret, sister and eventual heir of Ralph Croxton, of Croxton	
Mainwaring, Randle	5	d. 1456	John Mainwaring (d. 1410)		Margery Venables	John Mainwaring, William Mainwaring, Randle Mainwaring, Elizabeth Mainwaring, Cicely Mainwaring, Joan Mainwaring, Ellen Mainwaring, Agnes Mainwaring, Margaret Mainwaring, Hugh Mainwaring (illeg.), Thomas Mainwaring (illeg.), Randle Mainwaring (illeg.), 3 more daughters (illeg.)

Name	Chapters	Dates	Parents	Siblings	Spouse	Children
Marmion, Philip	5	d. 1291				4 legit daughters, Robert Marmion (illeg.)
Marmion, Robert	5		Philip Marmion		Isabel FitzRalph	
Martin, Joan	4		John Martin		John de Foxley (d. 1378)	Thomas Foxley (illeg.), Richard Foxley (illeg.), John Foxley (illeg.)
Martin, William	5					
Mauley, Peter de	3	d.c. 1348	Peter de Mauley (d. 1308) and Nichola de Gaunt		Eleanor Furnival	Peter de Mauley (d. 1355)
Mauny, Walter	5	1310–1372	Jean le Borgne, Lord of Masny and Jeanne de Jenlain	4 brothers, 1 sister, Mary	Margaret Brotherton	Ann, Mailosel (illeg.) and Malplesant (illeg.)
Meinill, Elizabeth	4		Nicholas Meinill (illeg.) and Alice Rous		John Darcy	
Meinill, Nicholas	3,5	d. 1299	John Meinill		Christine	Nicholas Meinill (d. 1322), John Meinill (d. 1337)
Meinill, Nicholas	Intro, 4, 6	d. 1322	Nicholas Meinill (d. 1299) and Christine	John de Meinill (d. 1337)		Nicholas Meinill (illeg.)

Name	Chapters	Dates	Parents	Siblings	Spouse	Children
Meinill, Nicholas (illeg.)	4	d. by Nov 1341	Nicholas Meinill (d. 1322) and Lucy Thweng		Alice Rous	Elizabeth Meinill
Merley, Isabella de	3	14th century	John Merley			
Mitchell, Ellen	1		John Mitchell		1. Michael Barre, 2 Ralph Sadler	Thomas Sadler (d. 1607), Henry Sadler (d. 1618), Edward Sadler, Anne Sadler (d. 1576), Jane Sadler (d. in or after 1587), Dorothy Sadler (d. in or after 1578). All legitimated by Parliament in 1547. Also 2 children with Barre.
Montagu, Alice	5		Thomas Montagu, Earl of Salisbury (d. 1428)	John Montagu (illeg.)	Richard Neville (d. 1460)	
Montagu, John (illeg.)	5		Thomas Montagu, Earl of Salisbury	Alice Montagu (half-sister)		

Name	Chapters	Dates	Parents	Siblings	Spouse	Children
Montagu, Thomas, Earl of Salisbury	5	1388–1428	John Montagu, 3rd Earl of Salisbury (d. 1400) and Maud Fraunceys		1. Eleanor Holland (d. of Thomas Holland and Alice FitzAlan), 2. Alice Chaucer	Alice Montagu, John Montagu (illeg.) 'Bastard of Salisbury'
Montfort, Alice (illeg.)	4		Peter de Montfort and Lora Astley	Guy Montfort (half-brother), Richard Montfort (illeg.), John Montfort (illeg.)		
Montfort, Guy	4		Peter de Montfort and Margaret Furnivall	John de Montfort (illeg.), Richard de Montfort (illeg.), Alice de Montfort (illeg.)	Margaret Beauchamp, d. of Thomas Beauchamp, Earl of Warwick	
Montfort, John (illeg.)	4		Peter de Montfort and Lora Astley	Guy Montfort (half-brother), Richard Montfort (illeg.), Alice Montfort (illeg.)	Joan de Clinton	Baldwin Montfort
Montfort, Peter de	Intro, 4	d. 1370	John de Montfort (d. 1296)		Margaret Furnivall	Guy Montfort, John Montfort (illeg.), Richard Montfort (illeg.), Alice Montfort (illeg.)

Name	Chapters	Dates	Parents	Siblings	Spouse	Children
Montfort, Richard (illeg.)	4		**Peter de Montfort** and Lora Astley	**Guy de Montfort (half-brother), John Montfort (illeg.), Alice Montfort (illeg.)**	Rose de Brandeston	
Mortimer, Thomas (illeg.)	5	d. 1403	Roger Mortimer, 2nd Earl of March (1328–1360)	Edmund Mortimer, 3rd Earl of March		
Multon, Hubert de	1	d. 1300	John Multon		1. **Ada le Brun** (annulled), 2. Margaret de Boys	**William le Brun,** John de Multon
Musard, Malcolm	4		**Nicholas Musard** and Christina			
Musard, Nicholas	4	d. 1300	Ralph Musard			Christiana (illeg.), **Malcolm (illeg.)**
Nanfan, Richard	3	d. 1507			Margaret	2 daughters, John (illeg.), William (illeg.)
Nash, James (illeg.)	5	d. 1400	**Richard Nash** (d. 1394/5)	Cecily (half-sister)		
Nash, Richard	5	d. 1394/5	Nicholas Nash and Lucy			Cecily, **James Nash** (illeg.)
Nerford, Maud	2,3		Sir William Nerford and Petronella Vaux	John, Thomas, Edmund	Simon de Driby?	John de Warenne (illeg), **Thomas de Warenne (illeg.)**

Name	Chapters	Dates	Parents	Siblings	Spouse	Children
Neville, Eilizabeth, Lady Scrope of Upshall and Masham	3	c.1464?– 1518	John Neville, Marquess of Montagu and Elizabeth Ingoldsthorpe		1. Thomas Scrope, Lord Scrope of Masham (d. 1493), 2. Henry Wentworth (d. 1500)	Alice Scrope, Mary (illeg.), d. of Thomas Grey, Marquess of Dorset
Neville, Ralph, Earl of Westmorland		c. 1364– 1425	John Neville (d. 1338) and Maud Percy		1. Margaret Stafford, 2. Joan Beaufort	22 children including Richard Neville, Earl of Salisbury (d. 1460) and William Neville (d. 1463)
Neville, Ralph (of Raby)	3	d. 1331	Robert Neville		1. Eupheme FitzRoger, 2. Margery Thweng	Robert Neville, Ralph Neville, Alexander Neville, John Neville, Thomas Neville, Mary Neville, Ida Neville, Euphemia Neville, Anastasia Neville
Neville, William, Lord Fauconberg	5	d. 1463	Ralph Neville (d. 1425) and Joan Beaufort		Joan Fauconberg	Joan, Elizabeth, Alice, Thomas Neville (illeg.) 'Bastard Fauconberg'

Name	Chapters	Dates	Parents	Siblings	Spouse	Children
Parr, William, Marquess of Northampton		1513–1571	Sir Thomas Parr of Kendal (d. 1517) and Maud Green	Katherine Parr	Anne Bourchier	
Paston, Edmund	Intro, 1	c.1450–c.1500	John Paston I and Margaret	John Paston II (d. 1479), John Paston III (d. 1504), Margery Paston (d.c. 1480), Anne Paston (d. 1494), Walter Paston (d. 1479), William Paston III (d.c. 1505)		Illeg. son with Mistress Dixon
Paston, Elizabeth	4	1429–1488	William Paston (d. 1444) and Agnes Barry (d. 1479)	John Paston I (d. 1466), Edmund Paston (d. 1449), William Paston II (d. 1496), Clement Paston (d. by 1479)	1. Robert Poynings (d. 1461), 2. George Browne (d. 1483)	Edward Poynings
Paston, John I	Intro	1421–1466	William Paston (d. 1444) and Agnes Barry (d. 1479)	Edmund Paston (d. 1449), Elizabeth Paston, (d. 1488), William Paston II (d. 1496), Clement Paston (d. by 1479)	Margaret Mautby	John Paston II (d. 1479), John Paston III (d. 1504), Margery Paston (d. 1480), Edmund Paston (d.c. 1500), Anne Paston (d. 1494), Walter Paston (d. 1479), William Paston III (d.c. 1505)

Name	Chapters	Dates	Parents	Siblings	Spouse	Children
Paston, John II	Intro, 4, 6	1442–1479	John Paston I and Margaret	John Paston III (d. 1504), Margery Paston (d.c. 1480), Edmund Paston (d.c. 1500), Anne Paston (d. 1494), Walter Paston (d. 1479), William Paston III (d.c. 1505)		Constance (illeg.)
Paston, John III	Intro, 3	d. 1504	John Paston I and Margaret	John Paston II (d. 1479), Margery Paston (d.c. 1480), Edmund Paston (d.c. 1500), Anne Paston (d. 1494), Walter Paston (d. 1479), William Paston III (d.c. 1505)	Margery Brews (d. 1495)	Christopher, William Paston IV, Elizabeth
Paston, Margaret (neé Mautby)	Intro, 3, 4, 6	c. 1422–1484			John Paston I	John Paston II (d. 1479), John Paston III (d. 1504), Margery Paston (d.c. 1480), Edmund Paston (d.c. 1500), Anne Paston (d. 1494), Walter Paston (d. 1479), William Paston III (d.c. 1505)

Name	Chapters	Dates	Parents	Siblings	Spouse	Children
Paston, Margery	3	d.c. 1480	John Paston I and Margaret	John Paston II (d. 1479), John Paston III (d. 1504), Edmund Paston (d.c. 1500), Anne Paston (d. 1494), Walter Paston (d. 1479), William Paston III (d.c. 1505)	Richard Calle	
Paston, William		1378–1444	Clement Paston (d. 1419) and Beatrice Goneld (d. 1409)		Agnes Barry (d. 1479)	John Paston I (d. 1466), Edmund Paston (d. 1449), Elizabeth Paston (d. 1488), William Paston II (d. 1496), Clement Paston (d. by 1479)
Paston, William II		1436–1496	William Paston (d. 1444) and Agnes Barry (d. 1479)	John Paston I (d. 1466), Edmund Paston (d. 1449), Elizabeth Paston (d. 1488), Clement Paston (d. by 1479)	Anne Beaufort (daughter of Edmund Beaufort, Duke of Somerset)	
Pelham, John	4	d. 1429	Thomas Pelham and Agnes Gensing		1. Margaret Grey, widow of Sir Thomas Shardlow, 2. Joan Bramshott, widow of Sir Hugh Zouche	John Pelham (illeg.)

Name	Chapters	Dates	Parents	Siblings	Spouse	Children
Pelham, John (illeg.)	4		**John Pelham (d. 1429)**			
Pierrepont, Henry	4	d. 1499	Henry Pierrepont (d. 1462)	Francis Pierrepont		? Edmund (illeg.), but paternity denied
Pigot, John	Intro, 4		John Pigot			John, Richard, Roger, Margaret, Joan, Matilda (illeg.)
Pilkington, John	4	d. 1478	Robert Pilkington	Charles	Jane Balderston	Edward, **Robert (illeg.)**
Pilkington, Robert (illeg.)	4		**John Pilkington (d. 1478)**	Edward (half-brother)	1. Alice Burrell, 2. Alice Bernard	Arthur
Plantagenet, Hamelin, Earl of Surrey (illeg.)	2	d. 1202	Geoffrey of Anjou	Henry II (half-brother)	Isabel de Warenne	**William IV de Warenne**
Pleasington, Henry	4	d. 1452				William, John (illeg.)
Plumpton, Elizabeth	1,3	d. 1507/7	**William Plumpton (d. 1461) and Elizabeth Clifford**	Margaret	John Sotehill (d. 1494)	Henry Sotehill
Plumpton, Margaret	1,3		**William Plumpton (d. 1461) and Elizabeth Clifford**	Elizabeth	John Rocliffe (d. 1533)	Brian Rocliffe

Name	Chapters	Dates	Parents	Siblings	Spouse	Children
Plumpton, Robert	Intro, 3	d. 1523	**William Plumpton** (d. **1480**) and Joan Wintringham	Robert (d. 1450), William (d. 1461), Joan, Elizabeth, Agnes, Margaret, Alice, Isabel, Catherine, **Robert** (illeg.), **William (illeg.)**	1. Agnes Gascoigne, 2. Isabelle Neville	
Plumpton, Robert (illeg.)	Intro		**William Plumpton** (d. **1480**)	Robert (d. 1450), William (d. 1461), Joan, Elizabeth, Agnes, Margaret, Alice, Isabel, Catherine, **Robert (d. 1523)**, **William (illeg.)**		
Plumpton, William	Intro, 1, 3	1404–1480	Robert Plumpton (d. 1421) and Alice Foljambe	Godfrey, Alice, Joan	1. Agnes Stapleton, 2. Joan Wintringham	Robert (d. 1450), William (d. 1461), Joan, Elizabeth, Agnes, Margaret, Alice, Isabel, Catherine, **Robert (d. 1523)**, Robert (illeg.), **William (illeg.)**
Plumpton, William	1	d. 1461	**William Plumpton** (d. **1480**) and Agnes Stapleton	Robert (d. 1450), Joan, Elizabeth, Agnes, Margaret, Alice, Isabel, Catherine, **Robert (d. 1523)**, **Robert (illeg.)**, **William (illeg.)**	Elizabeth Clifford	Margaret, Elizabeth

Name	Chapters	Dates	Parents	Siblings	Spouse	Children
Plumpton, William (illeg.)	Intro		William Plumpton (d. 1480)	Robert (d. 1450), William (d. 1461), Joan, Elizabeth, Agnes, Margaret, Alice, Isabel, Catherine, Robert (d. 1523), Robert (illeg.)		
Poynings, Edward		1459–1521	Robert Poynings (d. 1461) and Elizabeth Paston			John, Edward (illeg.), Thomas (illeg.), Adrian (illeg.), Joan (illeg.), 1 other illeg. son, 2 other illeg. daughters.
Poynings, Robert		d. 1461			Elizabeth Paston	Edward Poynings
Reynforth, Constance	6					Constance (illeg.) with John II Paston
Reynforth, Constance (illeg.)	6		John Paston II and Constance Reynforth			
Rocliffe, John	3	d. 1533	Brian Rocliffe (d. 1496)		Margaret Plumpton	Brian Rocliffe
Roos, Ellen	3	d. 1419	John Roos of Radwinter		Geoffrey Brokholes	Joan, Margery

Name	Chapters	Dates	Parents	Siblings	Spouse	Children
Roos, William (of Helmsley)	4, 5	d. 1414	Thomas Roos (d. 1384) and Beatrice Stafford	John Roos (d. 1394)	Margaret Arundel, d. of Sir John Arundel (d. 1379)	John, Thomas, William, Robert, Richard, Beatrice, Alice, Margaret (m. James Audley), Elizabeth (m. Robert Morley), Joan (illeg.)
Rous, Alice (illeg.)	5		John Rous I		William Pylehous	
Rous, John I (of Imber)	5, 6				Isolde FitzWaryn	William Rous, John Rous II, Richard (illeg.), Thomas (illeg.), Alice (illeg.), Margaret (illeg.)
Rous, John II	5, 6		John Rous I and Isolde Fitzwaryn	William Rous, Richard (illeg.), Thomas (illeg.), Alice (illeg.), Margaret (illeg.)	1. Joan Asshley, 2. Anne Gowayn	John Rous III (illeg.)
Rous, John III (illeg)	5		John Rous II and Joan Perot			
Rous, Margaret (illeg.)	5		John Rous I		John Wolley	
Rous, Richard (illeg.)	5		John Rous I and Alice Philips		Alice Percy or Pershay, d. of John Persy	

Name	Chapters	Dates	Parents	Siblings	Spouse	Children
Rous, Thomas (illeg.)	5		John Rous I			
Rous, William	3, 6		John Rous I and Isolde Fitzwaryn	John Rous II, Richard (illeg.), Thomas (illeg.), Alice (illeg.) Margaret (illeg.)	1. Margaret Thorpe, 2. Isabel Goodchild	William (illeg.), Janet (illeg.) Margaret (illeg.) and Isabel (illeg.)
Ryvere, Richard de la	4		William de la Ryvere (d. 1301) and Sara Middleton	John, Robert and Walter (half-brothers)		
Ryvere, William de la	4	d. 1301				John de la Ryvere, Robert de la Ryvere, Walter de la Ryvere, Richard de la Ryvere (illeg.)
Sackville, Alice (illeg.)	4		Andrew Sackville (d. 1369) and Joan Burgess	Andrew Sackville (half-brother), John Sackville (half-brother), Thomas Sackville (illeg.)		
Sackville, Andrew	Intro, 4, 6	d. 1369	John Sackville		1. Joan de la Beche, 2. Maud Lovat	Andrew Sackville, John Sackville, Thomas Sackville (illeg.), Alice Sackville (illeg.)

Name	Chapters	Dates	Parents	Siblings	Spouse	Children
Sackville, Thomas (illeg.)	Intro; 4, 5		**Sir Andrew Sackville (d. 1369) and Joan Burgess**	Andrew Sackville (half-brother), John Sackville (half-brother), **Alice Sackville (illeg.)**	Margaret Dallingridge	
Sadler, Ralph	1	1507–1587	Henry Sadler		Ellen Mitchell	Thomas Sadler (d. 1607), Henry Sadler (d. 1618), Edward Sadler, Anne Sadler (d. 1576), Jane Sadler (d. in or after 1587), Dorothy Sadler (d. in or after 1578). All legitimated by Parliament in 1547.
Saunford, John (illeg.)	Intro, 5		John Saunford			
Savage, John		d. 1492	John Savage and Katherine Stanley	Thomas Savage (d. 1507), Humphrey, Lawrence, James, Edmund, Christopher, William, George, Richard, Ellen, Katherine, Margaret, Alice and Elizabeth	Dorothy Vernon	Alice, Felicia, Ellen, Maud, George (illeg.)
Selman, John	5		John Selman (d. 1426)			
Shelton, William	4	d. 1421				John Shelton, Amice (illeg.)

Name	Chapters	Dates	Parents	Siblings	Spouse	Children
Smith, Richard	4	1455–1516			Agnes Justice	Richard (illeg.)
Sotehill, John	3	d. 1494	Henry Sotehill (d. after 1480)		**Elizabeth Plumpton**	Henry Sotehill
St Amand, Anthony	4		**Richard Beauchamp, Lord St Amand** (d. 1508) and Mary Wroughton		Anne West	Mary
Stafford (of Blatherwick), Humphrey junior	4		Humphrey Stafford of Blatherwick			
Stafford (of Blatherwick), Humphrey	4			Thomas Stafford of Tattenhoe (d. 1516)		Humphrey
Stafford William (illeg.)	4		Thomas Stafford of Tattenhoe and Alice Denton (widow of William Ingoldsby)		Eleanor	
Stafford, Humphrey (of Hooke)	4, 5	c.1379–1442	Humphrey Stafford (of Southwick and Hooke) and Alice Greville	**John Stafford, Bishop of Bath and Wells, later Archbishop of Canterbury** (illeg.)	Elizabeth Mautravers (d. and coheir of Sir John Mautravers by Elizabeth d'Aumarle)	John Stafford, William Stafford

Name	Chapters	Dates	Parents	Siblings	Spouse	Children
Stafford, Humphrey (of Southwick and Hooke)	Intro, 5	d. 1413	John Stafford and Margaret Stafford		1. Alice Greville, 2. Elizabeth d'Aumarle (widow of Sir John Mautravers)	Humphrey Stafford (d. 1442), John Stafford (illeg.)
Stafford, John (illeg.)	Intro, 5	d. 1452	Humphre Stafford (of Southwick and Hooke, d. 1413) and Emma of North Bradley (d. 1446)	Humphrey Stafford of Hooke (d. 1442)		
Stafford, Nicholas (illeg.)	Intro, 5	1331–1394	Richard, Lord Stafford of Clifton (d. 1380)		Elizabeth Meverel	
Stafford, Richard, Lord Stafford of Clifton	Intro	d. 1380	Edmund, Lord Stafford and Margaret Basset	Ralph Stafford (1st Earl of Stafford)		Nicolas Stafford (illeg.), John Stafford (illeg.), Richard Stafford (the younger), Edmund Stafford
Stafford, Thomas (of Tattenhoe)	4					William Stafford (illeg.)

Name	Chapters	Dates	Parents	Siblings	Spouse	Children
Stanley, Edward, Lord Monteagle	1,5	c. 1460–1523	Thomas Stanley, Earl of Derby (d. 1504) and Eleanor Neville	John Stanley, George Stanley, Richard Stanley, **James Stanley (d. 1515)**, Thomas Stanley (d. 1475), William Stanley, Anne Stanley, Alice Stanley, Katherine Stanley, Agnes Stanley	1. Anne Harrington, 2. Elizabeth Vaughan	Thomas Stanley, Jane Stanley, Edward Stanley (illeg.), **Thomas Stanley (illeg.) (d. 1569)**, Mary Stanley (illeg.)
Stanley, James, Bishop of Ely	1,5	d. 1515	Thomas Stanley, Earl of Derby (d. 1504) and Eleanor Neville	John Stanley, George Stanley, Richard Stanley, Edward Stanley (d. 1523), Thomas Stanley (d. 1475), William Stanley, Anne Stanley, Alice Stanley, Katherine Stanley, Agnes Stanley		**John Stanley (illeg.), Thomas Stanley (illeg.), Margaret Stanley (illeg.)**
Stanley, John (illeg.)	1,5		**James Stanley, Bishop of Ely**	**Thomas Stanley (illeg.), Margaret Stanley (illeg.)**		
Stanley, Margaret (illeg.)	1,5		**James Stanley, Bishop of Ely**	**John Stanley (illeg.), Thomas Stanley (illeg.)**	Sir Henry Halsall	John Stanley
Stanley, Thomas	1,5		**James Stanley, Bishop of Ely**	**John Stanley (illeg.), Margaret Stanley (illeg.)**		

Name	Chapters	Dates	Parents	Siblings	Spouse	Children
Stanley, Thomas, Earl of Derby	1	c. 1433–1504	Thomas Stanley, (1406–1459), and Joan Goushill		1. Eleanor Neville, d. of Richard Neville, Earl of Salisbury, 2. Margaret Beaufort	John Stanley, George Stanley, Richard Stanley, Edward Stanley (d. 1523), **James Stanley (d. 1515)**, Thomas Stanley (d. 1475), William Stanley, Anne Stanley, Alice Stanley, Katherine Stanley, Agnes Stanley
Stanley, Thomas, Bishop of Sodor and Man (illeg.)	1,5	d. 1569	**Edward Stanley (d. 1523)**	Edward Stanley (illeg.), Mary Stanley (illeg.)		
Stokes?, Constance	3	d.c. 1419		Robert Stokes	1. Sir Henry Percy, 2. John Percy, 3. Sir Robert Fitzwaryn, 4. Sir Henry de la River (d.c. 1400)	Isolde Fitzwaryn, Joan Fitzwaryn, Robert, (illeg.) with Robert Wyvill
Stonor, Thomas	5	d. 1474			Joan de la Pole (illeg.)?	

Name	Chapters	Dates	Parents	Siblings	Spouse	Children
Sturmy, William	Intro, 4	d. 1427	John Sturmy		Alice, widow of Hugh Hough of Shavington	Maud, Agnes, John Sturmy (illeg.)
Sumpter, Christine	3		John Sumpter and Margery Brokholes	John Sumpter (d. 1420), Ellen	2. Ralph Holt	
Sumpter, Ellen	3		John Sumpter and Margery Brokholes	John Sumpter (d. 1420), Christine		
Sumpter, John	3		John Sumpter		Margery Brokholes	John Sumpter (d. 1420), Christine, Ellen
Swillington, Robert	4					Roger Swillington, Thomas Hopton (illeg.)
Swynnerton, Maud	2		Robert Swynnerton and Elizabeth, daughter of Nicholas Beck		1. Humphrey Peshale, 2. William Ipstones	
Thickness, William	5	d. 1403	William Thickness (d. 1385) and Katherine Swynnerton			
Thornbury, Philip (illeg.)	5		John Thornbury	Philip Thornbury, Justan Thornbury (illeg.)		

Name	Chapters	Dates	Parents	Siblings	Spouse	Children
Thornbury, John	5					Philip Thornbury, Philip Thornbury (illeg.), Justan Thornbury (illeg.)
Thweng, Lucy	Intro, 3	c.1279–1346	Robert Thweng		1. **William Latimer,** 2. Robert de Everingham, 3. Bartholemew de Fanacourt	**William Latimer, Nicholas Meinill,** (with **Nicholas Meinill d. 1322**)
Trussell, Theobald	4	d. 1368			Katherine	Alfred (illeg.), John
Trussell, Alfred (illeg.)	5	d. after 1419	Theobald Trussell and Katherine	John Trussell	1. Katherine Trussell	William, Elizabeth
Tuddenham, Henry (illeg.)	5	1430–1461	**Thomas Tuddenham d. 1462**			
Tuddenham, Thomas	3	1401–1462	John Tuddenham		Alice Wodehouse	Henry (illeg.)
Tyrell, Edward (of Downham)	4	d. 1442	Walter Tyrell	John Tyrell (d. 1437)		Edward Tyrell, John Tyrell (illeg.)
Usflete, Gerard	Intro, 4		John Usflete			Gerard, Anne, Isabella, Leo (illeg.) John (illeg.)

Name	Chapters	Dates	Parents	Siblings	Spouse	Children
Valence, Aymer de, Earl of Pembroke	2, 5		John Valence			Henry (illeg.)
Valence, Henry (illeg.)	2, 5		Aymer de Valence, Earl of Pembroke			
Vescy, John de	4	1244–1289	William de Vescy (d. 1253) and Agnes Ferrers	William de Vescy (d. 1297)	1.Agnes, d. of Manfred of Saluzzo, 2.Isabel Beaumont	
Vescy, John de	4	1269–1295	William de Vescy (d. 1297) and Isabel de Periton	William de Vescy of Kildare (illeg.)	Clemence d'Avaugour	
Vescy, Richard de	5					
Vescy, William de	4	d. 1253	Eustace de Vescy		1. Isabel, d. of William Longspée, 2. Agnes Ferrers	
Vescy, William de	Intro, 3, 4, 5	1245–1297	William de Vescy (d. 1253) and Agnes Ferrers	John de Vescy (d. 1289)	Isabella de Periton	John de Vescy (d. 1289), William de Vescy (d. 1297)
Vescy, William (of Kildare) (illeg.)	Intro, 3, 4	d. 1314	William Vescy (d. 1297), Debforgaill, daughter of the lord of Desmond	John de Vescy (d. 1295)		John de Vescy (d. 1295) William de Vescy of Kildare (illeg.)

Name	Chapters	Dates	Parents	Siblings	Spouse	Children
Walsall, William	5	d. 1414	William Coleson		Margaret Zouche	
Warde, John	4		Jane Stapleton			Roger (illeg.)
Warenne, Alice de	2		William V de Warenne	John II de Warenne	Edmund FitzAlan, Earl of Arundel (d. 1326)	Richard FitzAlan (d. 1376)
Warenne, Edward de (illeg.)	2		John II de Warenne and Maud Nerford (?)	John de Warenne (illeg.), Thomas de Warenne (illeg.), William de Warenne (illeg.), Joan (illeg.), Katherine (illeg.), Isabel (illeg.), Prior William de Warenne (illeg.)		
Warenne, John de (illeg.)	2		John I de Warenne	William V de Warenne (half-brother), William de Warenne (illeg.)		
Warenne, John de (illeg.)	2		John II de Warenne and Maud Nerford	Thomas de Warenne (illeg.), William de Warenne (illeg.), Joan (illeg.), Katherine (illeg.), Isabel (illeg.), Prior William de Warenne (illeg.)		

Name	Chapters	Dates	Parents	Siblings	Spouse	Children
Warenne, John I de, Earl of Surrey	2	d. 1304	William IV de Warenne and Maud		Alice	William V de Warenne (d. 1286), John (illeg.), William (illeg.)
Warenne, John II de, Earl of Surrey	2, 3	d. 1347	William V de Warenne	Alice de Warenne	Joan de Bar	John de Warenne (illeg.), Thomas de Warenne (illeg.), William de Warenne (illeg.), Edward de Warenne (illeg.), Joan (illeg.), Katherine (illeg.), Isabel (illeg.), Prior William de Warenne (illeg.)
Warenne, Thomas de (illeg.)	2		John II de Warenne and Maud Nerford	John de Warenne (illeg.), William de Warenne (illeg.), Edward de Warenne (illeg.), Joan (illeg.), Katherine (illeg.), Isabel (illeg.), Prior William de Warenne (illeg.)		
Warenne, William de (illeg.)	2, 3		John I de Warenne	Warenne, William V de (half-brother), John de Warenne (illeg.)		

Name	Chapters	Dates	Parents	Siblings	Spouse	Children
Warenne, William de (illeg.), Prior of Castle Acre	2		John II de Warenne	John de Warenne (illeg.), Thomas de Warenne (illeg.), William de Warenne (illeg.), Edward de Warenne (illeg.), Joan (illeg.), Katherine (illeg.), Isabel (illeg.)		
Warenne, William de (illeg.)	2, 5		John II de Warenne	John de Warenne (illeg.), Thomas de Warenne (illeg.), Edward de Warenne (illeg.), Joan (illeg.), Katherine (illeg.), Isabel (illeg.), Prior William de Warenne (illeg.)	Margaret	
Warenne, William I de, Earl of Surrey	2		Rodulf de Warenne			William II de Warenne
Warenne, William II de, Earl of Surrey	2	d. 1138	William I de Warenne		Isabel, widow of Robert Beaumont, Earl of Leicester	William III de Warenne
Warenne, William III de, Earl of Surrey	2	d. 1147	William II de Warenne			Isabel de Warenne

Name	Chapters	Dates	Parents	Siblings	Spouse	Children
Warenne, William IV de, Earl of Surrey	2	d. 1240	Hamelin Plantagenet and Isabel de Warenne		1.?, 2. Maud, widow of Roger Bigod and one of the heiresses of William Marshal	John I de Warenne
Warenne, William V de	2	d. 1286	John I de Warenne and Alice			John II de Warenne
Wensley, John (illeg.)	Intro, 5		Sir Thomas Wensley			
Whittington, Richard,	Intro	d. 1423	Sir William Whittington	Robert Whittington		
Wilcotes, John	4	d. 1422		William Wilcotes	1. Alice, 2. Elizabeth Cheyne	Margaret Wilcotes, Elizabeth Wilcotes, Thomas Wilcotes (illeg.)
Wilcotes, Thomas (illeg.)	4	d. 1472	John Wilcotes (d. 1422)	Margaret Wilcotes, Elizabeth Wilcotes (half-sister)		
Winter, Eleanor	3		Edmund Winter		John Heydon	1 child (illeg.)
Winter, Thomas	5		Thomas Wolsey and 'Mistress Lark'	Dorothy (illeg.)		
Wodehouse, Alice	3	d. 1475	John Wodehouse		Thomas Tuddenham	
Wodehouse, John	3		John Wodehouse			Alice

Name	Chapters	Dates	Parents	Siblings	Spouse	Children
Wolsey, Thomas, Cardinal	5	d. 1530	Robert Wolsey and Joan Daundy			**Thomas Winter** (illeg.), Dorothy (illeg.)
Wood, John	5					
York, Richard	4	d. 1498		Joanna York, Elizabeth York		Richard York, Thomas York, William York, John York, George (illeg.), Guy (illeg.)

Bibilography

Acheson, Eric, *A Gentry Community: Leicestershire in the Fifteenth Century, c. 1422–c. 1485* (Cambridge, 1992)

Adams, Norma, '*Nullius Filius*: A Study of the Exception of Bastardy in the Law Courts of Medieval England', *The University of Toronto Law Journal* 6 (1946)

Anderson, Thomas, '"Legitimation, Name and All is Gone": Bastardy and Bureaucracy in Shakespeare's *King John*', *The Journal for Early Modern Cultural Studies* 4 (2004)

Barton, J. L., 'Nullity of Marriage and Illegitimacy in the England of the Middle Ages', in *Legal History Studies 1972: Papers presented to the Legal History Conference, Aberystwyth 1972*, (ed.) D. Jenkins (Cardiff, 1975)

Bean, J. M. W., 'The Percies' Acquisition of Alnwick', *Archaeologia Aeliana*, 4th series, xxxv (1954)

—, *The Estates of the Percy Family 1416–1537* (Oxford, 1958)

—, *The Decline of English Feudalism* (Manchester, 1968)

Beauclerk-Dewar, Peter and Roger Powell, *Royal Bastards: Illegitimate Children of the British Royal Family* (Stroud, 2008)

Bell, Charles G., 'Edward Fairfax, a Natural Son', *Modern Language Notes* 62 (1947)

Beltz, George Frederick, *Memorials of the Most Noble Order of the Garter from its Foundation to the Present Time* (London, 1841)

Bennett, Judith M., 'Writing Fornication: Medieval Leyrwite and its Historians', *Transactions of the Royal History Society* 13 (2003)

Bennett, M. J., 'Careerism in Late Medieval England', in *People, Politics and Community in the Late Middle Ages*, (eds) J. Rosenthal and C. Richmond (Gloucester, 1987)

Bestor, Jane Fair, 'Bastardy and Legitimacy in the Formation of a Regional State in Italy: The Estense Succession', *Comparative Studies in Society and History* 38 (1996)

Biancalana, Joseph: *The Fee Tail and the Common Recovery in Medieval England 1176–1502* (Cambridge, 2001)

Bindoff, S.T. (ed.) *History of Parliament: The Commons 1509–1558*, 3 vols. (London, 1982)

Blaauw, W.H., 'Warenniana—Ancient Letters and Notices Relating to the Earls of Warenne', *Sussex Archaeological Collections* vi (1853)

Blomefield, Francis, *An Essay Towards a Topographical History of Norfolk*, 11 vols. (London, 1805–10)

Blore, Thomas, *The History and Antiquities of the County of Rutland* (Stanford, 1811)

Boes, Maria R., '"Dishonourable" Youth, Guilds, and the Changed World View of Sex, Illegitimacy, and Women in Late-Sixteenth-Century Germany', *Continuity and Change* 18 (2003)

Brand, Paul A., 'The Origins of the English Legal Profession', *Law and History Review* 5 (1987)

—, 'New Light on the Anstey Case', *Essex Archaeology and History* 15 (1983)

—, '"Deserving" and "Undeserving" Wives: Earning and Forfeiting Dower in Medieval England', *The Journal of Legal History* 22 (2001)

Boutell, Charles, *Heraldry, Historical and Popular*, 3rd ed. (London, 1864)

Burckhardt, Jacob, *The Civilisation of the Renaissance in Italy*, (trans.) S. G. C. Middlemore (London, 1990)

Burrows, Montague, *The Family of Brocas of Beaurepaire and Roche Court: Hereditary Masters of the Royal Buckhounds, with Some Account of the English Rule in Aquitaine* (London,1886)

Carpenter, Christine, *Locality and Polity: A Study of Warwickshire Landed Society 1401–1499* (Cambridge, 1992)

Carpenter, David, *The Struggle for Mastery: Britain 1066–1284* (London, 2003)

Castor, Helen, *Blood and Roses: The Paston Family in the Fifteenth Century* (London, 2004)

Cheney, C. R., 'Legislation of the Medieval English Church', *English Historical Review* 50 (1935)

Cherewatuk, Karen, *Marriage, Adultery and Inheritance in Malory's Morte Darthur* (Woodbridge, 2006)

Chew, H. M., 'The Office of the Escheator in the City of London during the Middle Ages', *English Historical Review* 58 (1943)

Chojnacki, Stanley, *Women and Men in Renaissance Venice: Twelve Essays on Patrician Society* (Baltimore, 2000)

Clay, Charles, *Early Yorkshire Families*, Yorkshire Archaeological Society Record Series cxxv (1973)

Cockayne, G. E., *The Complete Peerage*, (eds) V. Gibbs *et al*, 12 vols. in 13 (London, 1912–50)

Collins, Hugh E. L., *The Order of the Garter: Chivalry and Politics in Late Medieval England 1348–1461* (Oxford, 2000)

Cooper, J. P., 'Patterns of Inheritance and Settlement by Great Landowners from the Fifteenth to the Eighteenth Centuries', in *Family and Inheritance: Rural Society in Western Europe 1200–1800*, (eds) Jack Goody, Joan Thirst and E. P. Thompson (Cambridge, 1978)

Cooper, W., *The Records of Beaudesert, Henley-in-Arden* (Leeds, 1931)

Crawford, Nicholas, 'Language, Duality and Bastardy in Renaissance Drama', *English Literary Renaissance* 34 (2004)

Cronin, H. S., 'Wycliffe's Canonry at Lincoln', *English Historical Review* 35 (1920)

Crossley, F., 'Medieval Monumental Effigies in Cheshire', *Transactions of the Historical Association of Lancashire and Cheshire New Series* 40 (1924)

Crouch, David, *The Birth of Nobility: Constructing Aristocracy in England and France 900–1300* (Harlow, 2005)

—, *The Image of Aristocracy in Britain, 1000–1300* (London, 1992)

Dart, John, *Westmonasterium* (vol. II, London, 1742)

Davis, Kingsley, 'Illegitimacy and the Social Structure', *American Journal of Sociology* 45 (1939–40)

d'Avray, David, 'Authentification of Marital Status: A Thirteenth-Century English Royal Annulment Process and Late Medieval Cases from the Papal Penitentiary', *English Historical Review* 120 (2005)

—, *Medieval Marriage: Symbolism and Society* (Oxford, 2005)

Denholm-Young, N., *The Country Gentry in the Fourteenth Century* (Oxford, 1969)

Dockray, Keith, 'Why did Fifteenth-Century English Gentry Marry?', in *Gentry and Lesser Nobility in Later Medieval Europe*, (ed.) Michael Jones (Gloucester, 1986)

Donahue, Charles, *Law, Marriage and Society in the Later Middle Ages* (New York, 2007)

Duby, Georges, *Medieval Marriage: Two Models from Twelfth-Century France*, (trans.) E. Foster (Baltimore, 1978)

Dugdale, William, *The Antiquities of Warwickshire*, 2nd ed. (London, 1730)

—, *The Baronage of England*, 2 vols. (London, 1675–6)

—, *Monasticon Anglicanum*, 6 vols. (London, 1846)

Earwaker, J. R., *East Cheshire Past and Present*, 2 vols. (London, 1877–80)

Emden, A. B., *A Biographical Register of the University of Oxford to A.D. 1500*, 3 vols. (Oxford, 1957–9)

Engdahl, David E., 'English Marriage Conflicts Law Before the Time of Bracton', *The American Journal of Comparative Law* 15 (1996–7)

Erdeswick, Sampson, *A Survey of Staffordshire: Containing the Antiquities of that County*, (ed.) Thomas Harwood (London, 1844)

Fairbanks, F. Royston, 'The Last Earl of Warenne and Surrey, and the Distributions of His Possessions', *Yorkshire Archaeological Journal* xxix (1907)

Findlay, Alison, *Illegitimate Power: Bastards in Renaissance Drama* (Manchester, 1994)

FitzPatrick, D., 'Legitimation by Subsequent Marriage', *Journal of the Society of Comparative Legislation* New Series 6 (1905)

Fraser, C. M., *A History of Anthony Bek, Bishop of Durham 1283–1311* (Oxford, 1957)

Gies, Frances and Joseph, *Marriage and the Family in the Middle Ages* (New York, 1987)

Given-Wilson, Chris, *Chronicles: The Writing of History in Medieval England* (London, 2004)

—, *The English Nobility in the Later Middle Ages*, 2nd ed. (London, 1996)

—, 'Wealth and Credit, Public and Private: The Earls of Arundel 1306–1397', *English Historical Review* 106 (1991)

— and Curteis, Alice, *The Royal Bastards of Medieval England* (London, 1984).

Gray, H. L., 'Incomes from Land in England in 1436', *English Historical Review* 49 (2003)

Grubb, James S., *Provincial Families of the Renaissance: Private and Public Life in the Veneto* (Baltimore, 1996)

Gwyn, Peter, *The King's Cardinal: The Rise and Fall of Thomas Wolsey* (London, 1990)

Hallas, G. M., 'Archiepiscopal Relations with the Clergy of the Diocese of York, 1279–99', *Yorkshire Archaeological Journal* 60 (1988)

Hamilton, J. S., 'Another Daughter for Piers Gaveston? Amie de Gaveston, Damsel of the Queen's Chamber', *Medieval Prosopography* 19 (1998)

Hanawalt, Barbara, *The Ties that Bound* (Oxford, 1986)

Hanham, Alison, *The Celys and Their World: An English Merchant Family of the Fifteenth Century* (Cambridge, 1985)

Hanshall, J. H., *History of the County Palatine of Chester* (Chester, 1817)

Harris, Barbara J., *English Aristocratic Women, 1450–1550: Marriage and Family, Property and Careers* (Oxford, 2002)

Harriss, G. L., *Cardinal Beaufort* (Oxford, 1988)

Helmholz, R. H., 'Bastardy Litigation in Medieval England', *American Journal of Legal History* 13 (1969)

—, *Canon Law and the Law of England* (London, 1987)

—, 'The Early Enforcement of Uses', *Columbia Law Review* 79 (1979)

—, 'Harboring Sexual Offenders: Ecclesiastical Courts and Controlling Sexual Misbehaviour', *Journal of British Studies* 37 (1998)

—, *The Oxford History of the Laws of England Volume I: The Canon Law and Ecclesiastical Jurisdiction from 597 to the 1640s* (Oxford, 2004)

Hicks, Michael, *Richard III* (Stroud, 2000)

Hicks, Michael, *Edward V: The Prince in the Tower* (Stroud, 2003)

Highfield, J. R. L., review of *Accounts Rendered by Papal Collectors in England, 1317–1378*, (ed.) William E. Lunt, in *English Historical Review* 85 (1970)

Hilton, R. H., *A Medieval Society: The West Midlands at the End of the Thirteenth Century* (Cambridge, 1983)

Hooper, W., *The Law of Illegitimacy* (London, 1911)

Hudleston, C. Roy and R. S. Boumphrey, *Cumberland Families and Heraldry*, Cumberland and Westmorland Antiquarian and Archaeological Society Extra Series 23 (1978)

Hunter, Joseph, *South Yorkshire: The History and Topography of the Deanery of Doncaster, in the Diocese and County of York*, 2 vols. (London, 1828–31)

Hurwich, Judith, 'Bastards in the German Nobility in the Fifteenth and Early Sixteenth Centuries: Evidence of the *Zimmerische Chronik*', *The Sixteenth Century Journal* 34 (2003)

Hyde Cassan, Stephen, *Lives and Memoirs of the Bishops of Sherborne and Salisbury* (Salisbury, 1824)

Ives, E. W., 'The Genesis of the Statute of Uses', *English Historical Review* 82 (1967)

Jacob, E. F., 'Archbishop John Stafford', *Transactions of the Royal Historical Society*, 5th series, 12 (1962)

Jones, Karen, *Gender and Petty Crime in Late Medieval England* (Woodbridge, 2006)

Karras, Ruth Mazo, *Sexuality in Medieval Europe: Doing Unto Others* (New York, 2005)

Kaeuper, Richard, 'Law and Order in Fourteenth-Century England: The Evidence of Special Commissions of *Oyer* and *Terminer*', *Speculum* 54 (1979)

Keen, Maurice, *English Society in the Later Middle Ages* (London, 1990)

—, *Origins of the English Gentleman* (Stroud, 2002)

Kermode, Jenny, *Medieval Merchants: York, Beverley and Hull in the Later Middle Ages* (Cambridge, 1998)

Kerry, C., *The History and Antiquities of the Hundred of Bray* (London, 1868)

King, Andy, 'Thomas of Lancaster's First Quarrel with Edward II', in *Fourteenth Century England III*, (ed.) W. Ormrod (Woodbridge, 2004)

King, E., 'Large and Small Landowners in Thirteenth-Century England', *Past and Present* 47 (1970)

Kirshner, Julius and Anthony Molho, 'The Dowry Fund and the Marriage Market in Early Quattrocento Florence', *Journal of Modern History* 50 (1978)

Kuehn, Thomas, '"As if Conceived within a Legitimate Marriage": A Dispute Concerning Legitimation in Quattrocento Florence', *American Journal of Legal History* 29 (1985)

—,'A Late Medieval Conflict of Laws: Inheritance by Illegitimates in *Ius Commune* and *Ius Proprium*', *Law and History Review* 15 (1997)

—, *Illegitimacy in Renaissance Florence* (Ann Arbor, 2001)

Lapsley, G., 'John De Warenne and the Quo Warranto Proceedings in 1279', *Cambridge Historical Journal* II (1927)

l'Anson, William M., 'Kilton Castle', *Yorkshire Archaeological Journal* xxii (1913)

Laslett, Peter, 'Comparing Illegitimacy Over Time and Between Cultures', in *Bastardy and its Comparative History*, (eds) Peter Laslett, Karla Oosterveen, and Richard M. Smith, (London, 1980)

Liebermann, F., 'The Annals of Lewes Priory', *English Historical Review* 17 (1902)

Lipscomb, George, *The History and Antiquities of the County of Buckingham*, 4 vols. (London, 1847)

Lloyd, M. E. H., 'John Wyclif and the Prebend of Lincoln', *English Historical Review* 61 (1946)

Lobel, M. D., *History of Dean and Chalford, Oxfordshire Record Society* 17 (1935)

Logan, F. Donald, *Runaway Religious in Medieval England* (Cambridge, 1996)

Lomas, Richard, *The Fall of the House of Percy, 1368–1408* (Edinburgh, 2007)

Lunt, William E., *Financial Relations of the Papacy with England, 1327–1534* (1962)

McCarthy, Conor, *Marriage in Medieval England: Law, Literature and Practice* (Woodbridge, 2004)

Maclean, Sir John, *The Parochial and Family History of the Deanery of Trigg Minor, in the County of Cornwall* (London, 1873)

McCree, Ben, 'Religious Gilds and Regulation of Behavior in Late Medieval Towns', in *People, Politics and Community in the Later Middle Ages*, (eds) Joel Rosenthal and Colin Richmond (Gloucester, 1987)

Macfarlane, Alan, 'Illegitimacy and Illegitimates in English History', in *Bastardy and its Comparative History*, (eds) Peter Laslett, Karla Oosterveen and Richard M. Smith (London, 1980)

McFarlane, K. B., *The Nobility of Later Medieval England* (Oxford, 1973)

—, 'Bishop Beaufort and the Red Hat', in *England in the Fifteenth Century: Collected Essays* (London, 1981)

McIntosh, Marjorie, *Controlling Misbehavior in England, 1370–1600* (Cambridge, 1998)

MacKay, Angus, 'The Lesser Nobility in the Kingdom of Castile', in *Gentry and Lesser Nobility in Late Medieval Europe*, (ed.) Michael Jones (Gloucester, 1986)

McSheffrey, Shannon, 'Men and Masculinity in Late Medieval London Civic Culture: Governance, Patriarchy and Reputation', in *Conflicted Identities and Multiple Masculinities: Men in the Medieval West*, (ed.) J. Murray (New York, 1999)

Maddern, Philippa, 'Gentility', in *Gentry Culture in Late Medieval England*, (eds) Raluca Radulescu and Alison Truelove (Manchester, 2005)

Maddicott, J. R., *Thomas of Lancaster, 1307–1322* (Oxford, 1970)

—, 'Thomas of Lancaster and Sir Robert Holland: A Study in Noble Patronage', *English Historical Review* 86 (1971)

Maitland, F. W., 'Canon Law in England', *English Historical Review* 11 (1896)

—, *Roman Canon Law in the Church of England* (London, 1898)

Middleton-Stewart, J., *Inward Purity and Outward Piety: Death and Remembrance in the Deanery of Dunwich, Suffolk, 1340–1547* (Woodbridge, 2001)

Morgan, D. A. L., 'The Individual Style of the English Gentleman', in *Gentry and Lesser Nobility in Late Medieval Europe*, (ed.) M. Jones (Gloucester, 1986)

Moor, C., *Knights of Edward I*, Harleian Society 80-84 (1929–32)

Musson, Anthony, 'Legal Culture: Medieval Lawyers' Aspirations and Pretensions', in *Fourteenth Century England III*, (ed.) W. Ormrod (Woodbridge, 2004)

Neal, Derek G., *The Masculine Self in Late Medieval England* (Chicago, 2008)

Neel, Carol (ed.), *Medieval Families: Perspectives on Marriage, Household, and Children* (Toronto, 2004)

Neill, Michael, '"In Everything Illegitimate": Imagining the Bastard in Renaissance Drama', *The Yearbook of English Studies* 23 (1993)

Newman, J. E. 'Greater and Lesser Landowners and Parochial Patronage: Yorkshire in the Thirteenth Century', *English Historical Review* 92 (1977)

Nicholas, David, 'Child and Adolescent Labour in the Late Medieval City: A Flemish Model in Regional Perspective', *English Historical Review* 110 (1995)

—*The Domestic Life of a Medieval City: Women, Children and the Family in Fourteenth-Century Ghent* (Lincoln, Nebraska, 1985)

Nichols, John, *History and Antiquities of the County of Leicester*, 4 vols (London, 1795–1815)

Nichols, J. G., 'Watson's Earls of Warren and Surrey', *Herald and Genealogist* 7 (1873)

Nicolas, Sir Nicholas Harris, *A Treatise on the Law of Adulterine Bastardy* (London, 1836)

Noble, Elizabeth, *The World of the Stonors: A Gentry Society* (Woodbridge, 2009)

Noy, David, 'Leyrwite, Marriage and Illegitimacy: Winslow Before the Black Death', *Records of Buckinghamshire* 47 (2007)

Ormerod, G., *The History of the County Palatine and City of Chester*, 3 vols. (London, 1882)

Oxford Dictionary of National Biography, 61 vols. (Oxford, 2004). Also available online via: http://www.oxforddnb.com/

Payling, Simon, 'Murder, Motive and Punishment in Fifteenth-Century England: Two Gentry Case-Studies', *English Historical Review* 113 (1998)

—, *Political Society in Lancastrian England: The Greater Gentry of Nottinghamshire* (Oxford, 1991)

—, 'Social Mobility, Demographic Change, and Landed Society in Late Medieval England', *Economic History Review New Series* 45 (1992)

Pedersen, Frederik, *Marriage Disputes in Medieval England* (London, 2000)

Phillips, J. R. S., *Aymer de Valence, Earl of Pembroke* (Oxford, 1992)

Phillips, Kim M., *Medieval Maidens: Young Women and Gender in England, 1270–1540* (Manchester, 2003)

Pole, Sir William, *Collections Towards a Description of the County of Devon* (London, 1791)

Pollard, A. F., *Wolsey* (London, 1929)

Pollock F. and F. W. Maitland, *The History of English Law before the Time of Edward I*, 2nd ed., 2 vols. (Cambridge, 1898)

Poos, L. R., 'Sex, Lies and the Church Courts of Pre-Reformation England', *Journal of Interdisciplinary History* 25 (1995)

Prestwich, Michael, 'An Everyday Story of Knightly Folk', in *Thirteenth Century England IX: Proceedings of the Durham Conference 2001*, (eds) Michael Prestwich, Richard Britnell and Robin Frame (Woodbridge, 2003)

Prince, John, *The Worthies of Devon* (London, 1810)

Pugh, T. B. and C. D. Ross, 'The English Baronage and the Income Tax of 1436', *Bulletin of the Institute of Historical Research* 26 (1953)

Ratcliffe, Marjorie, 'Adulteresses, Mistresses and Prostitutes: Extramarital Relationships in Medieval Castile', *Hispania* 67 (1984)

Rattray Taylor, G., *Sex in History*, revised ed. (London, 1953)

Razi, Z., *Life, Marriage and Death in a Medieval Parish* (Cambridge, 1980)

Richmond, Colin, 'East Anglian Politics and Society in the Fifteenth Century: Reflections 1956–2003', in *Medieval East Anglia*, (ed.) C. Harper-Bill (Woodbridge, 2005)

—, *John Hopton* (Cambridge, 1981)

—, *The Paston Family in the Fifteenth Century: Endings* (Manchester, 2000)

—, review of S. M. Wright, *The Derbyshire Gentry in the Fifteenth Century*, in *Medieval Prosopography* 6 (1985)

Rose, Alexander, *Kings in the North* (London, 2002)

Rosenthal, J., 'The Training of an Elite Group: English Bishops in the Fifteenth Century', *Transactions of the American Philosophical Society* 60 (1970)

Roskell, J. S. L. Clark and C. Rawcliffe (eds), *The History of Parliament: The House of Commons 1386–1421*, 4 volw (Stroud 1992). Also available online via: www.historyofparliamentonline.org/

Round, J. H., *King's Sergeants and Officers of State* (London, 1911)

Rousseau, Constance M., 'Kinship Ties, Behavioural Norms, and Family Counseling in the Pontificate of Innocent III', in *Women Marriage and Family in Medieval Christendom: Essays in Memory of Michael M. Sheehan, CSB*, (eds) Constance M. Rousseau and Joel T. Rosenthal (Kalamazoo, 1998)

Saul, Nigel, 'The Fragments of the Golafre Brass in Westminster Abbey', *Transactions of the Medieval Brass Society* 15 (1992)

—, *Knights and Esquires: The Gloucestershire Gentry in the Fourteenth Century* (Oxford, 1981)

—, *Scenes from Provincial Life: Knightly Families in Sussex 1280–1400* (Oxford, 1986)

—, *Richard II* (New Haven, 1997)

Schmugge, L., *Kirche, Kinder, Karrieren: Päpstliche Dispense von der Unehelichen Geburt im Spätmittelalter* (Zürich, 1995)

Scott, W. L., 'Nullity of Marriage in Canon Law and English Law', *University of Toronto Law Journal* 2 (1938)

Seacome, J, *Memoirs; Containing a Genealogical and Historical Account of the Ancient and Honorable House of Stanley From the Conquest to the Death of James Earl of Derby in the year 1735* (Manchester, 1783)

Searle, E., 'Seigneurial Control of Women's Marriage: The Antecedents and Function of Merchet in England', *Past and Present* 82 (1979)

Seipp, D. J., 'The Reception of Canon Law and Civil Law in the Common Law Courts before 1600', *Oxford Journal of Legal Studies* 13 (1993)

Sheehan, Michael, *Marriage, Family and Law in Medieval Europe: Collected Studies*, (ed.) J. K. Farge (Toronto, 1996)

Smith, Richard M., 'A Note on Network Analysis in Relation to the Bastardy Prone Sub-Society', in *Bastardy and its Comparative History*, (eds) Peter Laslett, Karla Oosterveen, and Richard M. Smith (Cambridge, 1980)

Spufford, Margaret, 'Puritanism and Social Control', in *Order and Disorder in Early Modern England*, (eds) A. Fletcher and John Stevenson (Cambridge, 1985)

Stringer, Keith, 'Nobility and Identity in Medieval Britain and Ireland: The de Vescy Family *c.* 1120–1314', in *Britain and Ireland 900–1300: Insular Responses to Medieval European Change*, (ed.) Brendan Smith (Cambridge, 1999)

Sweet, Alfred H., 'The Apostolic See and the Heads of English Religious Houses', *Speculum* 28 (1953)

Syme, Sir Ronald, 'Bastards in the Roman Aristocracy', *Proceedings of the American Philosophical Society* 104 (1960)

Teichmann, J., *The Meaning of Illegitimacy* (Cambridge, 1978)

Thornley, J. L., *Monumental Brasses of Lancashire and Cheshire* (Hull, 1893)

Thoroton, Robert, *History of Nottinghamshire*, 3 vols. (London, 1790–6)

Turner, Ralph V., 'Who was the author of Glanvill? Reflections on the Education of Henry II's Common Lawyers', *Law and History Review* 8 (1990)

Victoria History of the Counties of England (1900-). Also available through *British History Online*: http://www.british-history.ac.uk/

van Winter, Johanna Maria, 'Knighthood and Nobility in the Netherlands', in *Gentry and Lesser Nobility in Late Medieval Europe*, (ed.) Michael Jones (Gloucester, 1986)

Virgoe, Roger, 'The Divorce of Sir Thomas Tuddenham', in *East Anglian Society and the Political Community of Late Medieval England: Selected Papers of Roger Virgoe*, (eds) C. Barron, C. Rawcliffe and J. T. Rosenthal (Norwich, 1997)

Wagner, A., *English Genealogy* (Oxford, 1972)

—,'Heraldry', in *Medieval England*, (ed.) A. L. Poole (Oxford, 1958)

Walker, S. K., 'Lordship and Lawlessness in the Palatinate of Lancaster, 1370–1400', *Journal of British Studies* 28 (1989)

Watson, Jessica Lewis, *Bastardy as a Gifted Status in Chaucer and Malory*, *Studies in Mediaeval Literature* 14 (1996)

Watson, John, *Memoirs of the Ancient Earls of Warren and Surrey and their Descendants to the Present Time*, vol. 2 (Warrington, 1782)

Wedgwood, Josiah C., *History of Parliament: Biographies of the Members of the Commons House, 1439–1509* (London, 1936). Also available online via: www.historyofparliamentonline.org/

—, *Staffordshire Parliamentary History, from the Earliest Times to the Present Day*, William Salt Archaeological Society, *Collections for a History of Staffordshire* (1917)

Wells-Furby, Bridget, 'Sir Richard de la Ryvere (d. 1334–37): A Berkshire Bastard', *Southern History* 37 (2015)

Westcote, Thomas, *A View of Devonshire in MDCXXX, with a Pedigree of Most of its Gentry*, (eds) George Olwer and Pitman Jones (Exeter, 1845)

Wetter, J., *Bodrugans: A Study of a Cornish Medieval Knightly Family* (Lostwithiel, 1995)

White, J. D., 'Legitimation by Subsequent Marriage', *Legal Quarterly Review* 36 (1920)

Wright, S. M., *The Derbyshire Gentry in the Fifteenth Century*, *Derbyshire Record Society* viii (1983)

Wright, Thomas, *The History and Topography of the County of Essex*, 2 vols. (London, 1836)

Young, Charles R., *The Making of the Neville Family 1166–1400* (Woodbridge, 1996)

Zunshine, Lisa, *Bastards and Foundlings: Illegitimacy in Eighteenth-Century England* (Ohio, 2005)

Unpublished Theses

Astill, G. G., 'The Medieval Gentry: A Study in Leicestershire Society, 1350–1399' (University of Birmingham PhD thesis, 1977)

Beckerman, J. S., 'Customary Law in English Manorial Courts in the Thirteenth and Fourteenth Centuries' (University of London PhD thesis, 1972)

Gallagher, E., 'An Introduction to and Edition of the Suffolk Eyre Roll 1240—civil pleas' (King's College London PhD Thesis, 2005)

Warner, M. W., 'The Montagu Earls of Salisbury *c*. 1300–1428: A Study in Warfare, Politics and Political Culture' (University of London PhD Thesis, 1991)

Archives

London, The National Archives, particularly classes C1 Chancery, C47 Chancery Miscellanea, C139 Chancery Inquisitions Post Mortem, C143 Chancery: Inquisitions Ad Quod Damnum, CP 25/1 Court of Common Pleas, General Eyres and Court of King's Bench: Feet of Fines Files, Richard I – Henry VII, E 210 Exchequer King's Remembrancer: Ancient Deeds, Series D, PROB11 Prerogative Court of Canterbury and related Probate Jurisdictions: Will Registers and SC8 Special Collections: Ancient Petitions.

London, Lambeth Palace Library: Register of Walter Reynolds

Derbyshire Record Office, D77 Deeds and Estate papers, Gresley Family

Leicestershire Record Office, DE221 Peake (Nevill of Holt) MSS

Printed Primary Sources

Items indicated with an asterisk* are available online via *British History Online*: www.british-history.ac.uk

Accounts Rendered by Papal Collectors in England, 1317–1378, (eds) William E. Lunt and Edgar B. Graves (Philadelphia, 1968)

Annales Londoniensis in *Chronicles of the Reigns of Edward I and Edward II*, (ed.) W. Stubbs, vol I (Rolls Series, 1882)

Annales Paulini in *Chronicles of the Reigns of Edward I and Edward II*, (ed.) W. Stubbs, vol. I (Rolls Series, 1882)

The Armburgh Papers: The Brokholes Inheritance in Warwickshire, Hertfordshire and Essex, c. 1417–1453, (ed.) Christine Carpenter (Woodbridge, 1998)

Bedfordshire Wills Proved in the Prerogative Court of Canterbury 1383–1548, (ed.) Margaret McGregor, *Bedfordshire Historical Record Society* (1979)

Bracton de Legibus et Consuetudinae Angliae, (ed.) G. Woodbine, (trans.) S. E. Thorne, 4 vols. (Cambridge, Mass., 1968–77)

Bracton's Note Book, (ed.) F. W. Maitland, 3 vols. (London, 1887)

Britton: The French Text Carefully Revised, with an English Translation, Introduction and Notes, (ed.) Francis Morgan Nichols (Oxford, 1865)

Calendar of Close Rolls 1272–1509, 47 vols. (London, 1892–1963)*

Calendar of Documents Relating to Ireland, 5 vols. (London, 1875–86)

Calendar of Documents Relating to Scotland, 4 vols. (Edinburgh, 1881–88)

Calendar of Entries in the Papal Registers Relating to Great Britain and Ireland: Papal Letters, (eds) W. Bliss *et al*, i – vii (London, 1893–1906)*

Calendar of the Fine Rolls 1272–1509, 22 vols. (London, 1911–1962)

Calendar of Inquisitions Post Mortem 1236–1447, 26 vols. (London, 1904–2010)

Calendar of Letter Books Preserved among the Archives of the Corporation of the City of London … Letter Books A – L, (ed.) Reginald R. Sharpe (London, 1899–1912)*

Calendar of Patent Rolls 1232–1509, 52 vols. (London, 1891–1916)

Calendar of Wills Proved and Enrolled in the Court of Husting A.D. 1258–A.D. 1688, (ed.) Reginald R. Sharpe, 2 vols. (London, 1889–90)*

The Cely Letters 1472–1488, (ed.) Alison Hanham (Oxford, 1975)

Chartulary of Rievaulx, (ed.) J. C. Atkinson, *Surtees Society* lxxxiii (1889)

Chaucer, *Canterbury Tales* (Penguin ed., London, 1969)

Chronicle of the War between the English and the Scots in 1173 and 1174 by Jordan Fantosme, Spiritual Chancellor of the Diocese of Winchester, (ed.) F. Michel, *Surtees Society* xi (1840)

Collectanea Topographica et Genealogica, vii (London, 1841)*

Cornwall Feet of Fines, (ed.) J. H. Rowe, *Devon and Cornwall Record Society*, 2 vols. (1914–1950)

Corpus Iuris Canonici, (ed.) A. Friedberg (1879)

The Courts of the Archdeaconry of Buckingham 1483–1523, Buckinghamshire Record Society 19 (1975).

Coventry Leet Book, 1420–1555, (ed.) M. D. Harris, *Early English Text Society, Original Series* 134, 135, 138, 146 (1907–13)

Derbyshire Charters, (ed.) I. H. Jeayes (London, 1906)

Derbyshire Wills Proved in the Prerogative Court of Canterbury 1393–1574, (ed.) G. Edwards, *Derbyshire Record Society* (1998)

A Descriptive Catalogue of Ancient Deeds in the Public Record Office, (ed.) H. C. Maxwell-Lyte, 6 vols. (London 1890–1915)*

Dixon, W. H., *Fasti Eboracenses: Lives of the Archbishops of York*, (ed.) J. Raine (London, 1863)

Earliest English Law Reports, (ed.) Paul A. Brand,Selden Society 111, 112, 122, 123, (1995–2007)

Early Lincoln Wills: An Abstract of All the Wills and Administrations Recorded in the Old Diocese of Lincoln 1280–1547, (ed.) Alfred Gibbons (Lincoln, 1888)

Early Northampton Wills, (ed.) Dorothy Edwards, *Northants Record Society* xlii (2005)

English Historical Documents II: 1042–1189, (ed.) D. C. Douglas (London, 1981)

Feet of Fines for the County of Somerset, (ed.) Emmanuel Green, *Somerset Record Society* xxii (1905)

Feet of Fines for the County of York, *Yorkshire Arch Society Record Series*, 4 vols. (1910–2006)

The French Chronicle of London in *Chronicles of the Mayors and Sheriffs of London 1188–1274*, (ed.) H. T. Riley (London, 1863)

Gascoigne, T., *Loci e Libro Veritatum*, (ed.) J. E. Thorold Rogers (Oxford, 1881)

Gesta Edwardi de Carnarvon Auctore Canonico Bridlingtoniensis in *Chronicles of the Reigns of Edward I and Edward II*, vol. II, (ed.) W. Stubbs (Rolls Series, 1883)

Historiae Dunelmensis Sriptores Tres, (ed.) J. Raine, *Surtees Society* ix (1839)

Inquisitions and Assessments Relating to Feudal Aids: With Other Analogous Documents Preserved in the Public Record Office. A.D. 1284–1431, 6 vols. (London, 1899–1920)

Knighton's Chronicle, (ed.) G. H. Martin (Oxford, 1995)

Kingsford's Stonor Letters and Papers 1290–1483, (ed.) Christine Carpenter (Cambridge, 1996)

Letters and Papers, Foreign and Domestic, Henry VIII, (ed.) J. S. Brewer, 23 vols. in 35 (London, 1862–1932)*

Letters and Papers from the Northern Registers, (ed.) J. Raine (Rolls Series, 1873)

The Letters of Robert Grosseteste, Bishop of Lincoln, (trans.) F. A. C. Mantello and Joseph Goering (Toronto, 2010)

Lewes Chartulary, (ed.) L. F. Salzman, *Sussex Record Society* xxxviii (1932)

Liber Feodorum: The Book of Fees, Commonly Called Testa de Nevill, (ed.) H. C. Maxwell Lyte, 3 vols. (London, 1920–31)

London Plea and Memoranda Rolls 1437–57, (ed.) P. E. Jones (Cambridge, 1954)

Memorials of the Guild of Merchant Taylors: Of the Fraternity of St. John the Baptist in the City of London, (ed.) C. M. Clode (London, 1875)

Monachi cujusdam Malmesberiensis Vita Edwardi II in *Chronicles of the Reigns of Edward I and Edward II*, vol II, (ed.) W. Stubbs (Rolls Series, 1883)

Parliament Rolls of Medieval England, (eds) Chris Given-Wilson, Paul A. Brand, Seymour Phillips *et al*, 16 vols. (Woodbridge, 2005)*

The Parliamentary Writs and Writs of Military Summons, (ed.) F. Palgrave, 2 vols. in 4 parts (Record Commission, 1827–1834)

Paston Letters and Papers of the Fifteenth Century, (ed.) N. Davies (Oxford, 1971)

Pedigrees from the Plea Rolls, Collected from the Pleadings in the Various Courts of Law, A.D. 1200 to 1500, etc., (ed.) George Wrottesley (London, 1905)

Percy Chartulary, ed. M. T. Martin, *Surtees Society* cxvii (1911)

Petitions to the Crown from English Religious Houses c. 1272–c. 1485, (ed.) Gwilym Dodd and Alison K. McHardy (Woodbridge, 2010)

Petitions to the Pope 1342–1419, (ed.) W. H. Bliss (London,1896)*

Plumpton Letters, (ed.) J. Kirby, *Camden 5ᵗʰ Series* 8 (1996)

Proceedings and Ordinances of the Privy Council of England, (ed.) Sir Nicholas Harris Nicolas, 7 vols. (London, 1834–37)

Records of Nottingham, (eds) W. H. Stevenson *et al.* (London, 1882–)

The Register of Edmund Lacy, Bishop of Exeter, 1420–1455, (ed.) G. R. Dunstan, *Devon and Cornwall Record Society*, 4 vols. (1963–72)

The Register of Henry Chichele, Archbishop of Canterbury 1414–1443, (ed.) E. F. Jacob, *Canterbury and York Society* 43, 45–47 (1937–47)

The Register of John le Romeyn, Lord Archbishop of York 1286–1296, (ed.) W. Brown, *Surtees Society* cxxiii (1913)

The Register of John de Stratford, Bishop of Winchester 1323–1333, vol II, (ed.) Roy Martin Haines, *Surrey Record Society* xliii (2011)

The Register of John de Trilleck, Bishop of Hereford (A.D. 1344–1361), (ed.) J. H. Parry, *Cantilupe Society* (1910)

The Register, or Rolls, of Walter Gray, Lord Archbishop of York, (ed.) James Raine, *Surtees Society* 56 (1872)

The Register of Thomas Corbridge, Archbishop of York 1300–1304, (ed.) William Brown, *Surtees Society* 138 (1925)

The Register of Walter Giffard, Lord Archbishop of York 1266–1279, (ed.) William Brown, *Surtees Society* 119 (1904)

The Register of William Bateman, Bishop of Norwich 1344–1355, vol I, (ed.) Phyllis E. Pobst, *Canterbury and York Society* (1996)

The Register of William Greenfield, Lord Archbishop of York 1306–1315, (ed.) William Brown, *Surtees Society* 149 (1934)

The Register of William Melton, Archbishop of York 1370–1340, (ed.) R. M. T. Hill, *Canterbury and York Society* lxx (1977)

The Register of William Wickwane, Lord Archbishop of York 1279–1285, (ed.) W. Brown, *Surtees Society* 114 (1907)

The Registers of John de Sandale and Rigaud de Asserio, Bishops of Winchester (A.D. 1316–1323), (ed.) F. J. Baigent, *Hampshire Record Society* (1897)

Registrum Roberti Winchelsey Cantuariensis Archiepiscopi A.D. 1294–1313, (ed.) Rose Graham, *Canterbury and York Society* (1956)

Registrum Simoni de Gandavo Diocesis Sarebiriensis A.D. 1297–1315 (eds) C. T. Flower and M. C. B. Dawes (Oxford, 1934)

Roberti Grosseteste Epistolae, (ed.) J. R. Luard (Rolls Series, 1861)

'Roll of the Justices in Eyre at Bedford 1227', (ed.) Fowler, G. Herbert, *Publications of Bedfordshire Historical Record Society* 3 (1916)

Rotuli Parliamentorum, 6 vols. (London 1767–77)

Rymer, T., *Foedera*, 4 vols. in 7 (London, 1816–69)*

Select Cases Before the King's Council, (eds) I. S. Leadam and J. F. Baldwin, *Selden Society* 35 (1918)

Somerset Medieval Wills 1383–1500, (ed.) F. W. Weaver, *Somerset Record Society* 16 (1901)

Some Oxfordshire Wills: Proved in the Prerogative Court of Canterbury, 1393–1510, (eds) J. R. H. Weaver and A. Beardwood, *Oxfordshire Record Society* (1958)

Shakespeare, William, *Complete Works* (Oxford Shakespeare, 2nd ed.), eds. S.Wells, G.Taylor, J.Jowett and W.Montgomery (Oxford, 2005)

Statutes of the Realm, 11 vols. (London, 1810–28)

Taxatio Ecclesiastica Angliæ et Waliæ Auctoritate P. Nicholai IV : circa A.D. 1291 (London, 1802)

Testamenta Eboracensia, (ed.) J. Raine *et al*, *Surtees Society*, 4 vols. (1836–1869)

The Treatise on the Laws and Customs of the Realm of England Commonly Called Glanvill, (ed.) G. D. G. Hall (Oxford, reprinted, 1993)

Testamenta Vetusta, (ed.) Sir Nicolas Harris Nicolas, 2 vols. (London, 1836)

The Tropenell Cartulary, Being the Contents of an Old Wiltshire Muniment Chest, (ed.) J. Silvester Davies (Devizes, 1908)

The Usurpation of Richard the Third : Dominicus Mancinus ad Angelum Catonem de occupatione Regni Anglie per Riccardum Tercium libellus, Dominic Mancini, (trans.) C. A. J. Armstrong (1989)

Warwickshire Feet of Fines, (eds) E. Stokes, Frederick Wellstood and Lucy Drucker, *Dugdale Society*, 3 vols. (1932–1943)

Wells City Charters, (eds) Dorothy O. Shilton and Richard Holworthy, *Somerset Record Society* 46 (1932)

Wills of the Archdeaconry of Sudbury 1439–1474: Wills from the Register 'Baldwyne', (ed.) P. Northeast, *Suffolk Record Society* 44 (2001)

Wykeham's Register, ed. T. F. Kirby,*Hampshire Record Society* (1896–9)

Year Books, Selden Society 17, 19, 20, 22, 24, 26, 27, 29, 31, 33, 34, 36, 37, 38, 39, 41, 42, 43, 45, 47, 50, 52, 54, 61, 63, 65, 70, 81, 85, 86, 104 (1903–1988)

Year Books, Ames Foundation, 7 vols. (1914–1996)

Year Books, Rolls Series 31 (i)– (xx) (1863–1911)

Index